Women in

Reformation and

Counter-Reformation

Europe

Women in Reformation and Counter-Reformation Europe

PUBLIC AND PRIVATE WORLDS

Edited by Sherrin Marshall

Indiana
University
Press

Bloomington and Indianapolis

Library of Congress Cataloging-in-Publication Data

Women in reformation and counter reformation Europe.

Includes index.
1. Women—Europe—Religious life—History—16th
century.   2. Women—Europe—Religious life—History—17th
century.   3. Women—Europe—History—16th century.
4. Women—Europe—History—17th century.   I. Marshall,
Sherrin.
BV4527.W594   1989   274'.06'088042   88-45758
ISBN 0-253-33678-3
ISBN 0-253-20527-1 (pbk.)

1 2 3 4 5 93 92 91 90 89

CONTENTS

Women in

Reformation and

Counter-Reformation

Europe

SHERRIN MARSHALL

Introduction

The age of the Reformation and Counter Reformation, which encompassed the sixteenth and most of the seventeenth centuries, was a time of monumental change in institutional religion. Beginning with Martin Luther in 1517, religious leaders created a "reformation" of existing religious practices. Luther and the religious reformers broke with the Church of Rome, in succeeding waves of religious upheaval which encompassed much of the sixteenth century. By the second half of the century, Catholic response to these challenges was well underway, resulting in such institutional outcomes as the establishment of new religious orders and, theologically, in a reaffirmation of the Church's basic tenets of faith. These cataclysmic religious events in turn brought enormous social, economic, and political change as Europeans sought to establish a new stability. The leaders of these great movements—Protestant and Catholic alike—were men, almost without exception.

This book was written in the belief that history profits from being rewritten and revised—this time, from the viewpoint and experience of women rather than men. All the chapters in *Women in Reformation and Counter-Reformation Europe,* which was written for students, teachers, and scholars, raise new questions and use new evidence to answer them. What is clear is that the authors do not agree on either questions or answers—one sign of the coming of age of women's history. The goals of this book are to provoke discussion and contribute to the realization that differing conclusions with their nuances of meaning shape the general context of historical understanding. In many cases, the findings of individual chapters, valid for a particular country, locale, period of time, or social group, open up new possibilities for comparative study. Each chapter is based in large part on the author's archival research. But individual authors have not only drawn specific conclusions based on their own material, they have also attempted broader generalizations applicable to the whole study.

There are many ways to study history and analyze the past. The contributors to this volume all share the belief that, insofar as it is possible, we must examine historical sources that focus on women themselves. We have not scrutinized the great works of theology, such as the writings of the Protestant reformers Luther or Calvin or the Catholic leader Saint Ignatius Loyola, for these offer no insights into the actual lives and actions of women during this time. Chapters ignore, for the most part, political manifestos and activities, except for noting their impact on women. Court cases and trial records, on the other hand, often bring women visibility; such documents have been included.

This book is organized in three ways, each of which overlaps with the others. First, it is structured *geographically*, for our goal is to provide information on women in virtually every country of Europe during this period, from Iceland in the West to Hungary in the East. Second, it is ordered *chronologically*. Those chapters that deal with women in the Reformation begin with the coming of Protestantism, or even the antecedents of the reformers, such as the later Renaissance humanists. The chapters progress through the age of the Counter Reformation, the period of Catholicism's response to the challenge of Protestantism. In our opinion, a chronological approach aids students in thematic analysis. Third, the work is oriented *topically*. A number of common themes and issues appear throughout.

An initial important issue is the extent to which, and the ways in which, the great religious changes of this period affected the lives of women. Throughout Europe, confining and limiting norms were imposed on women. Women were instructed by church leaders and theologians to be "chaste, silent, and obedient." In many instances documented here, however, women either overcame such bounds or quite specifically ignored them. These women range from the exceptional, such as Elizabeth Bathory in Hungary and Luisa de Carvajal y Mendoza in Spain, to less visible women who would have considered themselves absolutely ordinary, such as Margaret Toftes in England. Religious changes affected the lives of women radically during this period, but often not in the ways men considered they should or would be affected. We discover that women had a significant role in shaping their own religious identity and destiny.

A second common theme has been the link among women, the family, and religious changes. A number of contributors observe that religion was not so private a matter in the age of Reformation and Counter Reformation as it is today. Religion was intermingled with familial concerns and has sometimes therefore been erroneously identified as a private concern. Yet because religion was also a prevailing political issue, religious decisions made within the family were never truly "private." Merry Wiesner believes that the more accurate distinction is really "public" as opposed to what she terms "personal," and she does not equate "personal" with "private." The implications of these spheres—private and public worlds—for women's history are powerful: the family was arguably the most important sphere of influence and most important focus of activity for women.

Historians have difficulty understanding, visualizing, and gaining access to information on activities that occurred behind closed doors within the family circle. Since the Reformation and Counter Reformation forced "household religion" into the open, it is precisely those previously invisible activities that can be glimpsed through the religious world of the family. And women's activities within the family are revealed to be different than earlier historians have supposed. Although strictures on female behavior were widely posited and apparently widely accepted in support of familial goals, women found personal satisfaction and social approbation—and just as often, their behavior defines and encompasses activist models.

In this book, however, we not only examine religion and the impact of religious change. We are also interested in women in Reformation and Counter-Reformation Europe, from about 1500 to 1700. By focusing on religious change, we also question whether such change functioned as a catalyst for other transformations, such as those which occurred simultaneously within the economy and the social order. Confining and negative behavioral norms *did* affect women adversely within the world of work, as is shown by the authors who study working women. Whereas the religious structure experienced renewal and revitalization during this period, the economic structure of European society became increasingly limiting for women. Work which had previously been open to women became closed; dependable opportunities for the economic autonomy of women through work became virtually nonexistent.

Several methodological approaches are employed in this book. The authors have been particularly sensitive to the question of "image" versus "reality" and also to the problem of drawing conclusions or generalizations on the basis of incomplete data. Specific case studies, or studies of individuals, have been used in some instances as the basis for broader generalization, particularly if these individuals can be identified as models or paradigms. The essays cross lines of class and status whenever possible and identify such differences. This enables comparison of elite women with, for example, working women. The authors consider the roles of women within the family and without, within the "private" as well as the "public" sphere. Feminine rather than masculine perspectives have been consciously incorporated.

Feminine as opposed to masculine perspectives are achieved in a number of ways. One way is to let the women in this book speak for themselves whenever possible, rather than allowing men to speak for them. Additionally, although authors discuss attitudes held toward women in the sixteenth and seventeenth centuries, their interest has been to expose the ways in which such attitudes shaped or reinforced the behavioral patterns of women.

For example, Grethe Jacobsen and Merry Wiesner both see what might be termed a "model of domesticity" as one result of the Reformation era. They regard this model as one which proved detrimental to women's position and self-actualization. To Jacobsen, the role of housewife and mother, with the clergyman's wife as model, became the all-important role for women in the Protestant churches of the Nordic countries. This was an "extension of the domestic aspect of their role in society at large." Wiesner uses lives of the reformers' wives to demonstrate how familial concerns became linked with those of the Reformation. She concludes that even when such women were allowed to undertake "good works" under their own initiative, and even when they were encouraged to share in theological dialogue with their husbands—the reformer Urbanus Rhegius published his discussions with his well-educated wife—they were still linked with traditional gender roles and norms for women: to be "chaste, silent, and obedient." "By the mid-seventeenth century," states Wiesner, "religion for all women in Germany, whether lay or clerical, had become much more closely tied to a household." In Germany and the Nordic countries, where the magisterial Reformation triumphed, both Wiesner and Jacobsen find that the identification of women within the family alone was limiting for women. Moreover, they see the role of pastors' wives as negative rather than positive, providing women with role models that emphasized and reaffirmed the passive and limiting behavioral models identified by Wiesner.

Working women as well as housewives were part of the larger society, and this model of domesticity had pernicious implications for women outside the home. Susan Karant-Nunn believes that women's work outside the family circle was often, to women's detriment, related to their work within the home. Studying women miners in Saxony, she finds that washing ore was a chore "considered suitable for women." The prevailing attitude toward women was that they were "inferior to and properly subordinate to men," and this sentiment reinforced the acceptability of such work for women. Washing, laundering, scrubbing, in whatever context, was women's work and, as such, poorly paid and marginal.

These models of feminine behavior and attitudes toward women had largely negative implications for women in Reformation and Counter-Reformation Europe. But the question of the existence of other possibilities, alternatives, and approaches still remains. Were women able to circumvent these restrictive models, and, if so, under what conditions and circumstances? Sherrin Marshall finds some contradiction in the expression and realization of such models in the Netherlands of the sixteenth and seventeenth centuries. There, as elsewhere throughout Europe, these confining and limiting ideals supposedly defined socially acceptable female behavior. The reality was that in periods of upheaval, such as the Revolt of the Netherlands or, in the case of Portuguese Jewish exiles, flight from the Spanish Inquisition, women were anything but obedient and silent. A number of women successfully assumed masculine roles, appearing publicly in a quasi-military or quasi-political function. When such activities were sanctioned by the woman's family or when they supported a socially acceptable cause, whether political or religious, the woman's behavior could be applauded as heroic. In riots, however, or in acting out roles defined as socially deviant—in other words, under different circumstances—the same behavior would be denigrated or actually prosecuted.

Beyond the delineation of these contrasting and sometimes conflicting attitudes toward women, Marshall reiterates the importance of familial ties, patterns, and bonds and regards them as significant for the course of religious history in a number of ways. Although the position of Reformed, Roman Catholic, and Jew differed in the Netherlands, Marshall shows that women of each group shared many religious patterns in common. Charitable functions provided an important outlet and leadership role for women, which familial patterns reinforced.

Diane Willen, in "Women and Religion in Early Modern England," concludes that under certain circumstances familial identification legitimized independent and autonomous activities for women. Willen's examples range from female Lollards who antedate the Reformation to the women radicals of the seventeenth century. She establishes that through household or family religion women not only dominated household management and child rearing, but also extended their roles beyond the household itself. In support of this conclusion, she discusses public activity linked with religion. Here again charity in the cause of religion, within and without the household, was important, and Willen finds that these newly endowed charitable institutions gave some women considerable autonomy. The norms for women that were articulated in England and the Netherlands were the same as those in Germany and Scandinavia, but these chapters draw a number of differing conclusions, indicating that the reality of women's lives within the family may have varied in different countries.

Sherrill Cohen, in "Asylums for Women in Counter-Reformation Italy," also identifies an "ideology of female inferiority and subordination." She concludes that although women did not articulate any challenges to this ideology, they did stave off attempts to enclose them in religious institutions against their will. To some extent, Cohen sees their success as based on public charitable support: charitable support for the new foundations she investigates matched and frequently surpassed more traditional institutions both in terms of successful care provided and in ability to attract financial contributions. These charitable houses of refuge filled quasi-familial functions, thereby legitimizing their own activities, which were in fact supportive of female self-actualization and independence.

Cohen, Willen, and Marshall all suggest that the enhanced role of charitable institutions following the Reformation and Counter Reformation helped legitimize activist roles for women. These roles may have been modeled on familial patterns, but they brought women into the public arena. Willen examines charitable institutions founded and maintained by Protestants; Cohen investigates Italian asylums founded by Catholics; and Marshall discusses charitable practices of Jews as well as those of Protestants and Catholics. Striking parallels exist in all three studies, with women's charitable activities as the connecting element.

Case studies of women allow us to examine in greater detail the experiences of women as individuals and compared with those of men. Wiesner finds the case of Argula von Grumbach instructive in that her pro-Lutheran stance was simply ignored by the authorities. Because she was a "mere woman," Wiesner concludes, her detractors failed to take her seriously and she died in obscurity. Argula von Grumbach's activism was punished, however, by attacks on her menfolk: her husband was deprived of his official position by the duke of Bavaria and was told to control her. Men could be prosecuted for their association with activist women. To Milagros Ortega Costa, male repudiation of such women shows the degree to which women accused of heresy, for example, *were* taken seriously in Spain.

Ortega Costa, in "Spanish Women in the Reformation," reveals the courage of Isabel Ortiz, who defied the inquisitors and survived, as well as the cowardice of her male allies who attempted to convince the inquisitors that their acquaintance with her was glancing. A number of Costa's conclusions are drawn from individual case studies and point up the religious eclecticism which women often typified. One of the *alumbrados,* or *illuminati,* she studies was Maria de Cazalla. Maria was greatly influenced by Erasmus and in the 1520s preached that the doctrine of pure love was more important than "good works." She considered marriage "more meritorious than virginity" and accepted sexual love (with her husband) as one of the highest forms of the pure love she and other *alumbrados* advocated. Costa mentions almost as an aside that many other members of her family, as well as friends, were implicated by Maria's activities.

The lives of individual women illustrate the ways in which women, who had considerably less formal education and thus typically little of the theological sophistication of men, might pick and choose from one or another religious credo or tenet. During a period of religious upheaval such as the sixteenth and seventeenth centuries, the lives of exemplary women can also illustrate change in the religious climate. Willen finds exemplary both the well-known Anne Askew, the noblewoman who was martyred for her Protestant faith in the early days of the English Reformation, and the more obscure Margaret Toftes, who made "heresy into a family affair," as did many women of this epoch. As Willen and Ortega Costa both demonstrate, women not only provided individual witness, they also served as a model for other family members: Toftes's mother and husband were also implicated for heretical activities.

After the Catholic or Counter Reformation, women appear in somewhat different roles. Argula von Grumbach, Maria de Cazalla, Anne Askew, and Margaret Toftes are representative of the many women who acted on their religious principles in the early days of the Reformation. Because of historical circumstances and national differences, the experience and fate of each individual also differed. The Jansenist women studied by F. Ellen Weaver were typical of this seventeenth-century reformist movement, which was never more than marginally accepted within the Catholic church. The majority of Weaver's female exemplars were literate and educated adherents of Jansenism. Weaver first discusses Mlle. de Joncoux, whose translation into French of the Latin notes of Pascal's *Provincial Letters* facilitated the work's popularization. A second important case study is that of Mme. de Fontpertuis, whose financial support of the convent and nuns of Port-Royal was a critical factor in its survival. To Weaver, these women illustrate the particular combination of "erudition and spirituality," offering evidence of the support of literary as well as pious endeavors that she identifies with Jansenist women. Through her study of individual lives, Weaver is able to generalize about the appeal of Jansenism to women.

Individual case studies also reveal the extent to which women either internalized or questioned social values. David Daniel describes three noblewomen in Reformation Hungary; all three exemplify behavior completely in accord with societal norms. Each woman relied on the social and political structure of dynasticism to further her political power, which was then used for either good or evil purposes in her society. The strength and independence of each was seriously inhibited; each found the attainment of personal autonomy impossible. For all three, gender shaped and limited destiny.

Ortega Costa's example of Luisa de Carvajal y Mendoza, however, illustrates that the limitations imposed by gender could also, ironically, be liberating. Luisa, she notes, "chose not to fit in either of the two alternatives open to [Spanish] women: marriage or convent." The vows of poverty, obedience, and finally martyrdom were made to herself; in search of this last, ultimately elusive, goal, Luisa traveled to England to bear witness to her Catholic faith. Ortega Costa concludes that this woman's example brought both new and backsliding Catholics into the fold and that Luisa personally considered her gender an asset, for her extraordinary conduct was simply unimaginable in a woman.

Women were thus liberated as well as enslaved during the age of Reformation and Counter Reformation. To the extent that they were forced to accept and fit into the stereotypes that shaped their behavioral options, women were confined. To the extent that they pursued—for themselves individually and collectively in the service of God—new activities and created definitions of spirituality not limited by gender, they were liberated. By the end of the sixteenth century, as within the world of work, women's options had become sharply limited. By the end of the early modern era, religion may also have ceased to provide an opportunity for women's self-actualization. Nevertheless, in the early period of the Reformation and Counter Reformation, women's lives demonstrate that they found social recognition and personal autonomy through activities which challenge our assumption that stereotypical limitations on behavior were accepted by women as well as men.

MERRY E. WIESNER

Nuns, Wives, and Mothers: Women and the Reformation in Germany

It is in many ways anachronistic even to use the word "Germany" when discussing the sixteenth century. At that time, modern-day East and West Germany were politically part of the Holy Roman Empire, a loose confederation of several hundred states, ranging from tiny knightships through free imperial cities to large territorial states. These states theoretically owed obedience to an elected emperor, but in reality they were quite independent and often pursued policies in opposition to the emperor. Indeed, the political diversity and lack of a strong central authority were extremely important to the early success of the Protestant Reformation in Germany. Had Luther been a Frenchman or a Spaniard, his voice would probably have been quickly silenced by the powerful monarchs in those countries.

Because of this diversity, studies of the Reformation in Germany are often limited to one particular area or one particular type of government, such as the free imperial cities. This limited focus is useful when looking at the impact of the Reformation on men, for male participation and leadership in religious change varied depending on whether a territory was ruled by a city council, a nobleman, or a bishop. Male leadership in the Reformation often came from university teachers, so the presence or absence of a university in an area was also an important factor.

When exploring the impact of religious change on women, however, these political and institutional factors are not as important. Except for a few noblewomen who ruled territories while their sons were still minors, women had no formal political voice in any territory of the empire. They did not vote or serve on city councils, and even abbesses were under the direct control of a male church official. Women could not attend universities, and thus did not come into contact with religious ideas through formal theological training. Their role in the Reformation was not so determined by what may be called "public" factors—political structures, educational institutions—as was that of men.

Women's role in the Reformation and the impact of religious change on them did vary throughout Germany, but that variation was largely determined by what might be termed "personal" factors—a woman's status as a nun or laywoman, her marital status, her social and economic class, her occupation. Many of these factors, particularly social and economic class, were also important in determining men's responses to religious change, but they were often secondary to political factors whereas for women they were of prime importance.

The Protestant and Catholic reformers recognized this. Although they generally spoke about and to women as an undifferentiated group and proposed the same ideals of behavior for all women, when the reformers did address distinct groups of women they distinguished them by marital or clerical status. Nuns, single women, mothers, wives, and widows all got special attention in the same way that special treatises were directed to male princes and members of city councils—men set apart from others by their public, political role.

It is important to keep in mind that although a woman's religious actions were largely determined by her personal status, they were not regarded as a private matter, even if they took place within the confines of her own household. No one in the sixteenth century regarded religion or the family as private, as that term is used today. One's inner relationship with God was perhaps a private matter (though even that is arguable), but one's outward religious practices were a matter of great concern for political authorities. Both Protestants and Catholics saw the family as the cornerstone of society, the cornerstone on which all other institutions were constructed, and every political authority meddled in family and domestic concerns. Thus a woman's choice to serve her family meat on Friday or attend the funeral of a friend whose religion was unacceptable was not to be overlooked or regarded as trivial.

Although "personal" is not the same as "private" in Reformation Germany, grouping women by their personal status is still the best way to analyze their role in religious change. This essay thus follows "personal" lines of division and begins with an exploration of the impact of the Reformation on nuns, Beguines, and other female religious. It then looks at single and married women, including a special group of married women, the wives of the Protestant reformers. Although the reformers did not have a special message for noblewomen, the situation of these women warrants separate consideration because their religious choices had the greatest effect on the course of the Reformation. The essay concludes with a discussion of several groups of working women whose labor was directly or indirectly affected by religious change.

FEMALE RELIGIOUS

Women in convents, both cloistered nuns and lay sisters, and other female religious, were the first to confront the Protestant Reformation. In areas becoming Protestant religious change meant both the closing of their houses and a negation of the value and worth of the life they had been living. The Protestant reformers encouraged nuns and sisters to leave their houses and marry, with harsh words concerning the level of morality in the convents, comparing it to that in brothels.[1] Some convents accepted the Protestant message and willingly gave up their houses and land to city and territorial authorities. The nuns renounced their vows, and those who were able to find husbands married, while the others returned to their families or found ways to support themselves on their own. Others did not accept the new religion but recognized the realities of political power and gave up their holdings; these women often continued living together after the Reformation, trying to remain as a religious community, though they often had to rely on their families for support. In some cases the nuns were given a pension. There is no record, however, of what happened to most of these women. Former priests and monks could become pastors in the new Protestant churches, but former nuns had no place in the new church structure.

Many convents, particularly those with high standards of learning and morality and whose members were noblewomen or women from wealthy patrician families, fought the religious change. A good example of this is the St. Clara convent in Nuremberg, whose nuns were all from wealthy Nuremberg families and whose reputation for learning had spread throughout Germany. The abbess at the time of the Reformation was Charitas Pirckheimer, a sister of the humanist Willibald Pirckheimer and herself an accomplished Latinist. In 1525, the Nuremberg city council ordered all the cloisters to close; four of the six male houses in the city dissolved themselves immediately, but both female houses refused. The council first sent official representatives to try to persuade the nuns and then began a program of intimidation. The women, denied confessors and Catholic communion, were forced to hear Protestant sermons four times a week; their servants had difficulty buying food; people threatened to burn the convent, threw stones over the walls, and sang profane songs when they heard the nuns singing. Charitas noted in her memoirs that women often led the attacks and were the most bitter opponents of the nuns. Three families physically dragged their daughters out of the convent, a scene of crying and wailing witnessed by many Nurembergers. The council questioned each nun separately to see if she had any complaints, hoping to find some who would leave voluntarily, and finally confiscated all of the convent's land. None of these measures was successful, and the council eventually left the convent alone, although it forbade the taking in of new novices. The last nun died in 1590.[2]

Charitas' firmness and the loyalty of the nuns to her were perhaps extraordinary, but other abbesses also publicly defended their faith. Elizabeth Gottgabs, the abbess of Oberwesel convent, published a tract against the Lutherans in 1550. Although she denigrated her own work as that of a "poor woman," she hardly held back in her language when evaluating the reformers: "The new evangelical preachers have tried to plug our ears with their abominable uproar . . . our gracious God will not tolerate their foolishness any longer." The letters of two sisters, Katherine and Veronica Rem, explaining why they would not leave their convent in Augsburg were later published without their knowledge by their brother; this pamphlet went through several editions, a sure sign it was being read or at least purchased.[3]

Nuns who chose to leave convents occasionally published works explaining their actions as well. Martha Elizabeth Zitterin published her letters to her mother explaining why she had left the convent at Erfurt; these were republished five times by Protestant authorities in Jena, who never mentioned that the author herself later decided to return to the convent.[4] Even if the former nuns did not publish their stories, these accounts often became part of Protestant hagiography, particularly if the women had left the convent surreptitiously or had been threatened. Katherine von Bora and eight other nuns were smuggled out of their convent at night after they had secretly made contact with Luther. The fact that this occurred on Easter and that they left in a wagon of herring barrels added drama to the story, and Katherine's later marriage to Luther assured that it would be retold many times.

The Jesuits and other leaders of the Catholic Reformation took the opposite position from the Protestants on the value of celibacy, encouraging young women to disobey their parents and enter convents to escape arranged marriages.[5] Although they did not encourage married women to leave their husbands, the Jesuits followed the pre-Reformation tradition in urging husbands to let their wives enter convents if they wished.

The Counter-Reformation church wanted all female religious strictly cloistered, however, and provided no orders for women who wanted to carry out an active apostolate; there was no female equivalent of the Jesuits.[6] The church also pressured Beguines, Franciscan tertiaries, and other sisters who had always moved about somewhat freely or worked out in the community to adopt strict rules of cloister and place themselves under the direct control of a bishop. The women concerned did not always submit meekly, however. The Beguines in Münster, for example, refused to follow the advice of their confessors, who wanted to reform the beguinage and turn it into a cloistered house of Poor Clares. The women, most of whom were members of the city's elite families, appealed to the city council for help in defending their civil rights and traditional liberties. The council appealed to the archbishop of Cologne, the cardinals, and eventually the pope, and, though the women were eventually cloistered, they were allowed to retain certain of their traditional practices.[7] In some ways, the women were caught in the middle of a power struggle between the archbishop and the city council, but they were still able to appeal to the city's pride in its traditional privileges to argue for their own liberties and privileges. Perhaps the fact that they had not been cloistered kept them aware of the realities and symbols of political power.

SINGLE AND MARRIED WOMEN

Of course most of the women in sixteenth-century Germany were not nuns or other female religious but laywomen who lived in families. Their first contact with the Reformation was often shared with the male members of their families. They heard the new teachings proclaimed from a city pulpit, read or looked at broadsides attacking the pope, and listened to traveling preachers attacking celibacy and the monasteries.

The reformers communicated their ideas to women in a variety of ways. Women who could read German might have read Luther's two marriage treatises or any number of Protestant marriage manuals, the first of which was published in Augsburg in 1522. They could have read tracts against celibacy by many reformers, which varied widely in their level of vituperation and criticism of convent life. Both Protestant and Catholic authors wrote books of commonplaces and examples, which contained numerous references to proper and improper female conduct attributed to classical authors, the church fathers, and more recent commentators.

The vast majority of women could not read but received the message orally and visually. Sermons, particularly marriage sermons but also regular Sunday sermons, emphasized the benefits of marriage and the proper roles of husband and wife. Sermons at women's funerals stressed their piety, devotion to family, and trust in God through great trials and tribulations and set up models for other women to follow. Vernacular dramas about marriage replaced pre-Reformation plays about virgin martyrs suffering death rather than losing their virginity. Woodcuts depicted pious married women (their marital status was clear because married women wore their hair covered) listening to sermons or reading the Bible. Protestant pamphlets portrayed the pope with the whore of Babylon, which communicated a message about both the pope and about women. Catholic pamphlets showed Luther as a lustful glutton, driven only by his sexual and bodily needs. Popular stories about Luther's home life and harsh attitudes toward female virginity circulated by word of mouth.

It may be somewhat misleading to focus only on works directed toward women, discussing marriage, or using female imagery, for women read, saw, and heard the more general message of the Reformation as well. Nevertheless, the majority of women probably paid most attention to works they could relate to their own experience, just as one would expect princes to listen more closely to works directed at them, and city council members likewise.

The Protestant reformers did not break sharply with tradition in their ideas about women. For both Luther and Calvin, women were created by God and could be saved through faith; spiritually women and men were equal. In every other respect, however, women were to be subordinate to men. Women's subjection was inherent in their very being and was present from creation—in this the reformers agreed with Aristotle and the classical tradition. It was made more brutal and harsh, however, because of Eve's responsibility for the Fall—in this Luther and Calvin agreed with patristic tradition and with their scholastic and humanist predecessors.[8]

There appears to be some novelty in their rejection of Catholic teachings on the merits of celibacy and championing of marriage as the proper state for all individuals. Though they disagreed on so much else, all Protestant reformers agreed on this point; the clauses discussing marriage in the various Protestant confessions show more similarities than do any other main articles of doctrine or discipline. Even this emphasis on marriage was not that new, however. Civic and Christian humanists also thought that "God had established marriage and family life as the best means for providing spiritual and moral discipline in this world," and they "emphasized marriage and the family as the basic social and economic unit which provided the paradigm for all social relations."[9]

The Protestant exhortation to marry was directed to both sexes, but particularly to women, for whom marriage and motherhood were a vocation as well as a living arrangement. Marriage was a woman's highest calling, the way she could fulfill God's will: in Luther's harsh words, "Let them bear children to death; they are created for that."[10] Unmarried women were suspect, both because they were fighting their natural sex drive, which everyone in the sixteenth century believed to be much stronger than men's, and because they were upsetting the divinely imposed order, which made woman subject to man. Even a woman as prominent and respected as Margaretha Blarer, the sister of Ambrosius Blarer, a reformer in Constance, was criticized for her decision to remain unmarried. Martin Bucer accused her of being "masterless," to which she answered, "Those who have Christ for a master are not masterless." Her brother defended her decision by pointing out that she was very close to his family and took care of the poor and plague victims "as a mother."[11]

The combination of women's spiritual equality, female subordination, and the idealization of marriage proved problematic for the reformers, for they were faced with the issue of women who converted while their husbands did not. What was to take precedence, the woman's religious convictions or her duty of obedience? Luther and Calvin were clear on this. Wives were to obey their husbands, even if they were not Christians; in Calvin's words, a woman "should not desert the partner who is hostile."[12] Marriage was a woman's "calling," her natural state, and she was to serve God through this calling.

Wives received a particularly ambiguous message from the radical reformers, ambiguity which is reflected in a sharp disagreement among historians about the impact of the Radical Reformation on the status of women.[13] Some radical groups allowed believers to leave their unbelieving spouses, but women who did so were expected to remarry quickly and thus come under the control of a male believer. The most radical Anabaptists were fascinated by Old Testament polygamy and accepted the statement in Revelations that the Last Judgment would only come if there were 144,000 "saints" in the world; they actually enforced polygamy for a short time at Münster, though the required number of saints were never born. In practical terms, Anabaptist women were equal only in martyrdom.

Although the leaders of the Counter Reformation continued to view celibacy as a state preferable to matrimony, they realized that most women in Germany would marry and began to publish their own marriage manuals to counter those published by Protestants. The ideal wives and mothers they described were, however, no different than those of the Protestants; both wanted women to be "chaste, silent, and obedient."[14]

The ideas of the reformers did not stay simply within the realm of theory but led to political and institutional changes. Some of these changes were the direct results of Protestant doctrine, and some of them had unintended, though not unforeseeable, consequences. We have already examined one of these changes—the closing of the convents—and there were a great many others which affected the lives of single and married laywomen.

Every Protestant territory passed a marriage ordinance that stressed wifely obedience and proper Christian virtues and set up a new court or broadened the jurisdiction of an existing court to handle marriage and morals cases which had previously been handled by church courts. They also passed sumptuary laws that regulated weddings and baptisms, thereby trying to make these ceremonies more purely Christian by limiting the number of guests and prohibiting profane activities such as dancing and singing.[15] Though such laws were never completely successful, the tone of these two ceremonies, which marked the two perhaps most important events in a woman's life, became much less exuberant. Religious processions, such as Corpus Christi parades, which had included both men and women, and in which even a city's prostitutes took part, were prohibited. The public processions that remained were generally those of guild masters and journeymen, at which women were onlookers only. Women's participation in rituals such as funerals was limited, for Protestant leaders wanted neither professional mourners nor relatives to take part in extravagant wailing and crying. Lay female confraternities, which had provided emotional and economic assistance for their members and charity for the needy, were also forbidden, and no similar all-female groups replaced them.

The Protestant reformers attempted to do away with the veneration of Mary and the saints. This affected both men and women, because some of the strongest adherents of the cult of the Virgin had been men. For women, the loss of St. Anne, Mary's mother, was particularly hard, for she was a patron saint of pregnant women; now they were instructed to pray during labor and childbirth to Christ, a celibate male, rather than to a woman who had also been a mother. The Protestant martyrs replaced the saints to some degree, at least as models worthy of emulation, but they were not to be prayed to and they did not give their names to any days of the year. The Protestant Reformation not only downplayed women's public ceremonial role; it also stripped the calendar of celebrations honoring women and ended the power female saints and their relics were believed to have over people's lives. Women who remained Catholic still had female saints to pray to, but the number of new female saints during the Counter Reformation was far fewer than the number of new male saints, for two important avenues to sanctity, missionary and pastoral work, were closed to women.[16]

Because of the importance Protestant reformers placed on Bible-reading in the vernacular, many of them advocated opening schools for girls as well as boys. The number of such schools which opened was far fewer than the reformers had originally hoped, and Luther in particular also muted his call for mass education after the turmoil of the Peasants' War.[17] The girls' schools that were opened stressed morality and decorum; in the words of the Memmingen school ordinance from 1587, the best female pupil was one noted for her "great diligence and application in learning her catechism, modesty, obedience, and excellent penmanship."[18] These schools taught sewing as well as reading and singing, and religious instruction was often limited to memorizing the catechism.

Along with these changes that related directly to Protestant doctrine, the Reformation brought with it an extended period of war and destruction in which individuals and families were forced to move frequently from one place to another. Women whose husbands were exiled for religious reasons might also have been forced to leave. Their houses and goods were usually confiscated whether they left town or not. If allowed to stay, they often had to support a family and were still held suspect by neighbors and authorities. A woman whose husband was away fighting could go years without hearing from him and never be allowed to marry again if there was some suspicion he might still be alive.

Women were not simply passive recipients of the Reformation and the ideas and changes it brought but indeed responded to them actively. Swept up by the enthusiasm of the first years of the Reformation, single and married women often stepped beyond what were considered acceptable roles for women. Taking literally Luther's idea of a priesthood of all believers, women as well as uneducated men began to preach and challenge religious authorities. In 1524 in Nuremberg, the city council took action against a certain Frau Voglin, who had set herself up in the hospital church and was preaching. In a discussion after a Sunday sermon by a Lutheran-leaning prior, a woman in Augsburg spoke to a bishop's representative who had been sent to hear the sermon and called the bishop a brothel manager because he had a large annual income from concubinage fees.[19] Several women in Zwickau, inspired by the preaching of Thomas Müntzer, also began to preach in 1521.[20]

All of these actions were viewed with alarm by civic authorities, who even objected to women's getting together to discuss religion. In their view, female preachers clearly disobeyed the Pauline injunction against women speaking in church and moved perilously close to claiming an official religious role. In 1529, the Zwickau city council banished several of the women who had gathered together and preached.[21] In the same year, the Memmingen city council forbade maids to discuss religion while drawing water at neighborhood wells. No German government forbade women outright to read the Bible, as Henry VIII of England did in 1543, but the authorities did attempt to prevent them from discussing it publicly.

After 1530, women's public witnessing of faith was more likely to be prophesying than preaching. In many ways, female prophets were much less threatening than female preachers, for the former had biblical parallels, clear biblical justification, and no permanent official function. Ursula Jost and Barbara Rebstock in Strasbourg began to have visions and revelations concerning the end of the world. When Melchior Hoffman, the Spiritualist, came to Strasbourg, they convinced him he was the prophet Elijah born again and thus one of the signs of the impending Apocalypse. He published seventy-two of Ursula's revelations, advising all Christians to read them. They were written in the style of Old Testament prophecy and became popular in the Rhineland and Netherlands.[22] Several other female Anabaptists also had visions that were spread by word of mouth and as broadsides or small pamphlets. Though these women were illiterate, their visions were full of biblical references, which indicates that, like Lollard women in England, they had memorized much of the Bible. Female prophecy was accepted in most radical sects, for they emphasized direct revelation and downplayed theological training. That these sects were small and loosely structured was also important for the continued acceptance of female revelation; in Münster, the one place where Anabaptism became the state religion, female prophecy was suppressed.

Not all female visionaries were radicals, however. Mysticism and ecstatic visions remained an acceptable path to God for Catholic women and increased in popularity in Germany after the works of Saint Theresa were translated and her ideas became known. Even Lutheran women reported miracles and visions. Catherine Binder, for example, asserted that her speech had been restored after seven years when a pastor gave her a copy of the Lutheran Catechism.[23] The Lutheran clergy were suspicious of such events, but did not reject them out of hand.

With the advent of the religious wars, female prophets began to see visions of war and destruction and to make political, as well as religious and eschatological, predictions. Susanna Rugerin had been driven far from her home by imperial armies and began to see an angel who revealed visions of Gustavus Adolphus. The visions of Juliana von Duchnik were even more dramatic. In 1628 she brought a warning from God to Duke Wallenstein, a commander of imperial troops, telling him to leave his estate because God would no longer protect him. Though Wallenstein's wife was very upset, his supporters joked about it, commenting that the emperor got letters from only the pope, while Wallenstein got them directly from God. Von Duchnik published this and other of her visions the following year and in 1634 returned to Wallenstein's camp warning him that she had seen a vision of him trying to climb a ladder into heaven; the ladder collapsed, and he fell to earth with blood and poison pouring out of his heart. Though Wallenstein himself continued to dismiss her predictions, others around him took her seriously. Her visions in this case proved accurate, for Wallenstein was assassinated less than a month later.[24] In general, female prophets were taken no less seriously than their male counterparts.

The most dramatic public affirmation of faith a woman could make was martyrdom. Most of the female martyrs in Germany were Anabaptists, and the law granted women no special treatment, except for occasionally delaying execution if they were pregnant. Women were more likely to be drowned than beheaded, for it was thought they would faint at the sight of the executioner's sword and make his job more difficult. Some of them were aware that this reduced the impact of their deaths and wanted a more public form of execution. A good indication of the high degree of religious understanding among many Anabaptist women comes from their interrogations. They could easily discuss the nature of Christ, the doctrine of the Real Presence, and baptism, quoting extensively from the Bible. As a woman known simply as Claesken put it, "Although I am a simple person before men, I am not unwise in the knowledge of the Lord." Her interrogators were particularly upset because she had converted many people: they commented, "Your condemnation will be greater than your husband's because you can read and have misled him."[25]

Although most of the women who published religious works during the Reformation were either nuns or noblewomen, a few middle-class women wrote hymns, religious poetry, and some polemics. Ursula Weide published a pamphlet against the abbot of Pegau, denouncing his support of celibacy.[26] The earliest Protestant hymnals include several works by women, often verse renditions of the Psalms or Gospels. Justitia Sanger, a blind woman from Braunschweig, published a commentary on ninety-six Psalms in 1593, dedicating it to King Frederick II of Denmark.[27] Female hymn-writing became even more common in the seventeenth century when the language of hymns shifted from aggressive and martial to emotional and pious; it was more acceptable for a woman to write of being washed in the blood of the Lamb than of strapping on the armor of God. Not all female religious poetry from the seventeenth century was meekly pious, however. Anna Oven Hoyer was driven from place to place during the Thirty Years' War, finally finding refuge in Sweden. She praised David Joris and Caspar von Schwenkfeld in her writings, which she published without submitting them for clerical approval. Some of them, including her "Spiritual Conversation between a Mother and Child about True Christianity," were later burned as heretical. In this dialogue she attacked the Lutheran clergy for laxness, greed, pride, and trust in wordly learning and largely blamed them for the horrors of the Thirty Years' War.[28]

Seventeenth-century women often wrote religious poems, hymns, and prose meditations for private purposes as well as for publication. They wrote to celebrate weddings, baptisms, and birthdays, to console friends, to praise deceased relatives, to instruct and provide examples for their children. If a woman's works were published while she was still alive, they included profuse apologies about her unworthiness and presumption. Many such works were published posthumously by husbands or fathers and include a note from these men that writing never distracted the author from her domestic tasks but was done only in her spare time. Unfortunately, similar works by sixteenth-century German women are rare. Thus, to examine the religious convictions of the majority of women who did not preach, prophesy, publish, or become martyrs, we must look at their actions within the context of their domestic and community life.

Married women whose religious convictions matched those of their husbands often shared equally in the results of those convictions. If these convictions conflicted with local authorities and the men were banished for religious reasons, their wives were expected to follow them. Because house and goods were generally confiscated, the wives had no choice in the matter anyway. Women whose husbands were in hiding, fighting religious wars, or assisting Protestant churches elsewhere supported the family and covered for their husbands, often sending them supplies as well. Wealthy women set up endowments for pastors and teachers and provided scholarships for students at Protestant, and later Jesuit, universities.

Many married women also responded to the Protestant call to make the home, in the words of the humanist Urbanus Rhegius, "a seminary for the church."[29] They carried out what might best be called domestic missionary activity, praying and reciting the catechism with their children and servants. Those who were literate might read some vernacular religious literature, and, because reading was done aloud in the sixteenth century, this was also a group activity. What they could read was limited by the level of their reading ability, the money available to buy books, and the effectiveness of the city censors at keeping out unwanted or questionable material. Women overcame some of the limitations on their reading material by paying for translations, thus continuing a tradition begun before the invention of the printing press.[30] The frequency of widowhood in the sixteenth century meant that women often carried religious ideas, and the pamphlets and books that contained them, to new households when they remarried, and a few men actually admitted to having been converted by their wives. The role of women as domestic missionaries was recognized more clearly by Catholics and English Protestants than it was by continental Protestants, who were obsessed with wifely obedience. Richard Hooker, a theorist for the Anglican church, commented that the Puritans made special efforts to convert women because they were "diligent in drawing away their husbands, children, servants, friends, and allies the same way."[31] Jesuits encouraged the students at their seminaries to urge their mothers to return to confession and begin Catholic practices in the home; in this way, an indifferent or even Lutheran father might be brought back into the fold.[32]

There are several spectacular examples among noble families of women whose quiet pressure eventually led to their husbands' conversions and certainly many among common people that are not recorded. But what about a married woman whose efforts failed? What could a woman do whose religious convictions differed from those of her husband? In some areas, the couple simply lived together as adherents of different religions. The records for Bamberg, for example, show that in 1595 about 25 percent of the households were mixed marriages, with one spouse Catholic and the other Lutheran. Among the members of the city council the proportion was even higher—43 percent had spouses of a different religion, so this was not something which simply went unnoticed by authorities.[33] Bamberg was one of the few cities in Germany which allowed two religions to worship freely; therefore, mixed marriages may have been only a local phenomenon. This, however, has not yet been investigated in other areas.

Continued cohabitation was more acceptable if the husband was of a religion considered acceptable in the area. In 1631, for example, the Strasbourg city council considered whether citizens should lose their citizenship if they married Calvinists. It decided that a man would not "because he can probably draw his spouse away from her false religion, and bring her on to the correct path." He would have to pay a fine, though, for "bringing an unacceptable person into the city." A woman who married a Calvinist would lose her citizenship, however, "because she would let herself easily be led into error in religion by her husband, and led astray."[34]

As a final resort, a married woman could leave her husband (and perhaps family) and move to an area where the religion agreed with her own. This was extremely difficult for women who were not wealthy, and most of the recorded cases involve noblewomen with independent incomes and sympathetic fathers. Even if a woman might gather enough resources to support herself, she was not always welcome, despite the strength of her religious convictions, for she had violated that most basic of norms, wifely obedience. Protestant city councils were suspicious of any woman who asked to be admitted to citizenship independently and questioned her intensely about her marital status. Catholic cities such as Munich were more concerned about whether the woman who wanted to immigrate had always been a good Catholic than whether or not she was married, particularly if she wished to enter a convent.[35]

Exceptions were always made for wives of Anabaptists. A tailor's wife in Nuremberg was allowed to stay in the city and keep her house as long as she recanted her Anabaptist beliefs and stayed away from all other Anabaptists, including her husband, who had been banished.[36] After the siege of Münster, Anabaptist women and children began to drift back into the city and were allowed to reside there if they abjured Anabaptism and swore an oath of allegiance to the bishop.[37] Both Protestant and Catholic authorities viewed Anabaptism as a heresy and a crime so horrible it broke the most essential human bonds.

It was somewhat easier for unmarried women and widows to leave a territory for religious reasons, and in many cases persecution or war forced them out. A widow wrote to the Nuremberg city council after the city had turned Lutheran that she wanted to move there "because of the respect and love she has for the word of God, which is preached here [that is, Nuremberg] truly and purely"; after a long discussion, the council allowed her to move into the city.[38] But women still had greater difficulties than men being accepted as residents in any city. Wealthier widows had to pay the normal citizenship fee and find male sponsors, both of which were difficult for women, who generally did not command as many financial resources or have as many contacts as men of their class. Because of this, and because innkeepers were forbidden to take in any woman traveling alone, no matter what her age or class, women's cities of refuge were often limited to those in which they had relatives.

Women who worked to support themselves generally had to make special supplications to city councils to be allowed to stay and work. Since they had not been trained in a guild in the city, the council often overrode guild objections in permitting them to make or sell small items to support themselves and was more likely to grant a woman's request if she was seen as particularly needy or if her story was especially pathetic. A woman whose husband had been killed in the Thirty Years' War asked permission in 1632 to live in Strasbourg and bake pretzels; this was granted to her and several others despite the objections of the bakers because, in the council's words, "all of the supplicants are poor people, that are particularly hard-pressed in these difficult times."[39] Another woman was allowed to make tonic and elixirs in Strasbourg after a city pastor assured the council that "she is a pious and godly woman who left everything to follow the true word of God."[40]

PASTORS' WIVES

One of the most dramatic changes brought about by the Protestant Reformation was the replacement of celibate priests by married pastors with wives and families. Many of the wives of the early reformers had themselves been nuns, and they were crossing one of society's most rigid borders by marrying, becoming brides of men rather than brides of Christ. During the first few years of the Reformation, they were still likened to priests' concubines in the public mind and had to create a respectable role for themselves. They were often living demonstrations of their husbands' convictions and were expected to be models of wifely obedience and Christian charity; the reformers had particularly harsh words for pastors who could not control their wives. Pastors' wives were frequently asked to be godmothers and thereby could be "important agents in the diffusion of evangelical domesticity from the household of the clergy to the rest of the population."[41] But they also had to bring the child a gift appropriate to its social standing from the meager pastoral treasury. The demands on pastors' wives were often exacerbated by their husbands' lack of concern for material matters. Often former priests or monks, these men had never before worried about an income and continued to leave such things in God's (or actually their wives') hands.

Pastors' wives opened up their homes to students and refugees, providing them with food, shelter, and medical care. This meant buying provisions, brewing beer, hiring servants, growing fruits and vegetables, and gathering herbs for a household that could expand overnight from ten to eighty. Katherine von Bora purchased and ran an orchard, personally overseeing the care of apple and pear trees and selling the fruit to provide income for the household. She occasionally took part in the theological discussions that went on after dinner in the Luther household and was teased by her husband for her intellectual interests; he called her "Professor Katie." Urbanus Rhegius had a slightly different attitude and published his discussions with his well-educated wife because he felt they could assist others without formal theological training in understanding Lutheran ideas. His wife also had a full round of duties and complained that she and her husband did not have as much time to discuss things as she would have wished.

Other pastors' wives assisted in running city hospitals, orphanages, and infirmaries, sometimes at the suggestion of their husbands and sometimes on their own initiative. Katherine Zell, the wife of Matthias Zell and a tireless worker for the Reformation in Strasbourg, inspected the local hospital and was appalled by what she found there. She demanded the hospital master be replaced because he served the patients putrid, fatty meat, "does not know the name of Christ," and mumbled the table grace "so you can't tell if it's a prayer or a fart."[42] Wealthy women set up endowments for pastors and teachers and provided scholarships for students at Protestant, and later Jesuit, universities.

NOBLEWOMEN

Neither the Protestant nor the Catholic reformers differentiated between noblewomen and commoners in their public advice to women; noblewomen, too, were to be "chaste, silent, and obedient." Privately, however, they recognized that such women often held a great deal of power and made special attempts to win them over. Luther corresponded regularly with a number of prominent noblewomen, and Calvin was even more assiduous at "courting ladies in high places."[43]

Noblewomen, both married and unmarried, religious and lay, had the most opportunity to express their religious convictions, and the consequences of their actions were more far-reaching than those of most women. Prominent noblewomen who left convents could create quite a sensation, particularly if, like Ursula of Münsterberg, they wrote a justification of why they had left and if their actions put them in opposition to their families. Disagreements between husband and wife over matters of religion could lead to the wife being exiled, as in the case of Elisabeth of Brandenburg. They could also lead to mutual toleration, however, as they did for Elisabeth's daughter, also named Elisabeth, who married Eric, the duke of Brunswick-Calenburg. She became a Lutheran while her husband remained a Catholic, to which his comment was: "My wife does not interfere with and molest us in our faith, and therefore we will leave her undisturbed and unmolested in hers."[44] After his death, she became regent and introduced the Reformation into Brunswick, with the assistance of Matthias Corvinus. Several other female rulers also promoted independently the Reformation in their territories, while others convinced their husbands to do so. Later in the century noble wives and widows were also influential in opening up territories to the Jesuits.

Most of these women were following paths of action that had been laid out by male rulers and had little consciousness of themselves as women carrying out a reformation. Others as well judged their actions on the basis of their inherited status and power, for, despite John Knox's bitter fulminations against "the monstrous regiment of women," female rulers were not regarded as unusual in the sixteenth century. Only if a noblewoman ventured beyond summoning and protecting a male reformer or signing church ordinances to commenting publicly on matters of theology was she open to criticism as a woman going beyond what was acceptable.

The best known example of such a noblewoman was Argula von Grumbach, who wrote to the faculty of the University of Ingolstadt in 1523 protesting the university's treatment of a young teacher accused of Lutheran leanings. She explained her reasons: "I am not unacquainted with the word of Paul that women should be silent in Church [1 Tim. 1:2] but, when no man will or can speak, I am driven by the word of the Lord when he said, 'He who confesses me on earth, him will I confess, and he who denies me, him will I deny' [Matt. 10, Luke 9] and I take comfort in the words of the prophet Isaiah [3:12, but not exact], I will send you children to be your princes and women to be your rulers."[45]

She also wrote to the duke of Bavaria, her overlord, about the matter. Neither the university nor the duke bothered to reply but instead ordered her husband or male relatives to control her and deprived her husband of an official position and its income as a show of displeasure. Instead of having the desired effect, these actions led her to write to the city council at Ingolstadt and to both Luther and Frederick the Wise of Saxony to request a hearing at the upcoming imperial diet at Nuremberg. Her letters were published without her knowledge, provoking a student at Ingolstadt to write an anonymous satirical poem telling her to stick to spinning and hinting that she was interested in the young teacher because she was sexually frustrated. She answered with a long poem that was both satirical and serious, calling the student a coward for writing anonymously and giving numerous biblical examples of women called on to give witness. This ended her public career, although she wrote to Luther and other reformers several times after this (the letters are no longer extant), received Luther's German works from Georg Spalatin, and visited Luther in 1530. Though she died in obscurity, her story was widely known and frequently reprinted as part of Lutheran books of witnesses and martyrs.

In the case of Argula von Grumbach, her sex was clearly more important than her noble status. Political authorities would not have ignored a man of similar status who was in contact with major reformers. Grumbach exhibited a strong sense of herself as a woman in her writings, even before her detractors dwelled on that point alone. Despite the extraordinary nature of her actions, she did not see herself as in any way unusual, commenting in her letter to the Ingolstadt city council that "if I die, a hundred women will write to you, for there are many who are more learned and adept than I am." She recognized that her religious training, which began with the German Bible her father gave her when she was ten, was shared by many other literate women and expected them to respond in the same way she did, proclaiming "the word of God as a member of the Christian church."[46]

WORKING WOMEN

Like noblewomen, women engaged in various occupations did not receive any special message from the reformers. Even Luther's harsh diatribe against the prostitutes of Wittenberg was addressed to the university students who used their services. This is because in the sixteenth century, women who carried out a certain occupation were rarely thought of as a group. A woman's work identity was generally tied to her family identity.

This can best be explained with an example. For a man to become a baker, he apprenticed himself to a master baker for a certain number of years, then spent several more years as a journeyman, and finally might be allowed to make his masterpiece—a loaf of bread or a fancy cake—open his own shop, marry, and hire his own apprentices and journeymen. He was then a full-fledged member of the bakers' guild, took part in parades, festivals, and celebrations with his guild brothers, lit candles at the guild altar in Catholic cities, and perhaps participated in city government as a guild representative. He was thus a baker his entire life and had a strong sense of work identity.

For a woman to become a baker, she had to marry a baker. She was not allowed to participate in the apprenticeship system, though she could do everything in the shop her husband could. If he died, she might carry on the shop a short time as a widow, but, if she was young enough, she generally married again and took on whatever her new husband's occupation was. She had no voice in guild decisionmaking and took no part in guild festivals, though she may have actually baked more than her husband. Changes in her status were not determined by her own level of training but by changes in her marital or family status. Thus, although in terms of actual work she was as much a baker as her husband, she, and her society, viewed her as a baker's wife. Her status as wife was what was important in the eyes of sixteenth-century society, and, as we have seen, many treatises and laws were directed to wives.

Although female occupations were not directly singled out in religious theory, several were directly affected by changes in religious practices. The demand for votive candles, which were often made and sold by women, dropped dramatically, and these women were forced to find other means of support. The demand for fish declined somewhat, creating difficulties for female fishmongers, although traditional eating habits did not change immediately when fast days were no longer required. Municipal brothels were closed in the sixteenth century, a change often linked with the Protestant Reformation. This occurred in Catholic cities as well, however, and may be more closely linked with general concerns for public order and morality and obsession with women's sexuality than with any specific religion.[47]

Charitable institutions were secularized and centralized, a process which had begun before the Reformation and was speeded up in the sixteenth century in both Protestant and Catholic territories. Many of the smaller charities were houses set up for elderly indigent women who lived off the original endowment and small fees they received for mourning or preparing bodies for burial. They had in many cases elected one of their number as head of the house but were now moved into large hospitals under the direction of a city official. The women who worked in these hospitals as cooks, nurses, maids, and cleaning women now became city, rather than church, employees. Outwardly their conditions of employment changed little, but the Protestant deemphasis on good works may have changed their conception of the value of their work, particularly given their minimal salaries and abysmal working conditions.

Midwives had long performed emergency baptisms if they or the parents believed the child would not live. This created few problems before the Reformation because Catholic doctrine taught that if there was some question about the regularity of this baptism and the child lived, the infant could be rebaptized "on the condition" it had not been baptized properly the first time; conditional baptism was also performed on foundlings. This assured the parents that their child had been baptized correctly while avoiding the snare of rebaptism, which was a crime in the Holy Roman Empire. In 1531, however, Luther rejected all baptisms "on condition" if it was known any baptism had already been carried out and called for a normal baptism in the case of foundlings. By 1540, most Lutheran areas were no longer baptizing "on condition," and those persons who still supported the practice were occasionally branded Anabaptists. This made it extremely important that midwives and other laypeople knew how to conduct correctly an emergency baptism.

Midwives were thus examined, along with pastors, church workers, and teachers, in the visitations conducted by pastors and city leaders in many cities, and "shocking irregularities" in baptismal practice were occasionally discovered. In one story, perhaps apocryphal, a pastor found one midwife confident in her reply that, yes, she certainly baptized infants in the name of the Holy Trinity—Caspar, Melchior, Balthazar! During the course of the sixteenth century, most Protestant cities included a long section on emergency baptisms in their general baptismal ordinance and even gave copies of this special section to the city's midwives. They also began to require midwives to report all illegitimate children and asked them to question any unmarried mother about who the father of the child was. If she refused to reveal his identity, midwives were to question her "when the pains of labor are greatest," for her resistance would probably be lowest at that point.[48]

In areas of Germany where Anabaptism flourished, Anabaptist midwives were charged with claiming they had baptized babies when they really had not, so that a regular church baptism would not be required.[49] In other areas the opposite seems to have been the case. Baptism was an important social occasion and a chance for the flaunting of wealth and social position, and parents paid the midwife to conveniently forget she had baptized a child so that the normal church ceremony could be carried out.

CONCLUSIONS

Despite the tremendous diversity of female experience in Germany during the Reformation, two factors are constant. First, a woman's ability to respond to the Reformation and the avenues her responses could take were determined more by her gender than by any other factor. The reformers—Catholic and Protestant, magisterial and radical—all agreed on the proper avenues for female response to their ideas. The responses judged acceptable were domestic, personal, and familial—prayer, meditation, teaching the catechism to children, singing or writing hymns, entering or leaving a convent. Public responses, either those presented publicly or those which concerned dogma or the church as a public institution, shocked and outraged authorities, even if they agreed with the ideas being expressed. A woman who backed the "wrong" religion was never as harshly criticized as a man; this was seen as simply evidence of her irrational and weak nature. One who supported the "right" religion too vigorously and vocally, however, might be censured by her male compatriots for "too much enthusiasm" and overstepping the bounds of proper female decorum. Thus, whatever a woman's status or class, her responses were judged according to both religious and sexual ideology. Since women of all classes heard this message from pamphlet and pulpit and felt its implications in laws and ordinances, it is not at all surprising that most of them accepted it.

Second, most women experienced the Reformation as individuals. Other than nuns in convents, women were not a distinct social class, economic category, or occupational group; thus, they had no opportunity for group action. They passed religious ideas along the networks of their family, friends, and neighbors, but these networks had no official voice in a society that was divided according to male groups. A woman who challenged her husband or other male authorities in matters of religion was challenging basic assumptions about gender roles, and doing this alone, with no official group to support her. Even women who reformed territories did so as individual rulers. Men, on the other hand, were preached to as members of groups and responded collectively. They combined with other men in city councils, guilds, consistories, cathedral chapters, university faculties, and many other bodies to effect or halt religious change. Their own individual religious ideas were affirmed by others, whether or not they were ultimately successful in establishing the religious system they desired.

The strongest female protest against the Reformation in Germany came from the convents, where women were used to expressing themselves on religious matters and thinking of themselves as members of a spiritual group. Thus, although the Protestant reformers did champion a woman's role as wife and mother by closing the convents and forbidding female lay confraternities, they cut off women's opportunities for expressing their spirituality in an all-female context. Catholic women could still enter convents, but those convents were increasingly cut off from society. By the mid-seventeenth century, religion for all women in Germany, whether lay or clerical, had become much more closely tied to a household.

NOTES

The research for this article was carried out in several archives in France and Germany and at the Newberry Library in Chicago. I wish to thank the Deutscher Akademischer Austauschdienst, the American Council of Learned Societies, and the Exxon Foundation for their support.

1. Lyndal Roper, "Discipline and Respectability: Prostitution and the Reformation in Augsburg," *History Workshop* 19 (Spring 1985):10.

2. Franz Binder, *Charitas Pirckheimer: Aebtissen von St. Clara zu Nürnberg* (Freiburg: Herder'sche Verlagshandlung, 1878).

3. "Litterarische Gegnerinnen Luthers," *Historische-politische Blätter für das Katholische Deutschland* 139 (1907).

4. C. F. Paullini, *Hoch- und Wohlgelehrtes Teutsches Frauenzimmer* (Frankfurt and Leipzig: Johann Michael Funcke, 1712), p. 166.

5. R. Po-Chia Hsia, *Society and Religion in Münster, 1535–1618* (New Haven: Yale University Press, 1984), p. 82.

6. Ruth Liebowitz, "Virgins in the Service of Christ: The Dispute over an Active Apostolate for Women during the Counter-Reformation," in *Women of Spirit*, ed. Rosemary Radford Ruether (New York: Simon and Schuster, 1979), p. 140.

7. Hsia, pp. 142–47.

8. Merry Wiesner, "Luther and Women: The Death of Two Marys," in *Disciplines of Faith: Religion, Patriarchy, and Politics,* ed. Raphael Samuel, James Obelkevich, and Lyndal Roper (London: Routledge and Kegan Paul, 1987); John H. Bratt, "The Role and Status of Women in the Writings of John Calvin," in *Renaissance, Reformation, Resurgence,* ed. Peter de Kierk (Grand Rapids, Mich.: Calvin Theological Seminary, 1976); Charmarie Jenkins Blaisdell, "Response to Bratt" in ibid.

9. John C. Yost, "Changing Attitudes toward Married Life in Civic and Christian Humanism," *ASRR Occasional Papers* 1 (December 1977):164.

10. *D. Martin Luthers sämmtliche Werke* (Erlangen and Frankfurt, 1826–57), 20:84.

11. Maria Heinsius, *Das unüberwindliche Wort: Frauen der Reformationszeit* (Munich: Chr. Kaiser, 1953), p. 45.

12. Quoted in Bratt, p. 9.

13. G. H. Williams in *The Radical Reformation* (Philadelphia: Westminster Press, 1962) states: "The Anabaptist insistence on the covenental principle of the freedom of conscience for all adult believers constituted a major breach in the patriarchalism and

a momentous step in the Western emancipation of women." (pp. 506–507) Claus-Peter Clasen, on the other hand, comments in *Anabaptism: A Social History, 1525–1618* (Ithaca, N.Y.: Cornell University Press, 1972): "Revolutionary as Anabaptism was in some respects, the sect showed no inclination to grant women a greater role than they customarily held in sixteenth-century society" (p. 207).

14. Suzanne Hull, *Chaste, Silent and Obedient: English Books for Women, 1475–1640* (San Marino, Calif.: Huntingdon Library, 1982).

15. Lyndal Roper, "Going to Church and Street: Weddings in Reformation Augsburg," *Past and Present* 106 (February 1985):62–101.

16. Peter Burke, "How To Be a Counter-Reformation Saint," in *Religion and Society in Early Modern Europe,* ed. Kaspar von Greyerz (London: George Allen and Unwin, 1984), pp. 45–55.

17. Gerald Strauss, "Lutheranism and Literacy: A Reassessment," in Greyerz, *Religion and Society,* p. 113.

18. Memmingen Stadtarchiv, Deutsches Schulwesen, 397/1, "Ordnung der Königen in der Mädchenschule" (1587).

19. Hans-Christoph Rublack, "Martin Luther and the Urban Social Experience," *Sixteenth Century Journal* 16/1 (1985):28.

20. Susan Karant-Nunn, "Continuity and Change: Some Effects of the Reformation on the Women of Zwickau," *Sixteenth Century Journal* 13/2 (1982):38.

21. Ibid., p. 40.

22. Williams, p. 263.

23. Johann Henry Feustking, *Gyneceum Haeritico Fanaticum* . . . (Frankfurt and Leipzig: Christian Gerdes, 1704), p. 178.

24. Gottfried Arnold, *Unpartheiische Kirchen und Ketzerhistorie* . . . (Frankfurt: Thomas Fritschens sel. Erben, 1729), pp. 232, 222–24.

25. T. J. Van Braght, *The Bloody Theatre or Martyrs' Mirror,* ed. Edward Underhill (London: Hanserd Knollys Society, 1850), 2:33, 202–17.

26. Robert Stupperich, "Die Frauen in der Publizistik der Reformation," *Archiv für Kulturgeschichte,* 37 (1927):227.

27. Paullini, p. 146.

28. Arnold, pp. 104–107.

29. Quoted in Gordon Rupp, "Protestant Spirituality in the first Age of the Reformation" in *Popular Belief and Practice,* ed. Derek Baker, Studies in Church History, 8 (Cambridge: Cambridge University Press, 1972), p. 169.

30. Susan Groag Bell, "Medieval Women Book Owners: Arbiters of Lay Piety and Ambassadors of Culture," *Signs* 7/4 (1982):766.

31. Quoted in Patrick Collinson, "The Role of Women in the English Reformation Illustrated by the Life and Friendships of Anne Locke," in *Studies in Church History,* vol. 2, ed. G. J. Cuming (London: Thomas Nelson, 1975), p. 259.

32. Hsia, p. 67.

33. Hans-Christoph Rublack, "Zur Sozialstruktur der protestantischen Minderheit in der geistlichen Residenz Bamberg am Ende des 16. Jahrhunderts," in *The Urban Classes, the Nobility and the Reformation: Studies on the Social History of the Reformation in England and Germany,* ed. Wolfgang Mommsen, with Peter Alter and Robert W. Scribner, Publications of the German Historical Institute, London, vol. 5 (Stuttgart: Klett-Cotta, 1979), pp. 140–46.

34. Strasbourg, Archives municipales, Akten der XXI, 1631, fol. 40.

35. Munich, Stadtarchiv, Ratsitszungsprotokolle, 1598, fol. 171; 1601, fol. 24.

36. Nuremberg, Staatsarchiv, Ratsbücher, Rep. 60b, 1541, fol. 230.

37. Hsia, p. 12.

38. Nuremberg, Staatsarchiv, Ratsbücher, Rep. 60b, 1526, fol. 150.

39. Strasbourg, Archives municipales, Akten der XV, 1634, fol. 34.

40. Strasbourg, Archives municipales, Akten der XV, 1636, fol. 242.

41. John Bossy, "Godparenthood: The Fortunes of a Social Institution in Early Modern Christianity," in Greyerz, *Religion and Society*, p. 200.

42. Otto Winckelmann, *Das Fürsorgewesen der Stadt Strassburg* (Leipzig: Heinsius, 1922), 2:76.

43. Charmarie Blaisdell, "Calvin's Letters to Women: The Courting of Ladies in High Places," *Sixteenth Century Journal* 13/3 (1982):67–84.

44. James Anderson, *Ladies of the Reformation* (London: Blackie and Sons, 1857), p. 123.

45. "Wie ain Christliche Fraw des Adels . . . Sendtbrieffe/die Hohenschul zu Ingolstadt (1523)," quoted and translated in Roland Bainton, *Women of the Reformation in Germany and Italy* (Minneapolis: Augsburg, 1971), pp. 97–98.

46. Ibid., p. 100.

47. Roper, "Discipline and Respectability," 21.

48. Merry E. Wiesner, "The Early Modern Midwife: A Case Study," *International Journal of Women's Studies* 6/2 (January/February 1983):26–43. For a more thorough discussion of working women during this period, see my *Working Women in Renaissance Germany* (New Brunswick, N.J.: Rutgers University Press, 1986).

49. Clasen, p. 149.

SUSAN C. KARANT-NUNN

The Women of the Saxon
Silver Mines

However ubiquitous they were, it is no easy task for the researcher to find the women who worked in and around the silver mines of the Erzgebirge (the Ore Mountains), that hilly region of southern Saxony and northern Bohemia that hardly seems mountainous to anyone who has seen the Rockies or the Alps. The Schneeberg, literally "snow mountain," is only 1,542 feet (470 meters) high. The major towns of this district in 1530 were Freiberg, the only one of mid-medieval foundation, given its first charter in 1186; Schneeberg, officially dating from 1479; Annaberg, 1496; Joachimsthal, 1516; and Marienberg, 1521. The silver rush that began about 1470 produced all of these except Freiberg. So eager were people—princes and paupers alike—to find silver that we almost forget that the Erzgebirge also yielded substantial quantities of copper, tin, lead, bismuth, and cobalt, and even a little gold and a few amethysts and topaz.

A duke of Albertine Saxony, George the Bearded, a tireless adversary of Martin Luther, named Annaberg after one of his favorite saints, a patroness of miners, a holy figure alleged to have the power to create silver ore for her supplicants. George had an imposing parish church built there to honor her. It is here that we can find pictorial evidence of the women of the mines, but only the informed visitor to this edifice is likely to spot it. To the left of the main altar and the chancel, over in a corner, stands the ancient Bergaltar, the altar of the silver miners. On its reverse side, and thus even farther back in the corner, is the "tetratych" commissioned of painter Hans Hesse in 1521 by the miners' brotherhood, the *knappschaft*. At the far right of the bottom panel—the viewer devoutly wishes for a flashlight—is the figure of a woman washing silver ore with a sieve over a great wooden tub like a barrel-half. She is the only female among thirty-four people depicted in the various stages of silver production. Her eyes are cast down upon her work, and she has a Mona Lisa smile on her face.[1]

In the woodcut illustrations for his classic work on mining techniques, *De re metallica,* the Saxon scientist, physician, and burgomaster Georgius Agricola[2] tries to convey to his readers the mundane realities of life around all the mines of the Erzgebirge, not just the silver mines.[3] We learn from his drawings, for example, that dogs were everywhere to be found, chewing on bones, lapping water from a stream, curled up on smelting hearths, tolerating the embrace of a small child. However roughly, Agricola tried to re-create the scenes that he had beheld during several decades of observation at shaft entryways, in ore-processing huts, and beside the smelters' ovens. Women were a part of that visual reality even if they were not, or were not regularly, employed about the mines, and Agricola included twenty-one of them in 289 illustrations. Some of the women are shown performing no duty essential to mining but are just part of the landscape; one walks by a processing hut with a covered basket on her back and the handle of another vessel visible in her hand (p. 289); the short skirt of another (p. 315) reveals her servant status, but we can only see her back; one, thinking to be unobserved, closely embraces a man in a hut, while outside a miner unloads ore and male washers wash it (p. 343); a lady, evident by her full sleeves, long skirt, headdress, and the peacock perched on the wall above her, leaves a yard where cakes of copper are being broken by an iron-shod stamping machine (p. 501); a servant girl sits barefoot on the foreground and eats her lunch while salt is boiled behind her (p. 553); a mother carries her clinging infant past a glassblower's furnace (p. 591).

As for their tasks that did have to do with mining, Hesse's and Agricola's artistry might lead us to think that the women engaged around the mines almost exclusively sorted or washed ore. Agricola depicts a table with decoratively carved legs at which stand (even though the text says they sit) four women supposed to be culling plain rock from metal-bearing mineral (p. 268). The author says, "The work of sorting the crude metal or the best ore is done not only by men, but also by boys and women." Whether the two beardless youths also at the table are intended to be boys is uncertain. They are as tall as the women. Two of the feminine workers seem to be arguing, for one points a finger accusatorily at the other; one of the other women holds a pointed implement in the face of one of the men and seems to speak animatedly to him. Did Agricola perhaps amuse his (male) audience with this stereotype of the quarrelsome and garrulous daughters of Eve? In all but two of the remaining woodcuts that include women (pp. 292–93, 317, 326, 332–33), Agricola has this gender at the task of washing ore, a natural transference of the traditional feminine household chore to the nondomestic sphere. Such jobs were thought suited to women. These laborers used sieves and tubs or troughs and rakes to swish away any mud or softer stone that clung to rich ore, or they tried to entrap waterborne flecks of gold or tinstone in the nap of rough cloths. More often than not, washing had to be done out-of-doors where water was available. In all seasons but summer, this could hardly have been a hand-warming occupation, and it was little likely to produce the angelic smile of Hans Hesse's lovely washerwoman. Indeed, in the deep mid-winter washing could not be carried out at all.

Pictures give us a beginning. They attest to women's presence around the mines. They inform us about some of these workers' activities. But only recourse to the few remaining documents can provide a more complete vision of women's various and changing roles where silver was dug and refined and of the conditions under which the women labored.

Were women themselves ever miners (*häuer*), diggers in the earth, wielders of picks and axes? The literature is nearly silent on this question. One recent writer says without citation, "Especially in the washing of ore and in smelting huts women worked by day. But also in prospecting and mining we find them."[4] Even the expert on early modern Saxon mining, Adolf Laube, only mentions women and children in passing.[5] Another researcher tells of individual prospectors in the "Middle Ages" working their own claims aided by their wives. One such wife sold her veil to help maintain the family until she and her husband struck it rich. This woman hurt her head on a projecting rock, and when her husband knocked the offending stone away, he found rich silver ore at last.[6] A fourth author brings forward an instance from the mid-sixteenth century of several women (*etzliche weiber*) doing their own prospecting and turning up some ore.[7]

More revealing on this question than these few documented examples is what we know about the labor relations of men and women in Germany

during the fifteenth and sixteenth centuries. As Merry Wiesner has recently shown, in the production of goods in general in western German cities, wives worked right alongside their husbands, until guild rules and pressure from journeymen restricted the wives' functions.[8] I hope to demonstrate on another occasion that Wiesner's conclusions are largely true of eastern German cities as well. Mining, however, is not usually thought of as a craft. We imagine wholly unskilled laborers hacking chunks of rock out of the earth and purveying them for refining to their necessarily more highly trained fellows, the smelters (*schmelzer*), who in turn saw their product, bars of silver, taken along to other true craftsmen, the minters (*müntzer*). Even a quick reading of Agricola's fat handbook will disabuse us of this notion. To prevent a potentially fatal accident, the wielders of the hammers and picks in tunnels penetrating ever deeper under the earth had to know how to recognize ore, how to extract it in safe and legal wise, how to deal with rain or ground water leaking into a shaft, how to tell if dangerous gases were present. From the time of the resumption of silver mining in Freiberg in the 1460s and the nearly simultaneous discovery of worthy veins on the Schneeberg, miners were increasingly organized in a guildlike manner and increasingly trained. Their brotherhoods, the knappschaften, were originally religious confraternities but came to possess many secular features.[9] In such a structure, the place for women was small.

The reasons for this were several. Previously mining could be done close to the surface and in pits open to the sky. Depictions of prospecting show men digging up the sod, and the half-myths of original discoverers, such as that of the angel and Daniel Knappe in what would become Annaberg, which is the central story of Hans Hesse's altarpiece, involve finding precious metal at the base of trees. Ordinary folk dreamed of such treasure as a means out of their impecunious drudgery at farming or piecework, and together with their wives and children they staked out and worked their claims. All capable family members dug, carried, broke up, and washed ore, if they were lucky enough to have some.

The presence of significant quantities of silver guaranteed that princes, investors, and hordes of treasure-seekers would quickly alter mining beyond recognition.[10] The amount of surface ore dwindled, and the costs of tunneling, bracing, ventilating, draining, providing tools and "frog lamps," supervising, and accounting could be met only through the investment of sizable amounts of capital. Territorial authorities, who took over the ultimate control and taxation of mining, continued to welcome family prospecting in case some promising veins close to the surface had been overlooked. But if these were found, the transformation from a kindred enterprise to large capitalist concern was swift. Many people, including women, and corporations, like cities that had money to spare, bought shares (*kuxe* or *berganteile*) in mines and hopefully christened their shafts with the names of influential saints like Anne, Mary, Wolfgang, and Barbara. If earthly women lacked power, beatified women were certainly believed to possess it, in the ore-bearing hills as in heaven itself.

Mining administration became highly structured, a sign of the princes' keen interest in its success as well as its growing scale. No *mark* or *lot* of silver was exempt from the ducal and electoral tenth. Both branches of the Wettin house were in need of money, and this need provided their chief incentive to cooperate in exploiting the mines. The administrative apparatus grew. From top to bottom it included the tithe gatherer (*zehntner*), who took in and registered all silver ingots, claiming the princely tenth; the overseer of production (*bergmeister*), in charge of shares, claims, and the incessant disputes over claims; his aides, the jurymen (*berggeschworenen*), the mining clerk (*bergschreiber*), the chief record keeper, and the share clerk (*gegenschreiber*), who kept track of investors' earnings and owings in writing; the foreman of the tunnel (*schichtmeister*), who paid the miners on Saturdays, provided them with tools and all necessary supplies, and rendered the investors (*gewerken*) a quarterly account of his expenditures; the manager of the tunnel (*steiger*), who watched over the miners in a single shaft and reported their shortcomings to the foreman; and the diggers (*häuer*), the unromantic counterparts of Snow White's seven dwarfs, who nevertheless did sometimes sing at their labors to help themselves keep a rhythm or stay awake.[11]

Beneath the miners in status and in pay were now apprentices (*lehrhäuer*).[12] Doubtless among them were some of the children alleged to be working in the mines, performing all manner of menial chores as they learned the methods of the experienced men. When mining became a skill to be taught by one generation of males to the next in a guild context, women stepped aside and occupied themselves with the unskilled pounding (*pauchen*) of rich ore apart from mere rock and with the washing of ore. They had pounded and washed before, but they had not been relegated to these activities alone. By the end of the sixteenth century, women were to be found only at these and other uncomplicated tasks.

It might be that women were glad not to risk their necks underground. The men themselves had no illusions about the perils of their profession. Mining has ever been one of the most dangerous occupations, one to which the ancient Greeks and Romans consigned insubordinate slaves. And, indeed, at all times numerous males, too, broke up the rock brought up from the mines and washed the ore. Hesse's altarpiece is as much proof of this as that women were present. The principal figure in the central panel, a young man wearing the miner's turban-style headdress, poises his hammer to strike a chunk of stone. In the background, not far behind Daniel Knappe's legendary tree, a distinctly male ore washer is at work over sieve and tub identical to those the woman is using. Agricola, too, depicts men at these jobs.[13]

A more indicative source concerning the position of women around the silver mines is the few surviving weekly paymasters' accounts. With rare exceptions all employees turned up on Saturdays at a designated spot, usually at the hut where implements for that shaft were stored and where the hutmaster and his family dwelled, to receive their wages. On the same day people engaged in the smelting huts were paid. Any shaft manager who allowed extra names (*blinde nahmen*) of men or women to be written in the accounts so that he could collect their pay was to be corporally punished, fired, and never employed in such a post again.[14] Even when particular mines were yielding little or no metal—and this was the case more often than not—the investors had to pay the workers out of their own pockets. The smelting staff was not so fortunate. If there was no ore, the refiners' fires went out.

From the paymasters' slender-folded bits of paper we learn several things.[15] First, when silver mining was organized as a capitalist enterprise, financed by more or less distant investors and run by their hired agents, women found employment chiefly as part-time breakers and launderers of ore. They worked alongside men, usually young men, and boys at the same tasks for the same low compensation. These men and boys were either day laborers and poor like themselves or, especially as mining came to function more as a guild, youths who might hope to leave the breaking bench and become, after a period of instruction underground, full-fledged and somewhat better remunerated miners.[16]

Second, women occasionally had other functions, especially in the late fifteenth and early sixteenth centuries. In one smelting hut, at the princes' own mine (*Erbstollen*) in Freiberg and probably from about 1517 up to at least 1540, one or more unnamed women (*gestubmacherinnen*) mixed coal dust with clay and formed this compound into briquets to be used in separating copper and silver.[17] They earned for their skilled performance between 10 and 18 groschen a week, up to twice as much as a miner.[18] These briquet makers may thus have earned between 25 and 45 florins a year if their employment was steady, a matter determined by the output of the mines that fed ore to this smelting furnace. With such an income in 1517, one could have maintained a family at a modest level. Twenty-five florins would go nowhere near as far by mid-century, after two or three decades of inflation.[19] In these same records, the ore breakers and washers are men.

Third, these highly paid smelters' helpers were a rarity, as far as extant documents allow one to judge. Another briquet maker in Schneeberg, a woman at the smelting furnaces of the very productive Saint George mine, usually made just 2½ groschen a week.[20] Far more representative are the pounders, washers, and servants. Poor women, often the widows of miners, went from shaft to shaft seeking a bit of work wherever they could find it. Part of our traditional concept of the lady is that she does not carry heavy loads, which men in our society have often hastened to relieve her of—at least in public. By contrast, the hungry wanderers from mine to mine were set to carrying anything that needed moving from one place to another: iron implements, rope, and baskets to the mine entrance; lead, ash, and coal to the smelting furnaces.[21] They could expect a few pfennigs or a groschen for their trouble, though sometimes we encounter a regular coal carrier or coal measurer who makes, depending on time put in, 9 to 15 groschen a week, a high wage for feminine and unskilled labor.[22]

Fourth, other than the wandering poor, who were members of the families of ill or deceased miners, the wives of living personnel were also awarded piecework by shaft foremen. Most frequently found in the accounts is the wife of the hutkeeper, guardian of supplies, who lived with his family in the hut near the entrance to the shaft. His wife (the *hutmannin*) had the advantage of being physically present when labor was needed. She could break up and sort one large container (*vas*) of ore without leaving home and earn 5 groschen, half or more of a miner's set wage.[23] When ore was plentiful and more help was needed, other wives were called in. These wives' occasional income greatly aided their families, who found it harder and harder to get by on the miners' 9 or 10½ groschen a week, a rate that was set by the princes in the fifteenth century without regard for cost of living and not raised throughout the sixteenth century.

Fifth, by the 1580s women could obtain nothing more than this temporary work around the mines, their places having been taken by men and boys. A century after the start of the great mining revival in the Erzgebirge, every regular position belonged to the masculine sex. The state of the economy and not a declining opinion of women was to blame for this. The prevailing attitude toward women both before and during the sixteenth century was that they were inferior to and properly subordinate to men. But opportunities for women in the world of commerce and manufacture were many until rapid demographic expansion and inflation made men desire any remunerative jobs held by women. The mines in particular were afflicted by the rapid exhaustion of their wealth, which made it difficult to earn a living there. For this reason, too, most available work went to men.

Sixth, some women made money through provisioning the miners and smelters. Lists of expenditures by shaft foremen and smelting supervisors contain regular payments to women, as well as to men, for the tallow (*unslitt*) that the diggers burned in the shallow bowl-lamps they wore on their heads; for the ash the smelters used in their fires along with coal, wood, and briquets; and for various other products like rope that appear in the records with less regularity. Wives of butchers often purveyed the tallow, and wives of bakers the ash. A schoolmistress and a bathhouse operator also sold ash—anybody who had quantities of it could find a buyer, it seems.[24] Women may have benefited from the preparation and sale of food for the miners. One of Agricola's illustrations (p. 340), albeit of tin rather than silver production, contains a woman preparing food next to a fire on which two pots simmer. The miners worked seven- to eight-hour shifts in locations that were often away from home, inn, or marketplace (although near Marienberg at mid-century some lived in huts and crude smithies near the mines[25]), and they needed at least bread and beverage to sustain them. In the early years, before the cities of Schneeberg, Annaberg, Joachimsthal, and Marienberg existed, there were hardly any markets to cater even to the miners' domestic needs. Under such favorable circumstances, tunnel managers exploited the miners and augmented their own incomes by selling food and drink at the mines. The Schneeberg brotherhood petitioned Dukes Ernst and Albrecht to forbid anyone to make a profit from such trade, though the "workers and miners might, if they wished, go together and buy a keg of beer for themselves."[26] A mining ordinance for Annaberg from the early sixteenth century forbids shaft managers and foremen to force the miners and other personnel to buy meals from them.[27] It appears that women, too, were being pressed to buy food; and where food was served, women most likely prepared it.

The women around the silver mines earned during their working lives much less than men. The few exceptions are not only remarkable but scarce as hens' teeth by mid-century. Wage rates set out by the princes in their periodic mining ordinances virtually never dictated amounts for women. Only the Bohemian ordinances stated what women could be paid, namely, the same amount as the lowest paid boys. In Schlaggenwald in 1548 this came to 9 white groschen for a six-day week of unstated, but definitely long, hours. Miners themselves may have worked only forty hours per week, but employees on the surface had to be in their places up to seventy-five hours.[28] Women do not appear in the Saxon mining ordinances because their labors were frankly considered to be temporary, part-time, and according to the needs and resources of each mine as judged by its foreman. If a woman were available to hammer, sort, and wash just when new wagons of rock were brought up, then she gained a few hours' work and a groschen or three the following Saturday. Likewise, if fresh finds of good ore set the smelting ovens in unaccustomed motion. If the hutman's wife were there, as she usually was, she got the first chance; if the smelter's wife, then she. What purpose would be served by setting salaries for women in the ordinances, their drafters must have thought.

Wherever wives worked directly alongside their husbands, the husband got a full wage and the wife a much smaller sum or a gratuity. In the late 1530s at an unnamed mine near Annaberg, month after month one "pastian" (Sebastian) made 16 groschen a week, and his wife got 8 or 4 groschen or nothing at all even though she is mentioned in the roster.[29] Every spring the Freiberg miners' brotherhood had a feast. In the accounts for 1529 and the years immediately following, we see that the treasurer paid the man who dispensed the brothers' wine and beer 10 groschen for his effort and gave his wife 2 groschen, which was simply a tip. The brotherhood paid the female cook who prepared the repast of beef, pork, veal, liver, kraut with chopped lungs, bread, and rolls 2 groschen. Yet it sent 30 groschen worth of beer or the cash to buy beer as a gift to the wives of the bergmeister and a certain officer of the brotherhood (the *zechmeister*).[30] Being on good terms with mining officials was paramount.

Women's work was less dangerous, normally part time, and low paying; men's was better compensated as long as the silver was not exhausted (as it soon became in the western Erzgebirge) and as long as the miners did not suffer any disability. The perils of work in the mines, however, were acknowledged by all. All too often greed for the gleaming mineral made officials careless in exerting the effort and expending the money that creating safer conditions in the shafts would have required. Tunnels often collapsed; lethal gases and water seeped into mines. In addition, miners were afflicted by illnesses brought on by their work. They breathed dust over long periods and handled lead and other toxic substances. Agricola knew of a woman who had lost seven husbands to "miners' sickness."[31] The diggers made a contribution from their pay every week of 1 to 6 pfennigs (*buchsenpfennige*) that they intended should assist sick or injured miners until they could work again. At least part of the money was so used after 1525, but it is obvious that the amounts produced, particularly as mining decreased and the ranks of the destitute burgeoned, were wholly inadequate.[32] Every Sunday, therefore, a plate was passed in the churches, and the money collected given out to miners' families for food and essential clothing. Miners died young leaving widows and children behind. "Stedtlein" Buchholz had only 350 hearths in 1555, when mining was in decline, yet the citizens had to support with alms 107 "poor widows, almost all with children."[33] Shafts that still operated were expected to give a few pfennigs on payday to the needy survivors of men who when alive had worked in that mine.[34] To this limited degree there was a sense of solidarity among the miners and the manager of each shaft.

All over the Wettin dynastic lands, whether metal-producing areas or not, poverty was familiar to more and more citizens from the 1520s on. But economic deterioration was more gradual and thus gentler away from the mines than near them. In Marienberg or Annaberg people did not know from one month to the next whether silver would continue to flow.

It is a wonder that people rushing to the prospectors' camps that became boom towns and then flourishing cities—people many of whom had been peasants or else artisans in crafts unrelated to mining—could quickly come to think of themselves proudly as members of a dignified, organized mining profession. To study Schneeberg, Annaberg, Buchholz, Joachimsthal, or Marienberg is to watch the forging of identity, the creation of tradition. The miners adopted the methods and customs of the Harz region, where Hans Luther was a self-made copper entrepreneur, and of Freiberg, whose early mining laws set the standard for the others of the Erzgebirge. One of the institutions appearing in the new mining cities was the miners' fraternity (knappschaft). Curiously, only the Freiberg association seems to have had female members. In 1521 it had 86 "old sisters" (*alte schwestern*) out of a total affiliation that year of 436.[35] It is not credible that one-fifth of the diggers were women. Although all diggers were eligible and expected to join, only the wives and other female relations of solid, respected miners took part. Most are identified in the register by their husband's name.[36] Nearly all are listed under the letter "d" for "dy," the feminine form of the article "the," as in "the Mrs. Laurence Stefan." Their belonging reflects identification with their husbands' craft and social cohesion among the members. Just what these women could and could not do in the brotherhood, we do not know. They were supposed to pay annual dues; they could not be officers; they were never chosen candle-bearers for the brotherhood's ceremonies and its annual procession. Those whose heirs could afford the fee of 15 groschen got their names inscribed on the list of dead members. From what we know about women's roles in religious confraternities in Saxony, we may surmise that the sisters entered into the social, spiritual, and welfare activities of the organization with some enthusiasm. Certainly this was true in Annaberg, where the Society of Saint Anne had a thousand members, with husband and wife counted as one member.[37]

The Lutheran Reformation brought with it an emphasis on women's place in the home. Duke Heinrich, George the Bearded's younger brother, inclined toward the Reformation throughout the early 1530s, as did many of Freiberg's citizens. The number of sisters in the brotherhood dropped steadily during these years. Heinrich proclaimed the Reformation in 1537; in the register of members for that year, a line is drawn through the name of each sister but one.[38] Over a decade passes without any women members being listed, and when female names appear again, they are exclusively those of the prioress (a cooperative local noblewoman) or a high ranking mining official's wife. Women seldom gained admittance, and, if they did, it was only through political advantage. The fraternity was rapidly transformed into an elite male club from which even poor miners were temporarily excluded. Noteworthy among the new members in 1542 are Elector Johann Friedrich, his brother Ernst, Duke Moritz, and his brother August.

We should not exaggerate the significance of this relegation of women from the Freiberg brotherhood in 1537. This act of exclusion seems dramatic, but it is only the most obvious manifestation of an attitude long developing. Evidence is accumulating of growing limitations on the sphere of women from the mid-fifteenth century on. All of Europe, probably including most women, consistently esteemed women less than men, and the Reformation articulated but did not bring about a marked change in this attitude. If the other miners' brotherhoods of the Erzgebirge did not include women, the reason may well lie in their having been founded after the middle of the fifteenth century—that is, during the era when the women of Germany were being nudged away from the public and into the private, domestic world.

There are few indications of a distinct mentality of the women of the silver mines. They lacked cohesion and produced no one to advance their collective economic interest. There is evidence of the male miners' outlook on the world—their superstitions, their restiveness, their inclination toward

Protestantism, if not necessarily toward Luther's version of it. But it would be unwise to assume that the women's *Weltanschauung* was the same as the men's. The bits of evidence that one would have to use—rhymes, lists of grievances, shaft names—are male in origin. I have found only two instances of women acting out, and these women were the wives of miners and not demonstrably workers themselves. In Buchholz the entire population hated the tyrannical magistrate of the mines (*bergvogt*) Matts Busch, who with electoral backing effectively ruled the town without resort to the city council (*richter* and *schoppen*).[39] Busch once exiled a citizen for two years for cutting grass on Sunday, and a young man for the same period for "sassing" his stepfather and cursing his mother.[40] In 1525 the wife of the bergmeister himself organized a protest against Busch in which thirty women took part. They hoisted a miner's protective leather garment (*grubenleder*) on a pole and marched on Busch's house.[41] This was a demonstration by elite women, however, largely on behalf of their just-as-elite husbands, against Busch's arrogance and limitless jurisdiction, and it was not successful. It is doubtful that ordinary ore pounders and washers took part.

In 1532 six widows of ordinary miners petitioned the elector against the alleged mining violations of a man named Christoff Meiner, whose negligence they believed had resulted in the death of their husbands. They had confronted Meiner personally, but he only cursed them.[42] The women of the mines were daily witnesses of the carelessness of the shaft foremen and those above them. The widows likely got no hearing, much less compensation for their loss.

We can also well imagine the crisis that the near-exhaustion of the silver mines during the sixteenth century brought with it for the families that lived from mining. Whatever attitudes toward women were, and whatever gainful occupations were now closed to them, as always before females adjusted. They found whatever means they could to put food in theirs and their children's mouths. Able-bodied miners, traditionally a peripatetic bunch, picked up household and kin and moved to where rich ores were still to be found. This wandering away explains the gradual but steady shrinking of the mining towns' population after mid-century. Until the Thirty Years' War there was no sudden slump in the numbers of urban inhabitants of the Erzgebirge. How did those remaining sustain themselves?

Some mining continued, more as one got closer to Freiberg. Also, Annaberg, Schneeberg, Marienberg, and the others had necessarily developed the panoply of trades needed to provide any large aggregation of people, and these trades, involved in the production of food and clothing, in carpentering and smithing, gained a momentum of their own independent of mining. The city marketplaces remained the transfer points of goods for rural folk as well. All of these activities together were nevertheless an insufficient substitute for the mining of the boom years, and people suffered.

Barbara Uttmann (1514–75), the wife and then widow of a powerful Annaberg patriarch, Christoph Uttmann, is reputed to have found a solution that enriched her still further and that gave relief to some of the deprived. She learned to make bobbin lace—from whom is not known—and taught it to dozens of housewives. This *klöppeln* occupied up to nine hundred Annaberg and Buchholz women, who sat at home over their hard lacemakers' cushions, throwing their bobbins so quickly that the eye could hardly detect the motion. They sold their ever more refined and varied pieces to Uttmann and the wives of other city magnates, who conveyed them to regional and continental markets.[43] Lacemaking, like spinning, was seen as a natural outgrowth of and compatible with women's duties in the home, and the handicraft spread throughout the Erzgebirge.[44] A number of fine examples of this bobbin lace, albeit of a later date, may be seen in the Freiberg City Museum. This industry lasted into the nineteenth century and is being revived today.

Some men did not sit idly by but took up the manufacture of decorative trims and braids, a nice accompaniment to the women's craft. These *borten* and *posament* makers formed a guild before the end of the sixteenth century which forbade women to cross the line between the manufacture of lace and of other decorative edgings.[45]

CONCLUSIONS

That women were ubiquitous around the silver mines in the late fifteenth and the sixteenth centuries is not to say that they were numerous. There was a woman or two at every shaft, at the very least the hutman's wife or a servant, but men far outnumbered women.

Women's position in the realm of artisanal production was declining from the second half of the fifteenth century.[46] As the organization of silver mining changed from a family enterprise to one in which distant investors employed through their hired officials persons whom they had never seen and as the miners developed a guild-style fraternity complete with apprenticeships, women ceased to dig for silver and mainly had to content themselves with breaking up and washing ore, tasks that required little expertise. Their wages were low, the same as the boys' who shared their menial occupations. Nevertheless, women were not wholly excluded from work around the mines until after the sixteenth century. The parallel between mining and urban manufacture reflects in part the strong influence of the city on the countryside: most mining shafts were outside of towns, indeed often well outside, and their personnel had a hybrid lifestyle made up of urban and peasant components. At least as many of the workers of both sexes lived outside the towns as lived in them, and numerous miners farmed on the side.

Economic developments did not favor women—or men, for that matter. Against a European background of rising inflation, the silver and other minerals of the Erzgebirge gave out. By mid-century the diggers themselves were looking for work. They imitated their wives' lacemaking and took up the fabrication of braids and trims. Men and women together created a new industry to sustain their region. Nevertheless, only the men formed guilds, and women were excluded from them. The Lutheran Reformation reinforced the conviction that women should care for home and family first and leave the public arena to men. Gradually, women's work outside the home came to indicate financial need and to have a social stigma attached to it. This evolution was complete soonest in the cities. In the countryside, on farms, and in mines located closer to villages than to city walls, the female presence persisted longer and with less prejudice.

The mysteries remain: Were women aware of the transformation that we detect? If so, did they mind? Did they accept the men's definitions of femininity and propriety? Until we can answer these questions about *le menu peuple,* we researchers have much to do.

NOTES

Research for this paper was funded by the International Research and Exchanges Board.

1. Wolfgang Buschmann, *Der Annaberger Bergaltar* (Berlin: Der Kinderbuch Verlag, 1982), a children's book, contains high quality, detailed photographs of the entire altar. I have counted the angel and Daniel Knappe, the alleged recipient of the angel's revelation, each time they appear.

2. For a brief account of Agricola's career, see Hans Prescher, "Georgius Agricola (24. 3. 1494–21. 11. 1555)—Leben und Werke," *Sächsische Heimatblätter* 2 (1981), 49–54; for greater detail consult Helmut Wilsdorf, *Georg Agricola und seine Zeit* (Berlin: Deutscher Verlag der Wissenschaften, 1956), vol. 1 of *Georgius Agricola, Ausgewählte Werke,* 10 vols., ed. Hans Prescher (1956–71).

3. *Georgii Agricolae De Re Metallica Libri XII. . . .* (Basel: Johannes Froben, 1556). The modern reader will be aided in understanding this very technical work by consulting, instead of the original, *De re metallica libri XII,* trans. and ed. Georg Fraustadt and Hans Prescher (Berlin: Deutscher Verlag der Wissenschaften, 1974), or, indispensable for the reader of English, *De re metallica,* trans. and ed. Herbert Clark Hoover and Lou Henry Hoover, first published by *The Mining Magazine* (London, 1912) and reprinted by Dover Publications (New York, 1950). All subsequent references in this paper are to the Dover edition. Fraustadt and Prescher think that Agricola made all the sketches of his illustrations and had them carved in wood for publication by Basilius Weffringer of Joachimsthal (Fraustadt and Prescher, p. 11).

4. Siegfried Sieber, *Zur Geschichte des erzgebirgischen Bergbaues* (Halle, Saale: Wilhelm Knapp Verlag, 1954), p. 99.

5. *Bergbau und Huttenwesen in Frankreich um die Mitte des 15. Jahrhunderts. Freiberger Forschungshefte* D38 (1964), p. 101. In contrast to Saxony, Laube was amazed to find no women at work in French mines (page 123).

6. Otto Hue, *Die Bergarbeiter. Historische Darstellung der Bergarbeiter-Verhältnisse von der ältesten bis in die neueste Zeit* (Stuttgart: J. H. W. Dietz Nachfolger, 1910), p. 154.

7. Joachim Vetter, *Die soziale und hygienische Lage der bergbauenden Bevölkerung des Erzgebirges in der ersten Hälfte des 16. Jahrhunderts,* Schriften für Heimatforschung, vol. 4 (Berlin: Wilhelm Limpert, 1940), p. 23.

8. *Working Women in Renaissance Germany* (New Brunswick, N.J.: Rutgers University Press, 1986), especially "Guilds, Crafts, and Market Production" (pp. 149–85) and "Conclusions" (pp. 187–98).

9. Hermann Löscher, "Die Anfänge der erzgebirgischen Knappschaft," *Zeitschrift der Savigny-Stiftung für Rechtsgeschichte,* Kanonische Abteilung, 71 (1954), 223–38.

10. Theodor Gustav Werner, "Das fremde Kapital im Annaberger Bergbau und Metallhandel des 16. Jahrhunderts," *Neues Archiv für sächsische Geschichte und Altertumskunde* 57 (1936), 113–79; 58 (1937), 1–47; 58 (1937), 136–201.

11. Laube gives a fuller description of the duties of these and other officials in *Studien über den erzgebirgischen Silberbergbau von 1470 bis 1546,* 2nd printing (Berlin: Akademie Verlag, 1976). Karl Marx University Library's copies were missing in 1986, and I was compelled to use Laube's dissertation of the same title (1971), pp. 104–11. On the *bergmeister* see Agricola, *De re metallica,* pp. 77–100. To accommodate English-speaking readers, I have adopted the Hoovers' translations (*De re metallica,* p. 78), but even they failed to come up with an apt rendering of bergmeister and retained the German word.

12. Hermann Löscher, *Die erzgebirgischen Berggebräuche des 16. Jahrhunderts und ihre Vorläufer seit etwa 1450* (Berlin: Akademie Verlag, n.d. [c. 1957]), p. 187: article 179 of Simon Bogner's Freiberger Berggebräuche.

13. *De re metallica,* pp. 270, 272, 288–89, 291, 301–303, 305–309, 311, 313–15, 317, 322–24, 326–29, 331–38, 340–43, 345–48, 387, 435.

14. Löscher, *Die erzgebirgischen Berggebräuche,* p. 187: article 178 of Simon Bogner's Freiberger Berggebräuche.

15. Most extant pay records (*Zechenrechnungen*) are at the Freiberg Bergarchiv (hereafter FBA), now a branch of the Dresden Staatsarchiv, and date from the latter sixteenth century up to the late eighteenth century. Early documents are scarce, but I found a few at the Weimar Staatsarchiv (WSA) and at the Dresden Staatsarchiv proper (DSA).

16. The princes' mining ordinances set weekly wages of 9 to 10½ groschen for häuer, not a high rate of pay. The häuer, however, were permitted to take on special one-time assignments (*gedinge*), in addition, at a prearranged fee. Many regularly did this. I myself think that many häuer were peasants on the side.

17. DSA, Loc. 4492, "Berg-Rechnungen de anno 1438–1538," vol. 1, passim; ". . . de anno 1538–1652," vol. 2, passim. See also Agricola, *De re metallica,* p. 374, for women preparing coal dust.

18. The Wettin monetary units at this time were florins or *gulden* made up of 21 groschen, each groschen containing 12 *pfennige* or pennies.

19. During the first half of the sixteenth century, a humble cottage could be bought for 20 or 25 florins. In 1522 in Annaberg, a pound of the best beef cost 5 pfennigs. In 1514 the same amount would buy $4^2/_3$ pound of bread. See Emil Finck, "Die Versorgung einer Stadt mit Fleisch und Brot vor 400 Jahren," *Mitteilungen des Vereins für Geschichte von Annaberg und Umgegend* 7 (1901), 103, 136–37.

20. DSA, Loc. 4508, "Schneebergische Berg-Rechnungen über den Silber-Kauff, Vorrath und Zehenden belangende 1516–34," vol. 2, passim.

21. FBA, Zechenrechnung G144, "Gnade Gottes . . . am goltberge," 1581–82, passim.

22. DSA, Loc 4492, "Berg-Rechnungen de anno 1538–1652," passim.

23. The Zechenrechnungen of the Freiberg Bergarchiv contain hundreds of references to the *hutmannin.*

24. For example, DSA, Loc. 4504, "6 Stück Marienbergische Hütten-Rechnungen de anno 1525, 32, 35, 36, 37, 38," passim. The schoolmistress appears on fol. 133.

25. DSA, Loc. 2001, "Visitation des Gebirgischen Kreisses 1555," fol. 242.

26. DSA, Loc. 4322, Wittenberg Archiv, "Bergwerks-Sachen Kapsel V, " fol. 19.

27. DSA, Loc. 4494, "Annabergische Berg-Ordnungen . . . 1499–1539," fol. 7. For evidence of a similar problem in Schneeberg, see WSA, Reg. T2, fol. 11; DSA, Loc. 4322, Wittenberg Archiv, fol. 63.

28. Wilsdorf, *Georg Agricola und seine Zeit,* pp. 55–58; Walter Bogsch, *Der Marienberger Bergbau in der ersten Hälfte des 16. Jahrhunderts* (Schwarzenberg, Saxony: E. M. Gartner, 1933), p. 113, 146n.; Ingrid Mittenzwei, *Der Joachimsthaler Aufstand 1525, seine Ursachen und Folgen* (Berlin: Akademie Verlag, 1968), pp. 64–66.

29. DSA, Loc. 4492, "Berg-Rechnungen de anno 1538–1652," vol. 2, passim.

30. FBA, no signature, "Ausgaben Verzeichnis der Knappschaft zu Freiberg," no pagination.

31. Vetter, *Die soziale und hygienische Lage,* p. 41. In 1523 the city physician of Joachimsthal Dr. Wenzel Beyer wrote about "schwinde, ferliche kranckheyten der brust" (Mittenzwei, *Joachimsthaler Aufstand,* p. 74).

32. The right to use the *buchsenpfennige* for relief was requested by knappschaften in the petitions during the Peasants' War. See Horst Carlowitz, "Die revolutionäre Bewegung der Bergleute in den Silberstädten Annaberg, Marienberg und Geyer während des Bauernaufstandes 1525," *Sächsische Heimatblätter* 16, 1 (1970), 18–20.

33. DSA, Loc. 10600, "Supplication Bericht vnnd Missiven an die herrn Visitator [sic] auss den Geburgischen Embtern Freibergk, Annabergk, Kempnitz, Zwickaw, Penick vnd Hartten Stein. 1557," [also contains other years], fol. 68. Another draft, fol. 69, says four hundred hearths. The widespread poverty is apparent nonetheless.

34. For example, FBA, Zechenrechnung B87, Brand Stolln, 1588–1589, passim.

35. Johannes Langer, "Die Freiberger Bergknappschaft," *Mitteilungen des Freiberger Altertumsvereins* 61 (1931), 20.

36. FBA, Brüderregister I, 1519–1545, no pagination.

37. Bernhard Wolf, "Aus dem kirchlichen Leben Annabergs in vorreformatorischer Zeit," *Mitteilungen des Vereins für Geschichte von Annaberg und Umgegend* 11 (1910), 77. The pope had limited this confraternity to a thousand members (page 81).

38. FBA, Brüderregister I, 1519–1545, no pagination.

39. WSA, Reg. T 374, "Gebrechen vnd Irrungen zwischen Mattes Puschen bergkvogt, Richter vnnd Schoppen an Einem vnnd dem Bergkmeister, Knapschaft vnnd gantzer gemein Im Buchholtz 1520–1525"; WSA, Reg. T 377–78. In the mining towns, with the exception of the older Freiberg, the city councils were referred to as "judge and jury," alluding to their limited powers. This limitation was owing to the presence of the princes' officials, the bergmeister, or in this case the bergvogt, whose jurisdictions were much greater. The tensions were constant between the councils and the officials.

40. Christian Meltzer, *Historische Beschreibung des St. Catharinenberges im Buchholz. Mitteilungen des Vereins für Geschichte von Annaberg und Umgebung,* year 17, vol. 6, no. 1 (n.d.), 326.

41. Laube, *Studien über den erzgebirgischen Silberbergbau,* p. 439.

42. WSA, Reg. T 63, fol. 48–50.

43. Max Grohmann, *Festschrift zur 400 jährigen Jubelfeier der Stadt Annaberg 1496–1896* (Annaberg: C. O. Schreiber, 1896), pp. 24–26.

44. See, for example, Christian Meltzer, *Historia Schneebergensis Renovata. . . .* (Schneeberg: Heinrich Fulde, 1716), pp. 882–83.

45. Herbert Zimmermann, "Die Posamenten im Erzgebirge," *Vom silbernen Erzgebirge,* ed. Friedrich Kohler (Schwarzenberg, Saxony: Glückauf Verlag, 1939), pp. 68–69.

46. Apart from Wiesner, *Working Women in Renaissance Germany,* see in the newer literature, Martha C. Howell, "Women, the Family Economy, and the Structures of Market Production in Cities of Northern Europe during the Late Middle Ages," *Women and Work in Preindustrial Europe,* ed. Barbara A. Hanawalt (Bloomington: Indiana University Press, 1986), pp. 198–222; Erika Uitz, "Zu den auf eine Verbesserung ihrer gesellschaftlichen Stellung hinzielenden Aktivitäten der Frauen in den deutschen Städten des Spätmittelalters," *Untersuchungen zur gesellschaftlichen Stellung*

der Frau im Feudalismus, Magdeburger Beiträge zur Städtegeschichte 3 (1981), 47–69; Kurt Wesoly, "Der weibliche Bevölkerungsanteil in spätmittelalterlichen und frühneuzeitlichen Städten und die Bestätigung von Frauen im zünftigen Handwerk (insbesondere am Mittel- und Oberrhein)," *Zeitschrift für die Geschichte des Oberrheins* 128 (1980), 69–117.

GRETHE JACOBSEN

Nordic Women and the Reformation

I

The institutional Reformation in the Nordic countries was begun shortly after 1520, had largely succeeded by 1536, and was completed in 1550 with the establishment of the Lutheran church in Iceland. The popular Reformation took much longer. Catholic rites and beliefs continued to exist, albeit underground, for several centuries. The institutional Reformation was carried out by men, who all belonged to the elite, owing to their birth or education. The church they established was for both sexes, but because women had no say in the shaping of the new church, it was men that determined proper religious behavior.

As an institution the medieval church had been nearly as closed to women; during the fourteenth and fifteenth centuries, however, lay piety shaped a religious culture in which women could and did have a say. The leaders of the Lutheran church realized fully the danger which this popular religion posed to their new ideas and did their utmost to suppress it. There were to be no opportunities for women to introduce a female element into the new religion or to express religious feelings on their own premises. After the Reformation, women could express religious feelings but only according to rules determined by men (attending services, singing authorized hymns). The Nordic Reformation caused a change in the relationship between the sexes which left the female sex at a disadvantage in one of the most important areas of contemporary life: religion.

II

When the first reform ideas were introduced in the North, the Nordic countries were divided into two political units, the Kingdom of Sweden, which included Finland under the leadership of Gustav Vasa (1523–60) and the Kingdom of Denmark and Norway, which included Iceland, under the kings Frederik I (1523–33) and his son Christian III (1536–59). A civil war (1534–36) preceded the establishment of the Lutheran church in Denmark in 1536, but the causes of it were political, social, and economic more than religious. Norway and Iceland attempted to break Danish hegemony and the protests of these countries against the new church had strong political overtones; factionalism, however, prevented either country from attaining independence. In Iceland, the Reformation arrived during a fight between two factions of chieftains, one controlling the see of Skálholt, the other the see of Hólar. Although the former became Lutheran in 1541, the other did not until 1550, after the execution of Bishop Jon Arason. In Sweden the gradual dismantling of the medieval church resulted in the Dacke Rebellion in 1542–43. This rebellion was comparable to the English Pilgrimage of Grace, but economic and political conditions were also behind the protests of the independent border population of Småland, center of the rebellion. By 1551 all of the Nordic countries had officially become Lutheran and had a national church, closely controlled by the Danish or Swedish king.[1]

The centralization of power, which took place during the sixteenth century and which was greatly aided (but not caused) by the Reformation, contributed significantly to the exclusion of women from the political sphere. Women did not participate in the councils of the realm or at the meetings of the Estates, nor did they occupy any posts close to the center of political action, in the royal chancery or treasury. Some aristocratic women did become part of the administration when as widows they took over their late husbands' positions as heads of an administrative unit, called the len, but their role in the royal administration was determined by their marital status, not their qualifications.[2]

An overwhelming majority of the population lived in the rural areas, though Denmark had become urbanized during the late Middle Ages and had over ninety cities while Sweden had about fifty, Norway, sixteen, Finland, six, and Iceland none. This meant that the preaching orders, especially the Franciscans, were important in the religious and social spheres in Denmark, whereas the parish church or the monasteries of the older orders remained the focus of religious activity in Sweden and Norway. In Iceland, where individual farms rather than villages determined the settlement pattern, the proprietary church was alive and well. The only two places with some central functions were the diocesan seats at Hólar and Skálholt.

The Nordic church as an ecclesiastical institution was by the late Middle Ages a man's world headed by a few learned and quite a number of not so learned men. Women were involved with individual office holders as mothers, sisters, cousins, and occasionally as mistresses, but they had no active and recognized role in the institutional church. The clergy was in theory celibate except in Iceland, where celibacy never was accepted. The last Catholic bishop in Iceland, Jon Arason, had a wife and several children, including two sons, who were captured and executed with him when they refused to accept Lutheranism and surrender the diocese to the Danish king. As wives of the bishops at Hólar and Skálholt, women were important and visible members of the episcopal households, which also served as political and cultural centers. They did not in any way perform the sacral duties of the bishops but administered the temporal property (lands, cattle, income) of the diocese. As these women often came from prominent and wealthy Icelandic families, they were accustomed to dealing with large households. As embroiderers they could and did express their piety in the altarcloths, copes, and vestments they produced for their husbands' cathedrals and staff.[3]

In Denmark, Norway, and Sweden the mistress or housekeeper of the parish priest, canon, or deacon was apparently not an uncommon sight. On the other hand, the higher clergy did not as a rule have concubines, and the ones who did created quite a scandal among their colleagues and their congregations. The women in the villages and the urban parishes might thus find a woman in the local rectory or vicarage with whom they could deal, but there were none in the houses and estates of the higher clergy.[4]

Women had more of a role in the monastic movement but, as elsewhere in Europe, they were disadvantaged in relation to men. The convents were fewer and poorer than the monasteries and the few extant sources tell little if anything of the intellectual activity of the convents, apart from the Birgittine motherhouse in Vadstena, where the first printing press in Sweden was installed. Most convents belonged to the Benedictine order, the remainder were the female Cistercians, the female Dominicans, the Poor Claires, or Birgittines.[5]

The Birgittine order was an innovation of the late Middle Ages, founded by the Swedish noblewoman, politician, preacher, and mystic Saint Bridget (Birgitta), who died in 1373. She wanted to create an order for women which would avoid the problems the existing female orders experienced in being restricted economically and physically by their brothers, who in turn came to view them as liabilities to the order. To ensure that her convents were economically sound, Saint Bridget demanded that each member of the first generation of nuns bring with her enough land and possessions to support a nun, in effect establishing an endowed chair for each female member of the community. Each convent was to house sixty nuns and twenty-five priests, deacons, and laymen who were to help the abbess with the practical and missionary affairs of the convent. To supply an institution with eighty-five people required large landholdings and connected labor, and for that reason only a few Birgittine houses were founded in Scandinavia. The motherhouse of Vadstena was the only one in her homeland, Sweden. In Denmark, two houses were founded during the early fifteenth century, in Finland one, and in Norway a former Benedictine monastery was converted into a Birgittine house.[6]

In the late fifteenth century, the daughter of St. Bridget, Catherine, was also canonized. Her cult, however, was never given a chance to spread, and one of the earliest signs of the Reformation in Sweden was the impoundment in 1524 of the silver given in her name to Vadstena convent by the king for payment of troops.

In spite of Saint Bridget's intention of having women from all layers of society join her order, the Birgittine convents remained aristocratic in Denmark; Vadstena, however, received many women from the urban patriciate during the fifteenth and early sixteenth centuries. The other convents in Scandinavia also recruited their members from the aristocracy, with the possible exception of the convents of Poor Claires in Roskilde and Copenhagen. The former convent was founded in 1257; the latter was founded in 1497 by Queen Christina and inaugurated in 1505. It was the only convent in the capital and may have provided shelter and religious life for women of the burgher classes and for poorer women. Until her death in 1522, Christina was an active supporter of the Franciscan order, especially the observant branch, and of the Poor Claires. She founded a second convent in Odense in 1521. There is some scattered evidence that Beguines existed in Danish and Swedish cities, but their number and popularity is not known. However scarce, the sources permit us to conclude that the medieval church offered Nordic women an alternative to the role of wife and mother, a model for a spiritual life, but we cannot tell how many were able to take advantage of it.[7]

Of popular religion we are better informed. Sermons of the Protestant preachers and writings of the reformers reveal that the saints, legends, and the holy sites of medieval Christianity were well known to the Nordic population. This is also demonstrated by the wall paintings of the Danish and Swedish churches, which also show that the cult of the Virgin and her family, especially her mother, Saint Anne, had reached Scandinavia during the late Middle Ages. The images of Anne, Mary, and the Christ Child must have looked like a female version of the Trinity to the women and men who could feast their eyes on the paintings during Mass. Together with the pictures of the female saints they stressed the female element in the religion. The wall paintings also contain several scenes depicting Adam and Eve. Although the Fall is clearly shown with Eve being tempted and in turn tempting Adam, the final image of Eve and Adam is that of a peasant couple hard at work, Adam in the field tilling the land and Eve at home spinning and taking care of her many children, who were either sitting on her lap or lying in their cradle.

Several wall paintings from the late fifteenth and early sixteenth centuries show one or several devils assisting or hindering women engaged in brewing beer or churning butter, indicating that continental demonology also reached Denmark and Sweden and helped prepare the way for the witchcraft craze.[8] The devils on the walls were to play an important role in the Danish witchcraft trials of the seventeenth century. The medieval Nordic laws refer to sorcery and the punishment for practicing sorcery. Although they indicate a popular belief that some people were capable of causing *maleficium*, such people were not associated with one gender only.

Confraternities provided another outlet for women's religious needs. They were especially important for those women who were not born or married into the craft and merchants' guilds of the city, who thus could not become members of these guilds as could eligible journeymen. Most of the confraternities were restricted to a specific social group, but one, the Saint Lucius guild in the diocesan town of Roskilde, had members drawn from all layers (except the very bottom) of society, from the bishop of Roskilde to female servants.

A final indication of the extent of popular religious feeling is the success the papal legate and indulgence dealer Arcimboldus had when he visited

Denmark and Sweden in 1517. Although he quarreled with the Danish king and enraged reform-minded Catholic leaders with his sale of indulgences, he apparently did a good business with the population at large in the two countries.[9]

Although the topic needs more exploration, it is clear from extant sources that the popular religion of the late Middle Ages offered women several opportunities to express their piety and find female models in the divine hierarchy.

III

There are very few references to women directly participating in reform activities. The wealthy Norwegian noblewoman Inger of Austråt played an important political role during the tumultuous years between 1532 and 1537 owing to her position as the widow of a large landowner and as the mother-in-law of the ambitious nobleman Vincent Lunge. Her household was already in 1529 rumored to have introduced Lutheran customs, such as the singing of psalms. Inger and Vincent led the opposition to the Norwegian archbishop, whose fight for the old church, as much from political and nationalistic as from religious motives, eventually cost the lives both of Vincent Lunge and another of Lady Inger's sons-in-law. In Iceland the daughter of Jon Arason, Thorunn, avenged her father and brothers by gathering a group of followers who slew the Danish official who had ordered their execution.[10]

The Danish and Swedish queens of the period seem to have served as models for housewives and mothers, the all-important roles for women in the new church. The belief in marriage as the highest, ideal state for men and women was avidly championed by the Danish queen Dorothea, married to Christian III. On several occasions she acted as matchmaker on behalf of her courtiers, citing Luther on the blessings of marriage. She also donated a brooch to the city of Copenhagen for the daughters of respectable citizens to wear on their wedding day.[11]

The activities of ordinary Danish women can only be glimpsed in the sources. In 1526 the reformer Hans Tausen was threatened during a sermon by servants of the bishop, but the male citizens protected him "after their wives had brought weapons from their homes." This account of the incident would confirm the traditional image of the role of Nordic women as bit players in the drama of the Reformation. The account was not, however, written down until fifty years later and may reflect a later generation's view of women's role in the Reformation. In 1530 a crowd stormed the collegiate church of Our Lady in Copenhagen and destroyed statues and altars, one of the few such incidents during the Reformation. Women might well have been part of the "rabble" that, according to the sources, made up the majority of the crowd, but the few people named are men.[12]

The wives of the urban magistrates, who supported the reformers, must also have been active in the Reformation, but their role has largely been ignored. One example is Citze Kortsdatter, whose father was a prominent citizen of Copenhagen and the secular guardian of the observant friary in the city. Her first husband, a merchant, was the warden of one of the churches. In the sources she appears in 1510 as a wealthy widow until her remarriage. Her second husband was the royal moneyer, merchant, and later mayor of Malmø, Jørgen Koch, who was active in the reform of that city. She died sometime before 1554. During her lifetime she experienced the religious change from the late medieval piety and lay involvement in the church to the establishment of the Lutheran church in Denmark. Alas, no letters or writings from her or from any other woman in her position have survived. The role of these women in providing care and support for their husbands and in linking together the urban patriciate can be glimpsed only indirectly through casual allusions in the sources.[13]

The wives of the first generation reformers, almost all former priests and monks, were instrumental in the fight for the new ideas. Most of the reformers married once they broke with the old church.[14] Clerical marriage became an important issue in theological debates and no doubt was one that the laity could understand and take sides on. The issue predated the reformers. In a Danish law from 1521, members of the clergy were prohibited from purchasing land "unless they would follow the teachings of St. Paul, who in his first letter to Timothy, chapter 3, advises them to take wives." The law was abolished in 1523 but the issue remained. In Stockholm, the leading Lutheran preacher married in February of 1525, which might have been the occasion for the first celebration of a new Swedish Lutheran mass. The marriage evidently took place with the blessing and support of the king, but it caused quite an uproar among the Catholics in the city.[15]

In Denmark, we find the first married priest in Malmø; by late 1525 Master Per Lauritsen had married a certain Mette. (Perhaps she had been a *præstedeje*, a concubine of the priest before their marriage and in that case not the only one, as a Bodil *præstedeje* is mentioned in 1532.) Because of their marriage, the couple was harassed by a fellow citizen. The couple complained to the city council, which told both parties to cease hostilities and specifically urged the citizen to stop harassing the couple until the archepiscopal court had legally separated them. Shortly afterward the first reformers arrived in the city and the magistrates refused to obey the archbishop. Neither Mette nor her husband appear later in the sources.

In Malmø the magistrates supported the marriage of the clergy, but elsewhere the first generation of priests' wives suffered the censure of relatives and of their superiors, who refused to go along with the new idea. For example, when Marine married the priest Søren Svendsen, his superior, the bishop of Børglum, declared the marriage illegal and the children illegitimate. The couple took their case to the provincial court of Viborg, which overturned the bishop's decision and pronounced them to be a properly married couple. By 1537 the Reformation had succeeded, the bishop was in jail, and the priest had died, leaving his widow and children with little support. Marine had to sell some of his land and was immediately hauled into court by her brother-in-law, who, on the basis of the bishop's verdict declared that, as the concubine of his late brother, she had no right to dispose of his lands and her children no right to inherit. Marine once more had to go to the provincial court, which confirmed its 1533 decision making her the proper wife of Søren and their children his legitimate heirs.

A register from the royal chancery lists a letter, issued in 1535 to a woman, Doritte Jensdatter, "concerning the inheritance after her husband, the late Niels, priest to Ørum." This indicates that Marine's fate was not uncommon among the first generation of ministers' wives. Even higher ranking clergymen were hesitant about marrying. In 1538 the canon Ivar Juel, a nobleman, feared that he might lose his benefices if he married. Therefore, he obtained a letter from the king confirming his right to keep the benefices after marriage.[16] Outside of Stockholm, clerical marriages were a rarity in Sweden, until the second phase of the Reformation, during the 1540s. In 1530, the parishioners of Kuddby complained of their pastor's marriage but were instructed by the king that "men, wise and learned in the Holy Scriptures had recently determined that the marriage of clergy was scriptural."[17]

After a generation, clerical marriages seem to have been generally accepted, except by a few incorrigible canons at the cathedral of Lund who apparently kept concubines in spite of exhortations to marry. Concurrently, standards for the wife of a minister were formulated by the leaders of the new church. She had to be respectable, well brought up, and in possession of good manners—in short she had to come from the middle and upper layers of society. The daughters of burghers and well-off peasants saw the number of eligible husbands considerably enlarged because it was the male members of their social class who filled the ranks of the Lutheran clergy. Although marriage to a Protestant minister offered an opportunity for women, primarily of the bourgeois class, to be a part of the church, their role was that of caring for the ministers and bringing up future generations of ministers and ministers' wives. This is clearly expressed in a royal letter of 1541, which provided support for the widow and children of one of the first Protestant bishops, or superintendents, as they were called. The widow received an annual pension, the sons money for studying, and the daughters money for dowries. Similarly, the wills probated in Malmø after the Reformation show that sons and stepsons of the reformers received books whereas daughters received money and household goods as their share of paternal inheritance.[18] One of the most influential of the first Danish superintendents, Peder Palladius, makes the same point in his sermons when he argues that bright boys should be put in school to become ministers whereas girls (and slow boys) should be taught the basic tenets of the faith.[19]

An example of the new role for women in the church is the decision of the widow of an early reformer in Malmø to marry his successor. This set a pattern of clerical marriage that was to become standard. She also embroidered some silk altarcloths for the church of the new hospital (the former Franciscan monastery), for which she received payment. Though she is referred to in several documents, we do not know her name. She remains the wife of Master Olof and of Master Hans and the mother of their children. The new ministers' wives could also serve as models for female parishioners exercising charity, as did Anne, wife of the superintendent of Ribe. In 1548 she marched into the city court, followed by the leading ladies of the town, to plead for mercy for a poor girl who had been seduced and abandoned and now stood accused of infanticide. The girl was convicted, but the sentence reduced from death to public penitence and banishment "on account of God and the pleas of the goodwomen of the town."[20]

Thus, by the Reformation women gained a visible and socially acceptable role in the institutional church. The new role was, however, an extension of the domestic aspect of their role in society at large. They were not given a voice in the affairs of the church or in the discussions of the faith. That remained a male prerogative. In the long run, this visibility and the emphasis on the domestic role of the minister's wife as a model for other women may have helped undermine the acceptability of women's public role and work outside the family.

IV

The advent of the Reformation gave some married women the opportunity to change their marital conditions. This was, however, more a by-product of the reformers' activities than an expressed goal. When the ecclesiastical courts were abolished, the need for a secular court arose, in which the cases previously determined by the canonical courts could be handled. In Denmark the urban magistrates proved more than willing to assume such responsibility, and in 1539 it was decided that such cases were to be heard in the urban secular court. In 1542, the king reversed himself and moved marital cases to a special ecclesiastical court, the *tamperret,* made up of the cathedral chapter, professors at the University of Copenhagen or of the local learned school, and the secular official in charge of the diocese with the superintendent advising on difficult cases. In 1582 an ordinance specifically dealing with marital cases, including divorce, was finally passed.[21]

The records only permit us to follow the actions of the urban magisterial court in Malmø during the period of transition, 1529–42. It appears that the magistrates were granting divorces in cases of desertion and impotence and at times were more liberal than the preachers who were consulted. The majority of marital cases brought before the court were not, however, petitions for divorce but requests for help in making a marriage work. The petitioner was almost always a woman who sought the assistance of the city council court to make her husband behave as an "honest, Christian goodman should towards his wife, with food, beer, and social intercourse," as the standard phrase goes. The earliest records of the *tamperret* from the seventeenth century also indicate that women preferred the enforcement of a promise of marriage or of the wedding vows to divorce except in cases of desertion or impotence, that is, when the husband was unable to fulfill his social, economic, and marital duties.

This was also the sentiment that guided the new leaders of the church. Although they allowed divorce, they strongly preferred to preserve a marriage. The advice of Peder Palladius in a case from 1546 concerning wife-beating is quite revealing. Palladius does not question the right of the husband to discipline his wife, but he strongly objects to the mistreatment evident in this case. He suggests that the authorities have the husband whipped "so he can feel himself how wonderful it is to beat and tear into a poor woman's body and limbs, especially the one towards whom he ought to show the best behaviour." If that does not help, the superintendent suggests that the couple be allowed to live separately, and, since the wife is the wronged party, she should get control over the largest portion of their joint property. He does not suggest divorce and advocates separation only as a second solution.[22] A similar solution was put forward by the Scanian superintendent in 1550 in another case of wife abuse.

Since the records from the medieval ecclesiastical courts have not survived, we cannot gauge how much of a change the new marital court procedures was for women. The Malmø cases seem to indicate that women eagerly sought the help of the magistrates of their town to improve marital conditions and that the magistrates encouraged this behavior as part of their strategy to exercise social control through their courts. Doubtless going into the local city court to men who were known to them and who, judging again from the Malmø records, were sympathetic to their plight encouraged more women to seek changes in unsatisfactory conditions than would an ecclesiastical court, which was physically and mentally further removed from women. On the other hand, not all secular courts condoned actions taken by women to obtain divorce. In 1536, the king's court convicted of adultery a woman who thought she had obtained a legal divorce, issued by the local reeve, from her husband. She had remarried in good faith, but her new husband was also found guilty of adultery and both were condemned to death. A similar case in Malmø, in which a woman had left her husband and for several years lived with another man with whom she had children, resulted in the husband being granted a divorce and the wife being indirectly declared the proper wife of her lover. In Sweden, the king had granted divorces as early as 1537 as part of a policy to undermine the authority of the church and to control where possible the lives and affairs of his subjects.[23]

The changes brought by the Reformation in matters concerning marital problems were, however, not major in the long run. After an interval the ecclesiastical courts of the old church were succeeded by the ecclesiastical courts of the new church. Divorce was allowed but only as an exception. What the extant records do make clear is that women who wanted changes in their marital conditions were quick to use the new venues that opened up during the period of transition.

The message given to women by the preachers was that marriage was now the highest and most desirable state. Since most women both before and after the Reformation did marry (convent life was for a small group only), this must have sounded pleasing to a large majority of women. But they could not have foreseen that the price for the elevation of the wife was paid by the women who, either voluntarily or involuntarily, did not marry or who were left as widows. And within marriage the superiority of the husband was stressed, perhaps more so than before. Palladius draws the picture of the husband as the strong and forbearing partner and the wife as the weaker spouse who should obey her husband in return for guidance and support. At the same time, the wife should also be the strong mistress of the household, specifically charged with the well-being of her female servants and responsible for their behavior.[24]

Opportunities for single women to lead a spiritual life disappeared with the Reformation. Convents could no longer accept new members, although the current population of nuns was allowed to remain in the convent if they so chose. When the property of Vadstena, motherhouse of the Birgittine order, was confiscated in the 1540s by the king, female as well as male adherents of the saint rallied to support her order and its first house. The motherhouse lived on for another couple of decades, literally in the shadow of the royal castle at Vadstena, which was built with stones taken from neighboring monasteries, convents, and churches when, according to the new order of things, they became superfluous.[25] The mendicant orders were violently expelled during the Reformation. The Danish friars wrote about their trials; their sister order, the Poor Claires, however, was doomed to suffer in silence. A letter of 1527 to the exiled king Christian II describes the poverty suffered by the Claires in Copenhagen but mentions also that they have sought to keep it a secret from their enemies. The sisters had received a box with money for safekeeping from Sigbrit, the female advisor of Christian II who had followed him in exile in 1523, and the writer asks the king if the sisters may use some of the money to survive, reminding him of the special devotion his mother had shown to the order. If indeed Christian did answer, his response has not survived. In 1532 the nuns are recorded as having left the city. The house in Roskilde survived until 1561, and one former nun still received a pension in the 1580s.[26]

For single women leading a secular life outside the household, life also became difficult. During the late Middle Ages urban society had offered a wide range of opportunities for women to make a living; the towns were also the first communities in which the new church and religion was firmly established along with new ideas of women's proper place. In 1549, an ordinance for Malmø directed "self-supporting maidens" either to become domestic servants or be banished from town.[27] Widows were allowed greater freedom, but actions by city magistrates and legislation from the second half of the sixteenth century show that women in the cities were increasingly restricted to marginal trades and crafts, which in turn had the effect of making them operate on the edge of the law in order to survive.[28]

In northern Norway, the drop in fish prices relative to grain prices during the early modern period hit women, especially single women engaged in the fishery, harder than the men because women were cut off from the actual catching of fish. They cleaned and salted the fish or catered to the fishermen as cooks, alewives, or prostitutes. With dropping fish prices, fishermen reduced costs by doing without paid women workers, relying instead on wives and daughters. Conditions were better for women in areas where the husband fished and the wife farmed, but this benefited married, not single, women.[29]

Some of these changes in women's work were caused by economic developments. Yet the new religion, which made women invisible except when in the role of wife, must have contributed not only to the change in the attitudes of the authorities toward single women's work but also must have undermined women's confidence in themselves and in their right to work outside the household setting.

V

Apparently the Reformation was accepted by the majority of the Danish people without major upheavals after the end of the civil war in 1536, even though on the surface the change was more drastic than in Sweden. There, a decision by the Estates in 1527 opened the way for a gradual dismantling of the medieval church and the takeover of its propertied institutions, but the wording expresses merely a desire to curb abuses in the church and to skim off "surplus wealth and luxury." Indeed, after a rebellion in 1528, the king had to promise that "all good old Christian customs may be confirmed and maintained and the Lutheran heresy and the evil communications that go with it be clean done away with." The king's own household remained partly Catholic, as Gustav Vasa's second wife, the Swedish noblewoman Margareta Leijonhufvud, remained a Catholic until her death in 1551.

In the major cities, where the city council, the king, or both actively supported the reformers, the abolishment of altars, confraternities, and Masses along with the expulsion of the mendicant orders made people immediately aware of what was happening. Protests against the new order were suppressed, as is shown from the following incident. In a letter signed "after evensong" on October 17, 1530, in Copenhagen, two prominent citizens admit to having received a silver crown from a citizen of Malmø, Kirstine Henrik Dringelbergs. The crown had been donated to the statue of the Virgin in the Church of Our Lady in Copenhagen by her late mother-in-law. Kirstine had decided that the crown had better be removed from the church and given to the two men for safekeeping "until the Church will recover and be allowed to enjoy the possessions that good people have given her." Should it happen "what God forbids that the Church will not recover and not be allowed to enjoy her donations," the crown had to be returned to the heirs of the donor. Two months later a crowd stormed into the church and destroyed the statues. In the earliest account book of St. Petri Church in Malmø from 1532, there is a reference to "income from rentals of Our Lady's crown," which shows that ten of the town's patrician women had rented it, most likely as a bridal crown for their daughters. The crown reappears in the accounts from 1539. If it is the same crown as the one that formerly adorned the statue of Our Lady in Copenhagen, the Dringelberg family had given up hope that the Church would "recover."[30]

Changes occurred less drastically in the countryside, where the large majority of the population lived. There, after an often skimpy lesson in the new teachings, the old parish priests continued to serve until a new generation of ministers could be educated in the Lutheran faith. The medieval wall paintings remained in the churches, echoing for another century the former popularity of the female and male saints as well as the former power of the Virgin. Peder Palladius recommended that side altars be removed and statues shorn of their adornment, which was to be sold for the benefit of the poor. But he allowed the pictures to remain "as a mirror for simple folks." He also stressed in sermons to the congregations of his diocese the futility of pilgrimages and the cult of the saints. Such beliefs were the work of the devil. Rather than running to the "dead James, Severin and Anne," his congregation should take care of the living James, Severin, and Anne in the parish, give them comfort, food, and clothes. Although he does not specify who among the parishioners should do so, from another sermon it is clear that charity of this kind was the responsibility of the housewives in the villages.

The condemnation of pilgrimages was not always immediately accepted or understood, as the poignant story of an anonymous Danish peasant-woman demonstrates. She dropped her child inadvertently and it broke its neck. In sorrow and in fear of her husband she ran with the dead child in her arms five miles to a church where a miracle-working host had been a popular goal for pilgrims during the fifteenth century. The Reformation, however, had intervened, the host was removed, and a Lutheran minister installed as parish priest, "and when he discovered her intentions, he taught her the proper faith and she laid down her child in the cemetery and went home."[31] Stories such as this may have had more of an impact on women than many sermons on faith. Palladius' message to Danish women was also conveyed to Norwegian and Icelandic women, when in 1541 he wrote a catechetical textbook for the Norwegian clergy, which in 1546 was translated into Icelandic.

In several sermons and writings, Palladius refers to popish agents who wanted to retain all altars and statues of saints "to await new times for their business and plunder to return." The same fear is echoed in the writings of other reformers, which would indicate that to some people the Reformation was a temporary phase which would pass. One woman we know of harbored just these feelings. When she died in 1571, it was discovered that among her belongings were "six chalices and patens with some books which the greyfriars who had lived there [in Elsinore] some years ago were said to have handed over to her for safekeeping."[32] If women especially held a secret hope for the return of the old church, the scarce evidence does not permit any firm conclusion. In Denmark, a woman was accused of thievery and of running around with a renegade monk, but the charges were denied and the case dismissed. Palladius also uses the term "popish monks' women" when referring to bad women. This might indicate a greater loyalty on the part of women to the Catholic clergy but may also be a common term of abuse aimed at women.[33] The earliest witchcraft trials in Denmark, however, did involve priests and women, so perhaps there were some bonds, now hidden to the historian.

Although the medieval laws of Denmark did refer to sorcery, not until the early sixteenth century did legislation specifically concerned with witches and sorcerers appear. The laws of Christian II from 1521–22 urge authorities to keep an eye on men and women who have a reputation for being sorcerers to see if they behave in an unusual manner or cause harm through sorcery. This attempt at an inquisitory process in cases of suspected witchcraft was halted when, after his flight, Christian II's legislation was abolished. Christian III responded to any signs of a witchcraft craze by issuing an ordinance in 1547 that prohibited the use of the testimony of "bad persons, including sorcerers," in a trial and the use of torture before the sentencing. Still, there are records of about one hundred witchcraft trials in Denmark before 1600; the majority of them took place in the 1560s and 1570s until stopped in 1576 by a royal decree which ordered that all witchcraft trials be appealed to the provincial courts. Legislation concerning the prosecution of and punishment for witchcraft did not come until 1617. The major concern of the authorities were persons, men as well as women, who used incantations and gestures for beneficial or evil purposes. They were seen as hidden agents for the Catholic church. The public did not, however, share this worry. It feared *maleficium*.[34]

The earliest known Danish trial is mentioned in a letter of 1523, which does not specify who or how many were tried for sorcery. In 1533, 1540, and 1543 witchcraft trials involving men and women took place in various Danish cities; some of the accused were priests who were charged with using white magic. Although these trials are relatively few, the psychological impact on women must not be underestimated, as is evident from a testimony issued in 1532 by the royal chancery. A Karine Laurisdotter (likely a single woman) had been accused by neighbors of using sorcery. Fearing the loss of her house and property, she had obtained a testimony from twenty-four goodmen of her parish declaring that they had known her since childhood and had never heard or known her to be using sorcery or engaging in similar evil deeds. Sensing that this was not enough to protect her, she went to the king and received a royal confirmation of the testimony.[35]

In Norway, old customs and rites remained in use publicly for quite a while after the Reformation. Indeed, Christian III had in 1537 advised his viceroy to proceed carefully with the Reformation and leave parish priests in their posts for the time being in order to prevent discord among the poor, simple, and ignorant people in Norway. In 1568, a Danish commission found that there were altogether too many pictures of saints in the churches of Bergen, but that the prompt removal of these by the superintendent caused a strong protest from the people and from the magistrates. The statutes passed at the synod in the diocese of Stavanger in 1573 also indicate that many of the rites and ceremonies of the medieval church were alive and well. That same year a woman was whipped for claiming to have received visions from the Virgin.[36]

During the 1560s the first documented witchcraft trials took place in Norway. Four trials took place between 1561 and 1570; the number rose to twenty-five between 1571 and 1580. The sources contain references to a witchcraft trial alleged to have taken place in 1539. The first major witchcraft legislation was issued in 1593, but the number of trials remained below twenty for each decade prior to 1611–20. The same pattern is found in Sweden and Finland. There, the records indicate that trials were few and scattered until the end of the sixteenth century, in spite of the fact that the medieval Swedish laws contain more references than the other Nordic laws to *maleficium* and white magic and make them peculiar female crimes.[37]

In Iceland, where the cult of the Virgin had dominated religious life during the fifteenth and the first half of the sixteenth centuries, Mary remained an important figure in popular beliefs and practices. In the nineteenth century, a collector of Icelandic folk and fairy tales noticed the survival of "popish prayers and verses," of which half were dedicated to the Virgin and read by ignorant folks, "especially women." The Feast of the Annunciation was officially abolished in 1770 but continued to be celebrated.[38] In the case of witchcraft, we see an interesting reversal of the standard European (and Scandinavian) pattern. Based on an old tradition of cunning men and of male magicians endowed with the power of special knowledge, men also became the victims of the witch hunts. During the 120 trials conducted between 1604 and 1720, twenty-two men and only one woman were burned as witches. The Icelandic word for witch was masculine, which was contrasted to the rest of Europe where, beginning with the *Malleus Maleficarum,* witch was defined as female.[39]

VI

One aspect of married life that gave women some control over their own lives was the period of pregnancy, childbirth, and recovery.[40] Childbirth was almost exclusively a female affair, a time when women came to rely on each other and when, as part of their wifely role, they could demand special privileges. It is also in the customs and rites connected with childbirth that the cult of the Virgin and Saint Margaret, patron saint of women in labor, survived. In Denmark a popular rhyme, "Mother Mary, mother Mary, lend me your key so I can open my loins," was taught by midwives to women in labor and was prohibited as "popish talk" as late as the early eighteenth century. The use of such rhymes or incantations worried the authorities who sought to suppress them by educating the midwives, who were to be examined by the local minister to make sure they could properly instruct the parturient women. Palladius inveighs against superstitious old "monks' women," whom he lumps together with witches, and he recommends that women seek the help of good midwives. He also gives examples of the incantations used by the "monks' women," revealing that these formulars have their origin in prayers to the Virgin, Saint Anne, and Saint Margaret. Palladius stresses that from now on women are dealing with God the Father and Christ the Son, who have ordained that women should bring up children with much sorrow and pain and "many nights awake." Women's response was apparently that these male figures were inadequate as birth helpers. Women continued, albeit partially hidden from male view (and thus unfortunately also from that of the historians), to seek the help of Mary and the saints during birth.

In Iceland a special cult of Saint Margaret has recently been uncovered through the many manuscripts of her *vita* that were written after the Reformation right down until the nineteenth century. The manuscripts are quite small and could easily be kept in a private place to be taken out when needed. Besides the *vita* of Saint Margaret, the manuscripts contain prayers for pregnant women and women in labor. Some of them also admonish the user to make sure that the manuscript is not soiled and, if it is, to copy it carefully and then burn it.[41]

Churching, which was the official church-sponsored celebration of the recovery of the parturient woman (if she was married), also provided an opportunity for women to take over the church, albeit for a brief moment. Palladius urges all female members of the congregation to join up behind the woman being churched and offer collects in her honor. He especially urges the richer women in the congregation to accompany the poorer, thus letting female solidarity override social barriers. An ordinance issued in Ribe in 1561 addresses the opposite problem, forbidding too many women to accompany the churching woman and urging those who do to give their collects at the same time, not one after the other "in order that the service not be delayed thereby".[42]

No such honor was accorded the unwed mother. For her, the churching was a humiliating public confession of her sins, one that the father also had to undergo, if he was around. The Reformation brought about a sharp change in attitudes toward unwed mothers. What had been a relatively relaxed attitude, in which the major concern was to make the father help support the child, became more severe, in which giving birth out of wedlock was seen as a grave insult to marriage and to society. Palladius talks at length against sinning, exhorting the young girls to say no until safely wed. Still, young women did become pregnant, and in 1555 the Danish king issued a letter declaring that he has heard that many girls in Copenhagen had let themselves be seduced, become pregnant, and then either killed their children or abandoned them at the church door. He urged that goodwomen of the city be appointed to examine servant girls or other unmarried women to see if they were pregnant. The purpose was to prevent the death of the infant either from neglect or from being killed deliberately by the desperate mother. In the seventeenth century, giving birth in secret was considered murder and was made a capital crime if the child died. In Iceland a severe lawcode, the *Storidomr,* which dealt with adultery, fornication, incest, and concubinage, was issued in 1564. Apparently the law was not strictly enforced until the seventeenth century, when many young women were executed for giving birth in secret even when pregnancy was the result of outright or incestuous rape.[43]

VII

In a discussion of the relationship between women and power in the North, the Swedish historian, Beata Losman, argues that women experienced a loss of political and economic power relative to men during the early modern period but that the loss took place over a long period and depended on class as well as gender. Only spiritual power was abruptly lost with the advent of the Reformation.[44] With the establishment of the Lutheran church in the Nordic countries, the secular and spiritual authorities were joined, thereby allowing no independent religious expression as had been possible during the Middle Ages. The female elements in religion were eliminated, as can be seen in the post-Reformation wall paintings. They depict Old Testament motives, primarily the (male) prophets, stress the maleness of Christ, and reduce Mary to a small person at the edge of the painting whose only role is to give birth to Christ. As women had no policymaking role in the church, they could not influence the new religious culture. Why, then, did they not protest? The question has not yet been asked because no one has thought to ask what the Reformation meant to women in the Nordic countries. In concluding, I shall attempt to provide some tentative answers.

The spiritual loss was not felt as keenly as a modern historian sees it. In spite of the hard work of the reformers, old rites and beliefs hung on. The medieval paintings, for example, were not covered for a century after their work; thus, women still saw images in the churches showing powerful female divine characters. In one peculiarly female aspect of their lives, during childbirth, a cult of the Virgin and the female saints was kept alive, albeit hidden from the clergy. Ironically, the increasing gap between public and private, along with the domestication of women, also meant that women could retain whatever they needed of the medieval religious culture in their private world.

The loss of the old religion also was a loss to men who preferred it to the new. Even though it was men who acquired a monopoly on shaping the new church, the large majority was also excluded from being heard. The change from predominantly noble to a predominantly bourgeois clergy did not make it easier for sons of poorer peasants, not to mention the male children from the growing rural and urban proletariat, to begin a clerical career. The structure of society and economic conditions made social distinctions more apparent than gender division. The same holds true for witchcraft. The early witchcraft trials generally involved an equal number of men and women, whereas the women dominated during the seventeenth century when the number of trials peaked. The Reformation did not introduce witchcraft as a peculiar female crime. The evidence shows, however, that accusations of witchcraft caused tension and anxiety among women during the early decades of the Reformation and perhaps a few women realized that being female made them more vulnerable.

On the surface, the elimination of spiritual space for single women concerned only a small group of upper-class women. Most women married and could approve the elevation of the wife. What women might forget, and what reformers and legislators certainly ignored, was the fact that demographic conditions made widowhood certain for many married women and eliminated eligible bachelors for a number of other women. The abolition of the single woman's spiritual space also caused her claim to secular space to be ignored by the authorities and society at large, even though the need for single women to find an existence outside the family and the household was very real.

The Reformation did indeed cause changes for both sexes in the Nordic societies, but the course of these changes varied in time and place and was dependent on class as well as gender. Only from a modern perspective does it become apparent that the end result was to place the female sex at a severe disadvantage relative to the male sex. This was first apparent in the area of religion.

NOTES

1. In spite of extensive research on the Nordic Reformation, little has been done on social and economic issues and nothing on women and the Reformation. My own research has focused on Denmark and, consequently, most examples in this article come from Danish sources. Useful works in English are: Michael Roberts, *The Early Vasas: A History of Sweden 1523–1611* (Cambridge: The University Press, 1968) and John C. F. Hood, *The Icelandic Church Saga* (London: Society for Promoting Christian Knowledge, 1946; repr. University Microfilm Reprint, 1973). No newer survey of the Danish and Norwegian Reformation exists in English. Martin Schwarz Lausten, *Reformationen i Danmark* (Copenhagen: Akademisk Forlag, 1987) is an excel-

lent survey in Danish; Schwarz Lausten has also produced voluminous and informative analyses of the crucial decades after 1536 in his *Christian d. 3. og kirken (1537–1559)*, Studier i den danske reformationskirke, 1 (Copenhagen: Akademisk Forlag, 1987) and *Biskop Peder Palladius og kirken (1537–1560)*, Studier i den danske reformationskirke, 2 (Copenhagen: Akademisk Forlag, 1987); both have German summaries. For Norway, *Norsk kirkehistorie*, vol. 1, (Oslo: Lutherstiftelsen, 1966) have been used. As the term Scandinavia refers only to Denmark, Norway, and Sweden, I have used the terms the North and Nordic to indicate all five Nordic countries.

2. For a discussion of the relationship between women and political, economic and social power in the preindustrial North, see Beata Losman, "Kvinnorna och makten eller Vart tog sköldmörna vägen?" in *Den dolda historien: 27 uppsatser om vårt okända förflutna*, ed. Ronny Ambjörnsson och David Gaunt (n.p.: Författarförlaget, 1984), pp. 13–32 and references there.

3. Elsa E. Gudjonsson, "Islandske broderier og broderersker i middelalderen," *Förändringar i kvinnors villkor under medeltiden. Uppsatser framlagda vid ett kvinnohistoriskt symposium i Skálholt, Island, 22.–25. juni 1981*, ed. Silja Adalsteinsdottir and Helgi Thorlaksson (Reykjavik: Sagnfrædistofnun Háskola Íslands, 1983), pp. 127–58; ibid., *Traditional Icelandic Embroidery* (Reykjavík: Icelandic Review, 1985), esp. pp. 55–57; Jonna Louis-Jensen, " 'Haldóra Sigurdardóttir á mig' " in *Sjötíu ritgerdir helgadar Jakobi Benediktssyni 20. juli 1977* (Reykjavík: Stofnun Árna Magnússonar, 1971), pp. 544–55. Both authors mention that the wife of a clergyman was called a *fylgikona*, indicating a status between a wife and a concubine, so formally the Icelandic clergy was not married. The social status of the *fylgikona* and her children depended, however, on her family background and that of her lover, so being a *fylgikona* did not in itself carry a social stigma. It can be mentioned, that the *fylgikona* of Jon Arason in 1526 made a special contract with her husband and his church that in return for an annual sum, she was to make embroideries for the cathedral.

4. Grethe Jacobsen, "Women, Marriage, and Magisterial Reformation: The Case of Malmø, Denmark," *Pietas et Societas: New Trends in Reformation Social History; Essays in Memory of Harold J. Grimm*, ed. by Kyle C. Session and Phillip N. Bebb, Sixteenth Century Essays and Studies, IV (Kirksville, Mo.: Sixteenth Century Journal Publishers, 1985), pp. 62–63, p. 65 n.41.

5. For information on the various orders and their houses in the Nordic countries see *Kulturhistorisk leksikon for nordisk middelalder fra vikingetid til reformationstid* (Copenhagen: Rosenkilde og Bagger, 1965–78), s.v. "Kloster" and individual orders. The number of Benedictine and Cistercian monasteries were thirty-seven to which must be added a small number of (male) houses from other orders, while Benedictine and Cistercian convents numbered twenty-nine. The convents were generally much smaller than the monasteries. Within the mendicant orders, the difference is greater: forty-five Franciscan and twenty-eight Dominican houses in Scandinavia (twenty-six and fifteen in Denmark) but only eight houses for Poor Claires or for Dominican nuns (five in Denmark, three in Sweden).

6. Tore Nyberg, *Birgittinische Klostergründungen des Mittelalters*, Bibliotheca Historica Lundensis, xv (Lund: Gleerup, 1965).

7. Thelma Jexlev, *Fra dansk senmiddelalder: nogle kildestudier* (Odense: Odense Universitetsforlag, 1976); Holger Fr. Rørdam, *Kjøbenhavns Kirker og Klostre i Middelalderen* (Copenhagen: Selskabet for Danmarks Kirkehistorie, 1859–63), pp. 287–90; Marianne Johansen, "Beginer i Danmark" in *Fromhed og verdslighed i middelalder og renaissance: festskrift til Thelma Jexlev*, ed. Ebba Waaben, et al. (Odense: Odense Universitetsforlag, 1985), pp. 18–23; *Kulturhistorisk leksikon for nordisk middelalder*, s.v. "Beginer".

8. *Kulturhistorisk leksikon for nordisk middelalder*, s.v. "Anna" and individual saints and motives. Jens Christian V. Johansen has discussed the connection between the devils on the Danish church walls and continental demonology during the late Middle Ages in "Hexen auf mittelalterlichen Wandmalereien: Zur Genese der Hexenproz-

esse in Dänemark," in Andreas Blauert, ed., *Die Anfänge der europäischen Hexenverfolgung im 15. Jahrhundert* (Frankfurt: Edition Suhrkamp, in press). For Danish witchcraft during the seventeenth century see his article on Denmark in *Witchhunting in Early Modern Europe: Centres and Peripheries,* ed. Bengt Ankarloo and Gustav Henningsen (London: Oxford University Press, in press). A Swedish edition has appeared as *Häxornas Europa, 1400–1700: Historiska och antropologiska studier* (Lund: Institutet för Rättshistorisk Forskning, 1987).

9. *Kulturhistorisk leksikon for nordisk middelalder,* s.v. "Brödraskap," "Gilde," "Indulgens," "Indulgensbrev."

10. *Norsk kirkehistorie,* 1:390, 394–96, 400; Hood, *Icelandic,* pp. 149–55.

11. E. Jørgensen and J. Skovgaard, *Danske Dronninger: Fortællinger og Karakteristikker* (Copenhagen: Hagerup, 1910) p. 109.

12. *Kirkehistoriske Samlinger,* 1 (1849–52), p. 376; Henrik Lundbak, . . . *Såfremt som vi skulle være deres lydige borgere": Rådene i København og Malmø 1516–1536 og deres politiske virksomhed i det feudale samfund* (Odense: Odense Universitetsforlag, 1985) pp. 97–102.

13. Information on Citse Kortsdatter and other Danish women during the Reformation in Grethe Jacobsen, *Kvindeskikkelser og kvindeliv i Danmarks middelalder* (Copenhagen: Gad, 1986), chapter 4. An English edition is planned.

14. The following is based on Jacobsen, "Women, Marriage" (n.4) pp. 62–67, except where noted.

15. Conrad Bergendoff, *Olavus Petri and the Ecclesiastical Transformation in Sweden (1521–1552): A Study in the Swedish Reformation* (New York: Macmillan, 1928), p. 220.

16. *Danske Kancelliregistranter, 1535–1550,* ed. Kr. Erslev and W. Mollerup (Copenhagen: Selskabet for Udgivelse af Kilder til Dansk Historie, 1881–82), pp. 1, 63, 123.

17. Bergendoff, *Olavus Petri,* p. 55; Herman Schück, *Ecclesia Lincopensis: Studier om Linköpingskyrkan under medeltiden och Gustav Vasa* (Stockholm: Almqvist och Wiksell, 1959), p. 568.

18. Bue Kaae, *Kvindekår og kvindeskæbner i reformationsårhundredet belyst ved eksempler fra Ribe* (Ribe: Historisk Samfund for Ribe Amt, 1981); *Danske Kancelliregistranter, 1535–1550,* p. 212; *Malmö Rådstueprotokol (Stadsbok) 1503–1548,* ed. Erik Kroman (Copenhagen: Selskabet for Udgivelse af Kilder til Dansk Historie, 1965), passim.

19. *Peder Palladius' Visitatsbog,* ed. Lis Jacobsen (Copenhagen: Gyldendal, 1925) pp. 89–96.

20. Malmö. Stadsarkivet. LIa:Räkenskaper för kyrka.Andliga godsens räkenskaper.l, fol. 20r (henceforth MSA. Räkenskaper); *Ribe rådstuedombøger 1527–1576 og 1580–99,* ed. Erik Kroman (Copenhagen: Selskabet for Udgivelse af Kilder til Dansk Historie, 1974) p. 22ff.

21. Following based on Jacobsen "Women, Marriage" (n.4) and same, *Kvindeskikkelser,* (n.13) chapter 5, except where noted.

22. *Breve til og fra Mogens Gyldenstjerne og Anne Sparre,* ed. E. Marquard (Copenhagen: Selskabet for Udgivelse af Kilder til Dansk Historie, 1929–36) pp. 129–32.

23. Roberts, *Early Vasas,* p. 168.

24. *Peder Palladius' Visitatsbog* pp. 50, 102, 112–13 (n.19). In the records of the marital cases in Malmø, there is a subtle shift during the 1530s toward stressing humility and obedience as important attributes of good wives (Jacobsen, "Women, Marriage," pp. 71–72).

25. Schück, *Ecclesia,* p. 591.

26. *Breve og Aktstykker til Oplysning af Christiern den Andens og Frederik den Førstes Historie, I,* ed. C.F. Allen (Copenhagen: Reitzel, 1854), pp. 477–79; *Kjøbenhavns Kirker og Klostre* (n.7) p. 290; Thelma Jexlev, "Nonneklostrene i Roskilde," *Historisk Årbog fra Roskilde Amt,* 1977, p. 38.

27. *Malmö Stadsbog 1549–1559, rådstuerettens, bytingets og toldbodrettens protokol,* ed. Erik Kroman (Copenhagen: Selskabet for Udgivelse af Kilder til Dansk Historie, 1972) p. 35. For a discussion of women in the medieval Danish cities see my

"Women's Work and Women's Role: Ideology and Reality in Danish Urban Society, 1300–1550," *Scandinavian Economic History Review*, 30:1 (1983), pp. 3–20; and "Economic Progress and the Sexual Division of Labor: The Role of Guilds in the Late-Medieval Danish City" in *Alltag und Fortschritt im Mittelalter: internationales Round-Table-Gespräch, Krems an der Donau 1. Oktober 1984*, Veröffentlichungen des Instituts für Mittelalterliche Realienkunde Österreichs, 8 (Vienna: Verlag der Österreichischen Akademie der Wissenschaften, 1986), pp. 223–36.

28. Jacobsen, *Kvindeskikkelser*, chapter 4 (n.13).

29. Ragnhild Aarsæther, "Kvinner som familieforsørgere og sjølforsørgende belyst ved nordnorske skattelister på 1500-tallet og 1600-tallet," *Kvinnans ekonomiska ställning under nordisk medeltid: Uppsatser framlagda vid ett kvinnohistoriskt symposium i Kungälv 8–12 oktober 1979*, ed. Hedda Gunneng and Birgit Strand (Göteborg: n.p., 1981), pp. 41–49.

30. *Kjøbenhavns Kirker og Klostre* pp. 188–90 (n.7); MSA. Räkenskaper, fols. 16v, 259v.

31. *Peder Palladius' Visitatsbog* pp. 36 (n.19), 130–32, 128–29.

32. *Helsingør i Sundtoldtiden 1426–1857*, ed. Laurits Pedersen, II (Copenhagen: Busck, 1927) pp. 47, 194.

33. *Det kgl. rettertings domme og rigens forfølgninger fra Christian III's tid*, ed. Troels Dahlerup (Copenhagen: Selskabet for Udgivelse af Kilder til Dansk Historie, 1959–69) I, pp. 207–208; *Peder Palladius' Visitatsbog*, p. 109.

34. Merete Birkelund, *Troldkvinden og hendes anklagere: Danske hekseprocesser i det 16. og 17. århundrede med et bilag om processerne i Østjylland* (Århus: Arusia–Historiske Skrifter, 1983), pp. 26–40; Karsten Sejr Jensen, *Trolddom i Danmark, 1500–1588* (Copenhagen: Arken-Tryk, 1982), pp. 36–54.

35. *Kong Frederik den Førstes danske Registranter*, ed. Kr. Erslev and W. Mollerup (Copenhagen: Selskabet for Udgivelse af Kilder til Dansk Historie, 1879), pp. 451–52; similar letters in *Danske Kancelliregistranter* p. 129, 130, (n.16).

36. *Norsk kirkehistorie*, pp. 417, 437–38, 445–46, 454. In the 1540s two peasants claimed to be Saint Olaf and Saint Nicholas bearing messages from the blessed mother of Christ (ibid).

37. Articles by Hans Eyvind Næss (Norway), Bengt Ankarloo (Sweden), Antero Heikkinen and Timo Kervinen (Finland) in *Witchhunting in Early Modern Europe: Centres and Peripheries* (n.8).

38. Stefan Einarsson, *A History of Icelandic Literature* (New York: The Johns Hopkins University Press, for the American-Scandinavian Foundation, 1957), pp. 76–78; Jón Árnason, *Islenzkar thjodsögur og æfintyri*, new ed. by Arni Bödvarsson and Bjarni Vilhjálmsson (Reykjavik: Bókaútgafan Thjodsaga Prentsmidjan Hólar, 1954–56, orig. publ. in Leipzig, 1862–64), II, pp. 57–58. The morning prayer seems to have been truly a prayer: "Mary Maiden, hear I pray / Hold me from all harms this day / . . . / thee I trust, God's own sweet maid / Pray for me alive and dead."

The evening prayer, however, seems more like an incantation: ". . . God keep the door and Crux the lock / Mary Maiden all within and Michael Angel all without . . ." English translation from *Ghosts, Witchcraft and the Other World: Icelandic Folktales I*, tr. Alan Boucher (Reykjavik: Icelandic Review Library, 1977), pp. 13, 88. Árni Björnsson, *Saga daganna: Hátídir og merkisdagar á Íslandi og úprúni theirra* (Reykjavik: Saga, 1977), p. 40.

39. See Kirsten Hastrup on Icelandic witchcraft in *Witchhunting in Early Modern Europe: Centres and Peripheries* (n.8).

40. Following is based on Grethe Jacobsen, "Pregnancy and Childbirth in the Medieval North: A Typology of Sources and a Preliminary Study," *Scandinavian Journal of History*, 9:2 (1984):91–111, except where noted.

41. *Kulturhistorisk leksikon for nordisk middelalder*, s.v. "Margareta (af Antiochia). Norge og Island"; Asdis Egilsdottir, " 'Margretar Saga' håndskrifter og deres brug

på Island som hjælpemiddel for fødende kvinder" to be published in *Kvinnors rosengård och örtagård,* Skrifter utgivna av Centrum för Kvinnoforskning (Stockholm: Stockholm University, 1989) containing papers from two Nordic symposia, held in 1985 and 1987, dealing with women's sexuality in the medieval North. In the 1970s a scholar sought to borrow one of them but was told that it could not be taken out of the county "in case the situation arose that there was a need for it." The story was related to me by Inga Huld Hákonardóttir, to whom I owe many thanks for useful information and references concerning Iceland.

42. *Peder Palladius' Visitatsbog* pp. 112–13, (n. 19); J. Kinch, *Ribe Bys Historie,* repr. ed. by Ole Degn (Århus: Jysk Selskab for Historie, Universitetsforlaget, 1985), pp. 93–96.

43. Beth Grothe Nielsen, *"Letfærdige Quindfolk": Fosterdrab og fødsel i dølgsmål i retshistorisk belysning* (Copenhagen: Kriminalistisk Institut, Københavns Universitet, 1980). The *Storidomr* is currently being studied by Inga Huld Hákonardóttir.

44. Losman, "Kvinnorna och makten" (n. 2).

DAVID P. DANIEL

Piety, Politics, and Perversion: Noblewomen in Reformation Hungary

Life was harsh in the troubled land of Hungary during the sixteenth and early seventeenth centuries. Brutality all too frequently strained and stained the fabric of Hungarian society. Rent asunder by the onslaught and continuing presence of the Turks, its governmental institutions sapped by the unabated political maneuvering of noble families seeking to secure their fortunes and influence during the seemingly perpetual struggle between the Habsburgs and their Transylvanian rivals for the Holy Crown of Hungary, the peoples of the partitioned nation became accustomed to violence and conflict. Religious controversy, slow economic decline, social and even ethnic tensions kept the wounds inflicted by war and party strife open and festering.[1]

The Hungarian "time of troubles" affected all elements of the population and was accentuated by the understandable but often destructive manifestations of the desire for self-preservation, barely bridled ambition, acquisitiveness, self-centeredness, and a remarkable propensity for self-delusion. Although estate and position did supply the nobility and the burghers with those ameliorating benefits of property, social status, and political influence, benefits denied the *miseria contribuens plebs,* the miserable, contributing peasantry, virtually no one in Hungary could feel truly secure, the master of one's own destiny.

If this was true for both male and female, it must likewise be admitted that in sixteenth-century Hungary, as throughout much of history, women endured the additional constraints imposed by law, custom, and biology. Women ultimately had little to say about how or with whom they would spend their lives: the cloister, the marriage bond, or servitude, whether involuntarily imposed or willingly assumed. To be sure, this did not mean that all necessarily were unhappy with their condition or position or that individual women did not prosper, experience fulfillment, and find contentment. There is evidence enough to indicate that some women found personal satisfaction and found prosperity within the constraints imposed from without or within on their gender. But when all is taken into consideration, women had few options. They were biological, economic, and political capital. Their primary obligation was to secure and insure the survival, position, and fortunes of the family into which they had been born or into which they married. Whatever their own personal desires or ambitions may have been, women, especially noblewomen, were reckoned as and had to consider themselves tools to be used for dynastic purposes. They had to be ready to sacrifice their own needs and desires in order to serve effectively as vessels carrying and agents securing the inheritance of their family, the means by which position was preserved, fortunes acquired, maintained, and enlarged.

Nevertheless, while only a very few women in sixteenth-century society had a determinative voice as to the conditions within which they would spend their days, women could and did attempt to obtain some control over their own lives. Within the boundaries imposed by family needs and interests, they sought to shape their fate and fortunes. Some were able to employ effectively their position and connections to obtain wealth, influence, and power for their families. Others, disregarding customary societal roles and mores, endangered the security of their own family and proved not only a threat to themselves, but to those around them as well. Some attained fame; others infamy.

Three individuals stand out as noteworthy examples of noblewomen who acted with considerable independence during this era and thereby emerged as influential figures in the history of Hungary: Mary of the house of Habsburg, the wife of King Louis II; Isabella, the wife of John Zápolya, the nemesis of Ferdinand I; and Elizabeth Nádasdy, née Báthory, the so-called Blood Countess of Čachtice, the only Magyar among them. Each became the wife of a leading Hungarian nobleman. Each possessed a forceful personality and demonstrated strength of will. Each attempted to carve out an independent sphere of action for herself after she was widowed but found that her destiny would be influenced, if not controlled, by others. Each of them, in her own way, affected the course of the Reformation in Hungary and, whether intentionally or unwittingly, fostered its development and expansion or threatened its gains and the position of its leaders. Finally, each had to sacrifice for the good of their respective families. For each, dynastic concerns and necessities limited the scope of her activity, circumscribed her position, beliefs, desires, and attitudes, and determined her effectiveness and fate.

Certainly, the majority of the biographers of the Habsburg born as Mary of Austria, briefly queen of Hungary and, for most of her life, regent of the Netherlands, characterize her as strong-willed, forceful, cultured, and learned.[2] Mary was a woman who clearly placed dynastic necessities above personal inclinations and interests. She possessed the determination and will to find room to maneuver and the means to reshape the circumstances into which she was thrust. In this she certainly equaled, perhaps surpassed, her siblings, who molded and often dominated the history of their century as few families had since the days of Imperial Rome.

During the sixteenth century, piety, passion, and ambition were seldom cloaked or checked. Mary not only possessed strong feelings, strength of will, confidence of purpose, and personal piety, but she also aroused strong emotions and responses in others, especially in those who came into personal contact with her or whose lives were affected by her presence. Although her stay in Hungary was brief—she was resident in the kingdom itself for not more than seven years—during her sojourn she attracted many devoted supporters. Among these were many of the humanists resident in Hungary, some of the most powerful Hungarian magnates, her advisor and confidant George of Brandenburg, and her sometime court preacher, John Henckel. During the troubled spring of 1525, Henckel declared his admiration for and confidence in the youthful but capable queen. "If only she could be changed into a king our affairs would be in better shape."[3] Later, in a letter of July 1528 to Erasmus, Henckel extolled her cultivated virtues: "If only you could see the Queen at home, you would think yourself not in a woman's apartment but in a school. She is always surrounded by books; she teaches and studies and consoles her widowhood with edifying reading."[4]

Nevertheless, although she had more than a few loyal supporters, in the eyes of many others, especially the Magyar nobility under the leadership of John Zápolya, Mary was the hated importer of "foreign ways." She was regarded as the patron of the pestiferous "German heresy" infecting the court and spreading through the land, the tool of her "Germanic" advisors and courtiers, a self-indulgent profligate who squandered the royal revenue on entertainments and costly adornments. But, most of all, they viewed her as the salient representative of the far from subtle designs of the Habsburgs on the land of the Holy Crown. If these plans were achieved, the precarious position of the lesser nobles would be further weakened. Mary, for her part, was quite aware of their animosity. She attempted to stiffen the backbone of her often weak-willed husband and reminded him frequently, if incorrectly, that according to the law of Hungary his rule was free and unlimited.

What was it about Mary that aroused such strong feelings of affection or animosity? Her personality, habits, physical and intellectual attributes were frequently invoked by admirers and opponents alike. She may not have been especially alluring physically, but, as the portraits by Hans Krell reveal, she was not unattractive, though she did possess the full lower lip inherited by the Habsburgs from the Polish princess Cymburga. On the other hand, some felt that her love of the hunt and horses, a predilection fostered by her beloved grandfather Maximilian, bespoke far too masculine an inclination. Riding was a passion early developed and long retained: as Roger Ascham later noted in his journal, "she is a Virago and is never so well as when she is flinging about on horseback and hunting all the night long."[5] While her physical attributes and athletic proclivities may have been lauded by her supporters or disparaged by her detractors, these criticisms of her were biting, yet essentially insignificant, barbs attached to the lance with which they sought to skewer her. Far stronger emotions were engendered by her habits, personality, and the strength of her commitment to the dynastic goals she represented and embodied.

Born in 1505, Mary was the daughter of Philip the Handsome of Burgundy and Joanna, heir to the crowns of Castile and Aragon. She was raised by influential women, Anna de Beaumont and Margaret, the duchess of Savoy, in the cultivated, stimulating surroundings of the Burgundian court. Music, the hunt, stimulating conversation, and extravagant, even ostentatious, entertainments were the mainstays of this, one of the great cosmopolitan courts of late medieval Europe. Impressions imbibed in Flanders were further nurtured in the less brilliant but no less stimulating environs of her grandfather's castles in Vienna and Innsbruck, to which she was taken in 1514. She was to be at hand as a ready pawn should the almost fantastic plans evolving in the brain and diplomacy of Maximilian be realized against all odds. At his court the adolescent Mary acquired the disregard for the prudent financial management that had become a Habsburg habit. She carried this profligacy with her to Hungary when the long-contracted and long-awaited marriage of the sixteen-year old Louis and the seventeen-year old Mary finally was celebrated and consummated in 1522.

Many of the Magyar nobles considered Mary to be willful, self-indulgent, and extravagant. Their accusations had some basis in fact. Almost one-third of the annual income of the nation was spent for maintaining the royal household in which Mary attempted to re-create the cultural brilliance she had known as a child. On the one hand, it is understandable that her expenditures were criticized roundly by the lesser Magyar nobles who begrudged her the income (already much reduced by existing encumbrances) from the mining cities of upper Hungary and from those estates that were the traditional wedding gift of a Hungarian king to his bride.[6] Even her supporters, some of whom were not above profiting from their sovereign's distress, were disquieted by her financial imprudence. Some, like Sigismund von Herberstein, the imperial ambassador, urged caution and moderation, especially since funds might be needed in the not too distant future for important enterprises. On the other hand, the anger of the queen and her supporters was justifiably aroused by the profligacy of the Magyar nobles who not infrequently financed their own extravagance in part by unabashedly siphoning funds from the royal treasury. The royal couple often had to borrow funds at usurous rates, mortgage their anticipated future income, or beg assistance from the members of their court. Considering such circumstances denunciations of the activities at the court ring hypocritical. Rather, the animosity showed toward Mary can best be ascribed to that purpose imposed on her at birth and her determination to fulfill it while, at the same time, maintaining her own personal independence of intellect, conscience, and action.

Mary was destined from birth to serve the interests of her family as the agent who would further the long-harbored designs of the Habsburgs for Hungary. The wily and tenacious Maximilian recognized that the imperial crown was prestigious and politically useful, if economically hollow. Vast sums were needed to secure and maintain possession of it, funds which could only be obtained from secure hereditary estates. Even as the infant Mary was still nursing, Maximilian conceived a plan which was as fantastic in its boldness as in its desperate, almost irrational confidence in the destiny of the house of Habsburg. In March of 1506 he and Vladislav Jagellon agreed that the then six-month-old Mary was to marry an as yet unborn Hungarian prince and one of his two grandsons would marry Anna, the daughter of the aging Vladislav and his French wife Anna. Such a double marriage bond would cement the dynastic relationships between the Jagellonian and the Habsburg dynasties. The emperor recognized that a union of flesh and blood created far more durable bonds between families than signed pieces of paper.[7]

The majority of the Magyar nobles rejected these agreements as infringing on the rights of the Hungarian diet to elect those who would govern the nation and were more than a little distressed as the Habsburg tendrils inexorably reached out toward the kingdom. They sought in vain to cancel or delay indefinitely the consummation of the contracted marriages. But, after Ferdinand had claimed Anna, Mary finally took the initiative and embarked in 1522 on the journey which would take her via Bratislava to Buda and her husband-to-be. The opposition was daunted by her strength of will and by the support given her cause—the Habsburg cause—by several of the leading magnates, most notably George of Brandenburg-Ansbach and members of the Thurzó family. Until the end of the decade, George and Mary were closely allied as they attempted to further the dynastic policy of Maximilian toward Hungary. Also gathered around them were many of those who were responsible for introducing Reformation teachings and practices into Hungary.

George was one of the most powerful magnates in Hungary.[8] Possessing numerous estates in the Kingdoms of Bohemia and Hungary, he was a force to be reckoned with, especially since he was also friendly with the already influential Thurzós, also supporters of the Habsburg cause. He had been appointed by Vladislav as one of the guardians and the military tutor of Louis. His exuberant personality and personal loyalty to Mary made him a fitting confidant for the queen. As the most influential defender of Mary, he shared in the animosity directed toward her person and cause. But not even George dominated the queen. She increasingly demonstrated her own fierce determination to maintain her personal independence while at the same time fulfilling her dynastic obligations.

During the years immediately preceding Mohács, George and Alexius Thurzó, the treasurer of the kingdom, seem to have lost some of their influence in the court. The latter was accused by the Magyarist party of embezzlement while George was often away, either managing his own numerous estates or engaged in a variety of diplomatic missions. This made it possible for the nativist party to slowly sap the influence of those advocating closer ties with the Habsburgs. Led by John Zápolya and other notables, the lesser Magyar nobility and the higher clergy formed an alliance to drive foreign, especially German, influences from the land. They attacked George and other Germans at court and even accused the queen of tolerating heretics. Among these George and Conrad Cordatus,[9] Mary's court preacher, were identified as ardent supporters of Luther. In April 1523 their opponents pushed through the Hungarian diet an edict that "all Lutherans and those favoring them . . . shall have their property confiscated and themselves be punished with death as heretics and foes of the most holy Virgin Mary."[10] The queen was forced to dismiss her chaplain. John Henckel from Levoèa succeeded Cordatus. Although no less committed to the cause of the evangelical reformers, Henckel was much more moderate and discreet in speech and action.

Several desultory and ineffective attempts were made to implement the law, but not until 1525 was the Magyarist-Church party strong enough to take what they hoped would be decisive action. In the diet of May 1525, they demanded that the king expel all foreigners from the court and from the retinue of the queen since they offended God and the Apostolic See by holding Lutheran ideas. The diet resolved that all Lutherans should be purged from the land, pursued, imprisoned, and burned by both the secular and clerical authorities. At the same time the Magyarist party assumed control of the Fugger-Thurzó operations in the mining cities owned by Mary. A boycott of Hungarian copper engineered by the Fuggers, however, worsened the economic position of the miners—already precarious because of inflation. Revolts erupted throughout the so-called *montana* mining district of northern Hungary,[11] where Cordatus and some other reform-minded humanists from Mary's court had preached after leaving her court. Hard on the heels of these uprisings came the long-awaited and feared advance of the Turks. Louis and Mary again and again appealed desperately for aid to Ferdinand, to Charles, and to anyone else who would receive or hear their representatives.

But little aid was forthcoming. On August 20, 1526, an ill-equipped and vastly outnumbered Hungarian force was slaughtered by the army of Suleiman. Among the casualties were numbered the king, 2 archbishops, 5 bishops, 28 magnates, 500 nobles, and nearly 20,000 soldiers. Mohács was perhaps the greatest disaster in the history of Hungary. For Mary it was a crushing personal catastrophe.

In the days following Mohács, as she was forced to flee Buda for Bratislava, she turned once again to George and those Germans still in her entourage. She openly sought consolation in her faith and manifested the piety of which, as she had once written George, she had too much. During the days following the loss of her husband and home she probably penned the hymn "Mag ich Unglueck nicht widerstehn," the acrostic title of which was to have signified "Mary in Ungarn, Nun Witwe" (Mary in Hungary, Now a Widow).[12] She also heeded the entreaties of her brother and marshaled her physical and emotional strength, force of will, and considerable political talents. These had been keenly honed by her experience during the tumultuous days she had endured since her arrival in Hungary, in Ferdinand's campaign to obtain that Holy Crown which had molded the course of both of their lives. She skillfully played the politician, Ferdinand the general. Together they succeeded in having Ferdinand elected king in 1526. The following year, after he defeated for the moment the forces of Zápolya, who by a most fortuitous delay had avoided the slaughter at Mohács, Ferdinand was crowned at Székesfehérvar.

But Zápolya and his supporters were only temporarily checked. Ferdinand confiscated his rival's estates in northern Hungary and distributed them to his loyal supporters, the Thurzós receiving the lion's share. The Magyar rival king withdrew to Siebenbürgen, or Transylvania, where he unrelentingly pursued his personal and political goal, the wresting of Hungary from the hands of the Habsburgs, even if it required an alliance with and obeisance before the sultan Suleiman.

Mary's days in Hungary were drawing rapidly to a close. While steadfastly serving her brother's cause, her personal relationships with Ferdinand deteriorated. They quarreled over the use of the income from her widow's inheritance,[13] her continued contacts with advocates of ecclesiastical and theological reform, and her obdurate refusal to consider marrying again. Forced to flee her adopted home when the Turks under Suleiman embarked on their determined but futile siege of Vienna in 1529, she slowly wended her way toward a reunion with her eldest brother, the emperor Charles. He too urged marriage on her. She again adamantly refused and implored him to help relieve her onerous financial burdens.

Within a year, however, Mary was needed for a new, important family matter. Charles had decided that she should leave that land for which she had been intended from her infancy and her friends and supporters there resident. She was to return to her childhood home to succeed their recently deceased Aunt Margaret as regent of the Netherlands. She had done her part, she had used her body, intellect, will, and spirit to help secure Hungary and Bohemia for the Habsburgs. She had done what was needed to bring to fruition her grandfather's grand design. She had done her part to secure Ferdinand's inheritance and cause. Now she must do the same for Charles.

Mary capably served the interests of her family in their Hungarian and Bohemian endeavors. She was to pursue the same ends in the Netherlands— but on her own terms, in her own way. She sought to retain, within the strictures imposed by dynastic politics, her own independence, even in matters of religion. While in Hungary, Mary had demonstrated considerable concern for and independence in the expression of her own religious faith, so much so that some have called her the patron of the early Reformation in Hungary. Was she?

On the one hand, there is clear and persuasive evidence that Mary's entourage during her Hungarian sojourn included many who were drawn to the teachings of Luther and vocal in their advocacy and practice of his teachings. First and foremost was her dear friend and confidant, George of Brandenburg, who would sign the confession presented in Augsburg by the Lutherans to her brother Charles in 1530. Conrad Cordatus, the court preacher whom she was forced to dismiss, seems to have contacted her again after Mohács.[14] His passionate attachment to Luther was widely known. She received works of consolation from both Luther and Erasmus. Shortly after Mohács, probably at the instigation of Cordatus, the Wittenberg reformer sent her his exposition of four psalms of consolation.[15] In 1529, after several entreaties by Henckel, Erasmus dispatched his tract *De vidua christiana* (Concerning a Christian Widow) to the queen, for which he requested some tangible sign of appreciation.[16] Although Henckel corresponded regularly with Erasmus, he was also in contact with the German reformers. Indeed, while at Augsburg Henckel met with the Lutheran party, probably with Mary's knowledge[17] and informed them of what transpired in the private consultations of the Catholic party. Melanchthon praised her piety;[18] Spalatin characterized her as being a friend of the Gospel and well versed in Scripture.[19]

To this contextual evidence must be added the more persuasive literary remains which testify to Mary's own religious attitudes. The hymn, which she prepared sometime after Mohács during the troubled days before her departure from Hungary, gives clear witness to the sincerity of her personal faith. Moreover, her correspondence with Ferdinand between the years 1527 to 1530 shows that she was unwilling to repudiate those in her courtly circle who were supporting Luther and other reformers or, more significantly, to categorically deny her sympathy for them or agree to expel those heretical influences from her retinue.[20] Her interest in the teachings of Luther seems to have persisted even during the meeting of the diet at Augsburg. While there, she sought, through Henckel and Melanchthon, the counsel of Luther on several questions concerning the reception of the Lord's Supper. In particular Mary wondered whether one necessarily had to receive both bread and wine for the reception of the sacrament to be valid. Could it not be valid and efficacious if one would receive only the bread, owing to necessities imposed by external circumstances?[21] Luther's answer, which uncompromisingly stated that one must receive both elements, must have disheartened her.[22]

For Mary, acceptance of Luther's ultimatum was an impossibility. She could only go so far in demonstrating sympathy for the cause advocated by the evangelical reformers. Her position and responsibilities did not allow her the liberty of identifying publicly with the reformers by openly receiving both bread and wine in taking the sacrament. Although there may have been one final letter from Luther to Mary in the summer following Augsburg,[23] Mary no longer was drawn to the Luther who had set before her this impossible demand and who would not provide her with a third option. Although she may have been sympathetic to the cause of reform, even her piety and faith was not hers alone. She was not and could not be a private person. She was a Habsburg. This made the expression of her piety and faith a public, political, and dynastic matter. In the final analysis, Mary placed above all else her responsibility to the dynastic aims and fortunes of her family.

As Mary dedicated her life to the cause of the Habsburgs, so Isabella Jagellion,[24] the Polish wife of John Zápolya, Ferdinand's nemesis, spent most of her adult life seeking to counter Habsburg influence in Hungary so that her son, John Sigismund, would someday reign as king of Hungary in his own right. She was as determined and as politically astute as the widowed Habsburg queen and, given the difficulties confronting her, was remarkably successful in attaining the goal to which she dedicated her life. Like Mary, she remained nominally a Roman Catholic for her entire life. At the same time, she criticized abuses in the established church, maintained an independence in her religious views and practices, allowed advocates of ecclesiastical reform to hold positions in her court and on her lands, eventually extended extensive liberties to the Protestants in Transylvania, and labored with determination to secure and protect the heritage of her family. After the widowed Mary left her adopted home for Flanders the Polish-born Isabella, first queen and later queen regent, became the single most influential woman in Hungary.

Mary and Isabella were similar in other respects. Both had grown up in stimulating courts and had been educated in surroundings where humanism flourished. Both enjoyed the hunt and court entertainments and were not noted for frugality. Both were characterized as strong willed, even willful, women. Both were widowed at an early age and refused to remarry. Both were queens of Hungary but were not native Magyars. Both evidenced sympathy for ecclesiastical reform and, while they never became open supporters of the reformation movement emanating from Wittenberg, more than few open advocates of the Reformation were to be found among their advisors. But they differed in at least one important respect. No grand dynastic design had shaped and governed Isabella's life from birth. Nevertheless, she was expected to fulfill her dynastic purpose of advancing her lineage and further familial goals.

Isabella was born in 1519, the firstborn child of Sigismund I of Poland and his second wife, the Milanese Bona Sforza. Raised primarily in Cracow, where Reformation influences were already spreading during the early 1520s among some of the humanists at the university and German townspeople, she may have been tutored briefly by John Honterus, later the humanist reformer of Brasov.[25] In light of her later performance, it seems she also learned from her father—who had the unenviable task of governing a nobility as contentious as that in Hungary—the art of political patience and compromise. As she was growing up, her future husband already was struggling to reclaim Hungarian land from the Habsburgs.

Having been elected by the poorly attended first post-Mohács Hungarian diet and crowned in November 1526, John Zápolya was supported primarily by the lesser Magyar nobility. As a result, he was unable to achieve a decisive victory in the several campaigns which he and Ferdinand waged against one another from 1527 to 1538. Force of arms changed little the emerging political geography of Hungary. While the center came increasingly under Turkish control, the Habsburgs controlled northern and western Hungary. In the east, Zápolya retained his lands in Transylvania and in the *Partium*, east of the Theiss River. In 1538, after a decade of indecisive armed encounters, Zápolya and Ferdinand secretly agreed to the treaty arranged by Bishop George Utjesenovics-Martinuzzi.[26] Ferdinand granted to the recently betrothed Zápolya the right to use the title King of Hungary for his lifetime; after his death, Transylvania and the Partium were to revert to Habsburg control. Zápolya's progeny, if there were any, would receive only the hereditary holdings of the family.

This settlement was short-lived. On March 2, 1539, the fifty-two-year-old Zápolya married the twenty-year-old Isabella in accordance with the wishes of her father, who was no more eager to see the eastward expansion of Habsburg influence than was his kinsman Zápolya. A little over one year later, two weeks before her husband's death, Isabella bore a son, John Sigismund. On his deathbed the father commanded his advisors and supporters never to recognize Ferdinand's claim to the crown but to insure that his son would reign as king of Hungary. To that end he named Isabella queen regent and, as child's guardians, Peter Petrovics, Valentine Török, and Bishop Martinuzzi, popularly referred to as "The Monk."

For the next decade, it was Martinuzzi who largely directed the affairs of the duchy and of Zápolya's child and widow. He believed that, whatever Zápolya's personal wishes might have been, a reunification of Hungary was necessary if the lands lost to the Turks ever were to be regained. But Isabella and the Transylvanian estates were suspicious of Martinuzzi's motives. At the Diet of Turda in 1542, the estates confirmed Isabella as queen regent and recognized Sigismund as their prince.

During the next five years Transylvania was troubled by the spread of the Reformation, conflicts between the various "nations" and classes, difficulties with the Roumanian inhabitants, who were excluded from the political life of the territory, and by the endemic triangular contest for hegemony between Ferdinand, the Turks, and the Transylvanians under Isabella. In 1547, after six years of desultory military activity, Ferdinand and the sultan agreed to a truce by which Ferdinand was recognized as king in exchange for the payment of a substantial indemnity.

Ferdinand, however, had not given up his attempts to obtain secure hold of Transylvania and the Partium lands. Meanwhile, by 1551, Isabella had grown weary of the increasingly haughty and presumptuous monk and agreed to recognize the earlier pact made with Ferdinand by which he promised to pay her—and her son—a handsome indemnity and bestow on them the territory of Opole, a fief of the Bohemian crown in Silesia. Martinuzzi, out of favor with the queen, once again threw his support to the Habsburgs but also continued to negotiate with the Turks. Ferdinand had had enough. Decisive action was needed. When the marquis de Castaldo entered Transylvania at the head of a Habsburg army, one of his first acts was to order the murder of Martinuzzi on December 17, 1551. For the next five years, the Habsburgs exercised at least nominal hegemony over Transylvania.

In accordance with their agreement, Isabella left with her young son for the estates Ferdinand had assigned them. En route, she demanded for her son freedom from all military responsibilities and from any taxes due the Bohemian crown. Ferdinand refused this petition and her later demand that John Sigismund be recognized as a sovereign prince in Opole, which Isabella insisted should be declared independent of the Bohemian crown. Although her persistent demands infuriated Ferdinand, he in turn alienated her. The estates he had assigned to her were in lamentable condition and economically strapped. He also failed to keep his financial commitments and by 1554 owed her nearly 122,000 gulden. Isabella began to prepare the way for a return to Transylvania. She negotiated with the sultan and the anti-Habsburg elements in Transylvania. The latter were on the rise owing to the undisciplined marauding of Habsburg forces there. She also sought assistance from her brother, Sigismund Augustus of Poland. Ferdinand was not unaware of her activities but could do little to counter her increasingly skillful political machinations. In 1555 she established a residence on the Polish-Hungarian border. After the estates of Transylvania reaffirmed her sixteen-year-old son as their prince in 1556, she returned to end Habsburg rule in the province. The Habsburgs did not regain control of Transylvania until the end of the eighteenth century.

For the next three years, until her death on September 20, 1559, she served as queen regent in the name of her son and actively governed Transylvania and the Partium lands, aided by her Lutheran chancellor Michael Csáki—a former tutor of her son—and, until his death in 1557, the Calvinist Peter Petrovic. Fearful that she would again be expelled, she trusted few, fought hard to maintain her extensive authority and independence of action, and proved willing to act decisively. Yet she was also willing to make necessary compromises to secure her own position and that of her son. She kept the office of *voivode* vacant so that none could challenge her authority as Martinuzzi had done. With the approval of the diet, she secularized the extensive estates of the vacant episcopal sees of Oradea and Alba Julia, using the income they produced for her own personal and political purposes. She herself exercised the formal episcopal right of confirming clerics in their position. In 1558 she sanctioned the election of Matthias Hebler as bishop of the Saxon Lutherans, granting him the extensive privileges and legal jurisdiction formerly held by the Roman clergy.

Isabella likewise extended limited toleration to her subjects, viewing this as a necessary concession to bring peace to the kingdom and strengthen her political influence and security. By the time she returned to Transylvania, the Reformation had taken firm root in Hungary. As early as 1546 the Lutherans had established their own church order. After this they so jealously guarded their privileges that in 1552 the "Saxon" and "Papal" parties were instructed by the diet to respect one another. Not only did difficulties between Lutherans and Catholics disturb the peace; alternate reformist views were taking root. During the regular synods of reformist clergy held during the 1550s, it became obvious that sacramentarian or Helvetic views were spreading. The Diet of 1558 reaffirmed the edict presented to them by Isabella the previous year. This edict decreed that

> each person maintain whatever religious faith he wishes, with old or new rituals, while We at the same time leave it to their judgement to do as they please in the matter of their faith, so long, however, as they bring no harm to bear on anyone at all, lest the followers of a new religion be a source of irritation to the old profession of faith or became, in some way, injurious to their followers.[27]

At the same time, the diet prohibited those sects of the sacramentarians which caused disturbances and brought disquietude and disorder, a provision which effectively limited toleration to the Lutherans and the old religion. Full religious toleration had to await the ascent of Isabella's son to the throne. John Sigismund became the first and only avowedly anti-Trinitarian king in European history.

That Isabella felt forced to concede limited religious toleration to the Lutherans in order to fulfill her dynastic and political responsibilities is understandable, especially after the Peace of Augsburg. But what was her personal attitude toward the Reformation? While she remained a nominal Catholic for her entire life there are more than a few indications (albeit largely circumstantial) that she sympathized with many aspects of the reformist movement, especially as advocated by evangelical humanist reformers. Like her brother, Sigismund Augustus, she had been raised in Cracow during the years when the Reformation movement emerged and gained strength. Both demonstrated a tolerance for those holding alternate religious views. As regent, she not only secularized the estates of the old church and declined to nominate candidates for the two vacant Roman Catholic sees under her jurisdiction, but she also assumed many of the ecclesiastical rights formerly exercised by those bishops and granted to the Lutheran superintendent extensive legal authority. Her councilors and faithful supporters included several open advocates of reformation, including the staunch Calvinist Peter Petrovic, the Lutheran Michael Csáki, and her sometime personal physician, Francis Stancarus. Stancarus taught publicly that Christ was the mediator between God and man only according to his human nature. In light of this circumstantial evidence it appears that Isabella, like Mary, sympathized with the cause of the evangelical humanist reformation as advocated by those around her. But she kept her own counsel and maintained her independence in religious matters. She used the Reformation and its advocates as she saw fit, on her own terms, for her own reasons, to secure for her son the rightful inheritance of the father he never knew.

Elizabeth Báthory,[28] on the other hand, had little regard for the structures of society or religion, for the security and position of her family, or even for her own gender. As the infamous "Blood Countess of Čachtice," she tortured and murdered between thirty and seventy women with the assistance of three other women and one male servant. Her actions threatened the position and property of her children and kinsmen and, through circumstance and family ties, the most influential patron of the Lutherans in upper Hungary, the Palatine George Thurzó. She is one of those complex, horrifying figures with which history is all too replete, a mass torturer and murderer. Based on the evidence of eye witnesses, she obtained emotional and sexual pleasure by inflicting gruesome torture on and then murdering other women. For nearly a decade, she gave free reign to her passion and perversion.

Elizabeth was born in 1560 into one of the most influential families in Hungary. The Báthory family held estates throughout Hungary and Transylvania and was, moreover, related by marriage to many of the most notable families in Hungary as well as to the Jagellions and Habsburgs. Not only was the family rich, influential, and powerful, it was also one in which behavioral aberrations were not uncommon. Cruelty was a trait evident in several of the Báthorys, and sexual problems were exhibited by both the impotent Gabriel and the promiscuous Gabriela, the sister of Elizabeth's father George. Of Elizabeth's childhood we know little,[29] although it does not appear that she received anything more than a rudimentary education and that she grew up in circumstances far less cultured and cultivated than those experienced by Mary or Isabella.

The family of her future husband, Francis Nádasdy, was equally illustrious. Although his mother, Ursula Kanizsa, was unable to read or write at the time of her marriage, his father, Thomas, was well educated and recognized as a capable, enthusiastic soldier. He served in the diplomatic service of King Vladislav, and, after supporting Zápolya for over a decade, he became a supporter of the Habsburgs in 1553. The following year Ferdinand named him Palatine of Hungary. Francis inherited his father's military abilities but was an indifferent student. Nevertheless, both father and son became staunch, if not particularly pious, supporters of the Reformation.[30]

The members of the Báthory and Nádasdy families, like so many others in Hungary, were inured to the cruelty of battle and the harsh habits of the era. Torture and violent death accompanied the frequent armed encounters which plagued the nation for most of the sixteenth century. It was reported that after his wife began to exhibit sadistic tendencies, Francis did not think her actions particularly unusual. At least he made no efforts to restrain her.

Francis and Elizabeth were married in 1575; he was twenty-one, she not yet sixteen. He was athletic and a ladies' man but lacked the education of his father. She was pretty, haughty, and temperamental. During their years together, Elizabeth gave birth to five children, of whom three survived. Illustrious marriages were arranged for their offspring. Thus, by birth and through her own marriage as well as those of her children, Elizabeth was related to many of the major families in Hungary. These dynastic links would surely assure the material well-being, social status, political influence, and future security of Elizabeth and her children.

Few specific details of the home life of the couple are available, although it is reported that the castle often resembled a soldiers' camp and was governed with military efficiency and discipline, even during the frequent absences of Francis. Around 1600, Helena Jó, a widow, was engaged as a wet nurse. About the same time a washmaid, Katherine Beneczky, entered the household, to be followed a few years later by Dorothea Szentes, who was to care for Catherine. Also employed since 1594 was John Ujváry, also called Ficzko. These four became accomplices in the systematic tortures and murders directed by Elizabeth.

According to their later testimony,[31] Elizabeth's open manifestations of cruelty began when she was thirty-four. This would place it about 1594, near the time of the birth of her first child after almost two decades of marriage. It was reported that she began to abuse her servants for the slightest breach in their demeanor or responsibilities. During one summer, Elizabeth, exercising her right as a noblewoman to execute household justice, condemned a serving girl to stand naked outdoors for twenty-four hours, covered with honey to attract the flies and insects. Yet as harshly as she punished her servants while her husband lived, her actions did not equal those which followed his death in July 1604, shortly after entrusting the care of his family and estates to George Thurzó.[32] Elizabeth subsequently initiated the torture and then murder of others of her sex.

It was then that one more important figure in this cast of female sadists appeared, the mysterious Anna Darvula from Sárvár, who became Elizabeth's confidant and tutor in torture. A heartless, hideous, and irascible woman, she was called a wild beast in a woman's guise. It was she who first instructed Elizabeth in the use of instruments of torture to prolong her victim's pain and her pleasure and who fostered and intensified her interest in witchcraft. During the next six years, scores of women, including several of noble birth, were lured or brought to Elizabeth in Sárvár, Čachtice, Bratislava, Piešt'any, and Vienna. Elizabeth and her accomplices systematically tortured these unfortunates to death. As the protocols of the various legal hearings conducted during 1611 reveal, the intended victims were first accused of neglecting their responsibilities, which could be as simple as failing to have neatly ironed aprons. Then they were taken to the room which was often used, the laundry, frequently stripped and beaten with clubs or with the hand by Elizabeth and, when she grew weary, by the others in her coterie until blood flowed freely. Scissors or blades were used to slash the upper bodies, the jaw might be pulled apart, pins inserted, most usually in the fingers and lips, hot irons applied, sometimes to the genitals. In winter, ice water was poured over the naked victim and she was made to stand for hours in the cold until she froze to death. These occurrences increased in frequency during late 1609 and 1610, when at least fifteen women were killed. Even though rumors soon began to spread about the atrocities taking place, those responsible for imposing justice were slow to act. Why?

On the one hand, Hungary was in turmoil. During the fifteen years of war with the Turk, the Calvinist Stephen Bocskay from Transylvania gained control of much of upper Hungary in his struggles with the Habsburgs and as part of his attempt to secure legal recognition for Hungarian Protestantism. By the twin treaties of Zsitvatörök and Vienna, which brought both conflicts to a close, the reformist parties were promised toleration in Hungary. This was not, however, incorporated into the Hungarian legal code until the Diet of 1608, when the Protestants received the right to establish their own independent church. During this struggle, moreover, Matthias replaced his brother Rudolf as the de facto Habsburg ruler of Hungary.[33] Given the internal chaos, it was not unusual for rumors to be conveniently ignored. Moreover, Elizabeth was related to the most powerful families in Hungary, and witnesses, especially from the lower classes, were not eager to come forth to accuse one so well connected and highborn. They knew, as was indeed proven by the disposition of the case, that there were two levels of justice under the Tripartitum: one for the nobility, another for its subjects.

Notwithstanding, reports in late 1609 of the countess's activities, having reached Matthias' ears, could not be ignored. Early in 1610, the Bratislava tabular court took testimony from fifty-eight witnesses. The dispositions provided sufficient grounds to indict Elizabeth as a mass murderer. But this presented problems, not only for the president of the court, Palatine Thurzó, who was related to Elizabeth through his wife, Elizabeth Czobor, but also for the sons-in-law of Elizabeth and her other relatives, many of whom were Protestants. Not only would they be disgraced, but, if Elizabeth were executed as a common criminal, her property would be forfeited to the crown. Moreover, if they did not cooperate in her prosecution, they could be charged with obstructing or failing to secure justice and their own lands could be confiscated. The loss of these lands to the Habsburgs and the potential diminution of their own influence could endanger the Lutheran movement in northwestern Hungary, which had just established its own legal ecclesiastical organization. In light of these circumstances, Thurzó, Nicholas Zrínsky, and George Drugeth, Elizabeth's sons-in-law, agreed to a secret compact. They would seek to save her from standing trial, save her life, and preserve her lands for the family. To attain this end they agreed to imprison her in the fortress above the town of Čachtice and prosecute her accomplices.

On the night of December 29, 1610, Thurzó arrived with an armed force at the manor house of Čachtice and surprised the countess, "that accursed woman," as he put it in a letter to his wife, almost *in flagranti* since at the door was the body of a servant, Doricza, who had just been tortured to death. In the house were found two servants, tortured but not yet dead. Although immediately incarcerated in the fortress of Čachtice, where she would die on August 21, 1614 at the age of fifty-four, Elizabeth was never formally brought to trial. Justice would be visited instead on her accomplices.

On January 2, a hastily summoned court convened in Bytèa, and twenty judges representing the Bratislava tabular court heard evidence. No attempt was made to verify the statements of the four accused or the thirteen witnesses. The court had been convened primarily to gather such information as to justify a verdict conforming to the agreement between Thurzó and Elizabeth's sons-in-law. Among the thirteen witnesses nine were men, three were the widows of farmers, and one was an unmarried woman. The four accused accomplices were asked the same eleven questions: How long had they been in the service of the countess, how many were murdered, where were they killed, who were they, how were they killed, where were their bodies, had their mistress tortured and killed with her own hands, where did the torture take place, who else in the household knew about what was going on, and when did Elizabeth begin the atrocities? On January 7 the verdict was handed down. Dorothea Szentes and Helena Jó were to have their fingers cut off and then be burned at the stake. John Ficzka was to be beheaded while Katharine Beneczky, judged least guilty, was to be imprisoned until more precise information could be ascertained concerning her guilt.

Although Thurzó reported the conclusion to the affair to Matthias on March 30, 1611, the latter was not satisfied. In one fell swoop he could greatly enlarge his holdings in Hungary, humble those Protestant magnates who had caused him so much trouble, and present himself as the true defender of Hungarian law.[34] He therefore ordered another investigation. Two protonotaries of the Bratislava court heard 236 witnesses from the various estates held by Elizabeth, during which time it became clear that many individuals had known about what was happening but failed to act or looked the other way. Yet, nothing more was done. The powerful and influential magnates wanted this "unfortunate" affair closed and forgotten. Elizabeth remained incarcerated. The inheritance of her family, which she had threatened by her actions, had been secured by her kinsmen, even if at the expense of an equitable and full execution of the law. But, after all, Elizabeth was a noblewoman, and, no matter how famous or infamous, pious or perverse, noblewomen performed one fundamental, one essential function in sixteenth-century society: they were the vessels, the agents by which dynastic capital was transmitted from generation to generation.

In their own way, then, each of these three individuals demonstrates the importance of the dynastic role assigned to noblewomen during the era of the Reformation and Counter Reformation. The primary function and role of noblewomen was to serve passively, through marriage, as vessels which carried the progeny of a family and the embodiment of familial alliances or actively as agents of family policy who were expected to further the interests, influence, and fortunes of the particular family into which they were born or into which they were married. Yet, within these roles imposed on them by biology, law, and societal mores, noblewomen could use their position, influence, and wealth to carve out for themselves a sphere within which they could act with considerable independence and assert their own individuality.

Moreover, since family ties and alliances were also the foundations for political alliances, noblewomen were not and could not consider themselves private individuals. They were political as well as dynastic capital and were expected to acquiesce in the familial goals and strategies normally drafted by their male relatives. Yet, at the same time, being raised with privileges denied most women, and often achieving even more influence and authority on the death of their husbands, widowed noblewomen could utilize the very responsibilities imposed on them to their advantage. They viewed them as a means to acquire personal independence and fulfillment. Nevertheless, no matter which path noblewomen might follow, they could not escape the dynastic implications their gender role imposed, nor could they cast off completely the constraints on their sex. Most noblewomen understood this and, like Mary and Isabella, recognized and accepted the particular role they were expected to play in society, devoting themselves both to fulfilling the responsibilities their position imposed and serving the interests of their families. Elizabeth Báthory, on the other hand, used her position for her own benefit, repudiated her expected function and role, and thereby forfeited her own independence and endangered the security of her family. Elizabeth demonstrated no religious devotion or concern and jeopardized not only her family's inheritance, but also the faith to which many of them subscribed. Both Isabella and Mary, however, seem to have taken their religious faith seriously, even if they prudently avoided expressing publicly their personal religious views. Moreover, because of their positions, both Mary and Isabella had considerable influence on the religious life of others—members of their families, their entourages, and their tenants. Both seemed sympathetic to and were tolerant of elements of the program of theological and ecclesiastical reform espoused by the evangelical humanist reformers. Their households and courts included many who were supporters of the Reformation, and they took few steps to inhibit or check its advance in the lands under their control. On the other hand, even in the practice of the faith they confessed, they could not forget or evade the constraints imposed by their expected role. While in private they might have been able to believe as they wished, in public they had to consider the implications their actions might have on their families.

Individual women could attain a degree of freedom, exercise considerable influence, and achieve personal fulfillment. Nevertheless, a noblewoman ultimately could not evade the constraints which her gender role imposed or reject its contingent responsibilities without endangering herself or the fate of the family to which she belonged.

NOTES

1. For an introduction to the considerable body of literature on the sixteenth century in Hungary see David P. Daniel, *The Historiography of the Reformation in Slovakia*, number 10 in the series Sixteenth Century Bibliography (St. Louis: Center for Reformation Research, 1977) and also Charles H. O'Brien, "Recent American Doctoral Dissertations and Articles concerning Protestantism in the Austrian Habsburg Lands," *Jahrbuch für die Geschichte des Protestantismus in Österreich* 99/100 (1983/84):30–40. For an introduction to the political history of the region examined see: Robert A. Kann, *A History of the Habsburg Empire, 1526–1918* (Berkeley: University of California Press, 1974), R. J. W. Evans, *The Making of the Habsburg Monarchy, 1550–1700* (Oxford: Clarendon Press, 1979), Peter F. Sugar, *Southeastern Europe under Ottoman Rule 1354–1804* (Seattle: University of Washington Press, 1977), Ervin Pamlényi et al., *Die Geschichte Ungarns* (Budapest: Corvina, 1971), Denis Sinor, *History of Hungary* (New York: Frederick A. Praeger, 1959), and Victor S. Mamatey, *Rise of the Habsburg Empire 1526–1815* (New York: Holt, Rinehart andd Winston, 1971). The establishment of Habsburg rule in Hungary during the first half of the sixteenth century has been treated in the excellent study by Paula Sutter Fichtner, *Ferdinand I of Austria: The Politics of Dynasticism in the Age of the Reformation*. (Boulder, Colo.: East European Monographs; distributed by Columbia University Press, 1982), while the most recent survey of the Reformation in all of Hungary is Mihaly Bucsay, *Geschichte des Protestantismus in Ungarn, 1521–1978. Ungarns Reformkirchen in Geschichte und Gegenwart, I. Im Zeitalter der Reformation, Gegenreformation und katholischen Reform* (Wien: Hermann Böhlaus, 1977). See also Jeno Sólyom, *Luther és Magyarország, A Reformátor Kapcsolata Hazánkkal Haláláig* (Budapest: Kiadja a Luther-Társaság, 1924), Kalman Benda, "La reforme en Hongrie," *Bulletin de la Société de l'Histoire du Protestantisme Français* 122 (1976):1–53, David P. Daniel, "The Lutheran Reformation in Slovakia, 1517–1620," (Ph.D. diss., Pennsylvania State University, 1972), Mathias Szlávik, *Die Reformation in Ungarn* (Halle: Buchdruckerei des Waisenhauses, 1884), William Toth, "Highlights of the Hungarian Reformation," *Church History* 9 (1940):141–56 and also his "Luther's Frontier in Hungary," pp. 75–91 in *Reformation Studies, Essays in Honor of Roland H. Bainton*, edited by Franklin H. Littell (Richmond: John Knox Press, 1962).

2. Mary has been the subject of much more extensive study than the other two individuals covered in this essay, and among the biographical studies the following are particularly useful: Jane de Iongh, *Mary of Hungary, Second Regent of the Netherlands*, trans. M. D. Herter Norton (London: Faber and Faber, 1958), Ghislaine de Boom, *Marie de Hongrie* (Brussels: La Renaissance du Livre, 1956), Gernot Heiss, "Königin Maria von Ungarn und Böhmen (1505–1558)," (Ph.D. diss., University of Vienna, 1971), from which two articles were extracted, "Politik und Ratgeber der Königin Maria von Ungarn in den Jahren 1521–1531," *Mitteilungen des Instituts für österreichische Geschichtsforschung* 82 (1974): 119–80 and "Die ungarischen, böhmischen Besitzungen der Königin Maria (1505–1558)," *Mitteilungen des österreichischen Staatsarchiv* 27 (1974): 61–100, 29 (1976):52–121. Also extremely useful are the earlier studies by Wilhelm Stracke, "Die Anfänge der Königin Maria von Ungarn, späteren Statthälterin Karls V," (Ph.D. diss., University of Göttingen, 1940); Jan Kvačala, "Král'ovná Mária a jej účast' v dejoch reformácie," *Viera a Veda* 1 (1930):10–22, 59–72, 97–105; Théodore Ortvay, *Maria II Lajos magyar kîrály neje, 1505–1558* (Budapest:

Magyar. tört. Társulat, 1914); Louis Neustadt, *Ungarns Verfall und Maria von Ungarn* (Budapest: Killan, 1885); Louis Sacher-Masoch, *Ungarns Untergang und Maria von Österreich zum Theil nach Urkunden des k. k. Staats-archivs zu Wien* (Leipzig: Wiegel, 1862); and Théodore Juste, *Les Pays-Bas sous Charles-Quint. Vie de Marie de Hongrie* (Brussels: Decq, 1855) and also his *Mária magyar királyné II Lajos özvegye* (Pest: Rath, 1866).

3. Iongh, *Mary of Hungary*, p. 93. For the role of John Henckel in the court of Mary see Adalbert Hudak, "Der Hofprediger Johannes Henckel und seine Beziehungen zu Erasmus von Rotterdam," *Kirche im Osten* 2 (1959):106–13; Gustav Bauch, "Dr. Johann Henckel, der Hofprediger der Königin Maria von Ungarn," *Ungarische Revue* 4 (1884):599–627 and Lajos Nyikos, "Erasmus und der bömisch-ungarische Königshof," *Zwingliana* 7 (1937):346–74.

4. Henckel to Erasmus, July 18, 1528, No. 2011 in P. S. Allen (editor), *Opus Epistolarum Des. Erasmi Roterdami,* volume 7 (Oxford: Clarendon, 1928), pp. 418–20.

5. William Bradford, *Correspondence of Charles V* (London: Richard Bentley, 1850; photo-mechanical reprint New York: AMS, 1971), p. 124.

6. On the relationship of Mary to the mining cities of the *montana* region, today in central Slovakia, see the numerous studies of Günther Frhr. von Probszt, and especially "Königin Maria und die niederungarischen Bergstädte," *Zeitschrift für Ostforschung* 15 (1966):621–703 and *Die niederungarischen Bergstädte. Ihre Entwicklung und wirtschaftliche Bedeutung bis zum Übergang an das Haus Habsburg (1546),* volume 15 in the series Buchreihe der Südostdeutschen Historischen Kommission (München: R. Oldenbourg, 1966).

7. Otto Frass, *Quellenbuch zur österreichischen Geschichte I* (Wien: Birken, 1956), pp. 262–64; Neustadt, *Ungarns Verfall und Maria von Ungarn*, pp. 31–35, Sinor, pp. 123–41.

8. On the role of George in Hungary see Louis Neustadt, *Markgraf Georg von Brandenburg als Erzieher am ungarischen Hofe* (Breslau: T. Schatzky, 1883). Also helpful is Konrad Müller, "Markgraf Georg von Brandenburg-Ansbach-Jägerndorf. Ein Gestalt aus der fränkischen und schlesischen Reformationszeit," *Jahrbuch für schlesische Kirche und Kirchengeschichte,* N.F. 34 (1955):7–31; Theodor Kolde, "Der Briefwechsel Luthers und Melanchthons mit Markgrafen Georg und Friederick von Brandenburg," *Zeitschrift für Kirchengeschichte* 13 (1892):318–87; and Sacher-Masoch, *Ungarns Untergang.*

9. The influence of the Reformation within the retinue of Mary has been examined by Gustav Hammann in "Conrad Cordatus Leombachensis: Sein Leben in Österreich," *Jahrbuch des oberösterreichischen Musealvereins* 109 (1964):250–78; "Johannes Kresling," *Jahrbuch für schlesische Kirchengeschichte* 44 (1965):7–12; and "Bartholomeus Francfordinus Pannonius, Simon Grynäus in Ungarn," *Zeitschrift für Ostforschung* 14 (1965):228–42. The influence of Cordatus is likewise treated by Igor Kišš, "Konrad Cordatus, der Reformator der mittleren Slowakei," *Lutherische Rundschau* 10 (1960–61):252–59; H. Wrampelmeyer, *Festschrift des königlichen Gymnasiums zu Clausthal zum Luther-Jubiläum am 10. November 1883* (Halle: Niemeyer, 1883) and by Sándor Payr, *Cordatus Konrád budai pap Luther jó barátja* (Budapest: Luther-Társ, 1944). In addition to the groundbreaking work of Sólyom the recent studies of Tibor Fabiny are also helpful, especially his "Luthers Beziehungen zu Ungarn und Siebenbürgen," pp. 641–46 in *Leben und Werk Martin Luthers von 1526 bis 1546. Festgabe zu seinem 500. Geburtstag I,* edited by Helmar Junghans (Berlin: Evangelische Verlagsanstalt, 1983).

10. Imre Révész, *Dévay Biró Mátyás, első magyar reformátor életrajza és irodalmi müvei* (Pest: Osterlamm Károly 1863), p. 22. See also Article 54, 1523, *Corpus Juris Hungarici: Decretum Generale inclyti regni Hungariae Partiumque eidem annexarum Tomus Primus Continens Opus Tripartitum Juris Consuetudinarii ejusdem Regni auctore Stephano de Werbőczy . . . ,* Volume 1 (Budae: Reg. Universitatis Hungaricae, 1844).

11. The revolt of the miners and the Reformation in the *montana* mining cities has been extensively examined. For the revolt the following are the most significant studies: Peter Ratkoš, *Povstanie baníkov na Slovensku roku 1525–1526* (Bratislava: Slovenská Akadémie Vied, 1963) and its companion volume, *Dokumenty k baníckemu povstaniu na Slovensku, 1525–1526* (Bratislava: Slovenská Akadémie Vied, 1957). Also helpful is Günther Frhr. von Probszt, "Die sozialen Ursachen des ungarischen Bergarbeiteraufstandes von 1525–1526," *Zeitschrift für Ostforschung* 10 (1961):401–32 and Gustáv Heckenast, "A besztercebányai banyászfelkelés, 1525–1526," *Századok* 86 (1952):354–96, which appeared also in Slovak as "Banskobystrické banícke povstanie, 1525–1526," *Historický Časopis* 2 (1954):71–104. For the Reformation in these cities see especially Pavol Križko, *Dejiny banskomestkého Senioratu* (Lipt. sv. Mikuláš: Tranoscius, 1948), and Alžběta Göllnerová, "Počátky reformace v Banské Bystrici," *Bratislava* 4 (1930):580–612.

12. For a discussion of Mary's authorship of this hymn see J. Mgebroff, "Schriftstellernde deutsche Frauen der Reformationszeit," *Kirchliche Zeitschrift der ev. luth. Synode von Iowa und anderen Staaten* 31 (1906):264–83 and Theodore Kolde, "Markgraf Georg von Brandenburg und das Glaubenslied der Königin Maria von Ungarn," *Beiträge zur Bayerischen Kirchengeschichte* 2 (1896):62–89. Concerning Mary's evangelical sympathies see also Georg Loesche, "Die evangelischen Fürstinnen im Hause Habsburg," *Jahrbuch der Gesellschaft für die Geschichte des Protestantismus in Österreich* 15 (1904):5–21.

13. See Probszt, "Königin Maria und die niederungarischen Bergstädte."

14. Kíšš, p. 221.

15. WA 19, 542–615. An English translation of his letter is in Theodore G. Tappert, ed. and trans., *Luther: Letters of Spiritual Counsel,* volume 18 in the series Library of Christian Classics (Philadelphia: Westminster, 1955), pp. 57–58.

16. See the works of Nyikos and Hudak for the circumstances surrounding the appearance of the work of Erasmus. The text of *De Vidua Christiana* is in Desiderius Erasmus, *Opera Omnia* 5 (Lugundi Batavorum: Petri Vander, 1704): 723–66.

17. See Mgebroff, pp. 273–75 and WA Br V:512.

18. CR II, 770, p. 178 and 808, p. 233.

19. WA Br V:425–426.

20. The well-known exchange of letters between Ferdinand and Mary has been published in Wilhelm Bauer and Robert Lacroix, eds., *Die Korrespondenz Ferdinands I,* Vol. 2 (Wien: 1938). See especially pp. 57–59, 63–64, 70–71, 214–21, 268–70, 271–72.

21. WA Br V:510–511.

22. WA Br V:525–530.

23. WA Br VI:196–197.

24. The two most significant biographies of Isabella are Endre Veress, *Izabella Kiralyné* (Budapest: A Magyar Történelmi Társulat, 1901), which was abridged and appeared in Italian as *Isabella regina d'Ungheria* (Rome, 1903) and Lajos Szádecky, *Isabella és János Zsigmond Lenyelorszagban, 1552–1556* (Budapest: Athenaum, 1888), which examines in detail her sojourn in Poland. See also Endre Veress, *Izabella Királyne diplomacziai müködése, 1551–1556* (Pest: Magzar Tudománzos Akadémia, 1899).

25. Oskar Wittstock, *Johannes Honterus der Siebenbürger Humanist und Reformator. Der Mann, Das Werk, Die Zeit* (Göttingen: Vandenhoeck und Ruprecht, 1970), p. 76. For a brief introduction to the era of the Reformation in Poland see Oscar Halecki, *Borderlands of Western Civilization: A History of East Central Europe* (New York: The Ronald Press, 1952), pp. 177–90; Francis Dvornik, *The Slavs in European History and Civilization* (New Brunswick: Rutgers University Press, 1962); Gy. Székely and E. Fügedi, *La Renaissance et La Reformation en Pologne et en Hongrie 1450–1650* (Budapest: Akadémiai Kiadó, 1963); Bernhard Stasiewski, *Reformation und Gegen Reformation in Polen* (Münster: Aschendorf, 1960); Stanislaw Lubieniecki, *Historia Reformationis Po-*

Ionicae (Warsaw: Panstwe Wydawnictwo Naukewe, 1971); Paul Fox, *The Reformation in Poland: Some Social and Economic Aspects* (Baltimore: Johns Hopkins University Press, 1924). For the history of the Reformation in Poland and Transylvania with a special emphasis on anti-Trinitarianism see George Hunston Williams, *The Radical Reformation* (Philadelphia: Westminster Press, 1962), pp. 404–16, 639–69, 708–63; and Earl Morse Wilbur, *A History of Unitarianism in Transylvania, England, and America* (Cambridge: Harvard University Press, 1952), pp. 3–80.

26. For the career of Martinuzzi and the reign of Isabella, see especially Laszló Makkai, *Histoire de Transylvanie* (Paris: Les Presses Universitaires de France, 1946); Sinor, pp. 152–71; Fichtner, pp. 118–139; Alfons Huber, "Die Erwerbung Siebenbürgens durch Ferdinand I im Jahre 1551 und Bruder Georgs Ende," *Archiv für österreichische Geschichte* 75 (1889): 483–545; and also his "Die Verhandlungen Ferdinands I. mit Isabella von Siebenbürgen 1551–1555," *Archiv für österreichische Geschichte* 78 (1893): 181–247.

27. There exists a rich literature on the history of the Reformation in Transylvania. Among the most significant publications in Western languages are: Karl Reinerth, *Die Gründung der evangelischen Kirchen in Siebenbürgen,* volume 5 in the series Studia Transylvanica (Köln: Böhlau Verlag, 1956), based on his earlier briefer study, *Die Reformation der siebenbürgisch-sächsischen Kirche* (Gütersloh: Carl Bertelsmann, 1956); Erich Roth, *Die Reformation in Siebenbürgen und der Schweiz II. Von Honterus zur Augustana,* volume 4 in the series Siebenbürgisches Archiv (Köln: Böhlau Verlag, 1964); Ludwig Binder, *Grundlagen und Formen der Toleranz in Siebenbürgen bis zur Mitte des 17. Jahrhunderts,* volume 11 in the series Siebenbürgisches Archiv (Köln: Böhlau Verlag, 1976); and Friedrich Teutsch, *Geschichte der ev. Kirche in Siebenbürgen* (Hermannstadt: W. Krafft, 1921).

28. Although there have been several fictional or semifictional accounts of the life of Elizabeth Bathory, the most reliable early scholarly investigation was that of R. A. Elsberg, *Elisabeth Báthory (Die Blutgräfin). Ein Sitten-und Charakterbild* (Breslau: S. Schottlaender, 1904). Most recently two new scholarly studies of the circumstances and implications of the trial have appeared: Jozef Kočiš, *Alžbeta Báthoryova a palatín Thurzo* (Martin: Osveta, 1984) and Péter Katalin, *A csejtei várúrno: Báthory Erzsét* (Budapest: Helikon Kiadó, 1985).

29. Kočiš, pp. 9–17.

30. Elsberg, pp. 20–34, 77–104.

31. Most of the documents pertaining to the case, including the protocols of the various hearings held during the years 1610 and 1611 are housed in either the National Archive in Budapest or in the Regional Archive in Bytča. Summary extracts are included in both Elsberg and Kočiš.

32. The best biography of Thurzó is that of Pavel Kolárovský, "Palatín Juraj Thurzo, jeho doba, život a dielo," Ph.D. diss. citation, Evangelical Theological Faculty Bratislava, 1972. His correspondence with his second wife, Elizabeth Czobor, has been published by Edmund Zichy, *Bethlenfalvi gróf Thurzó György levelei nejéhez Czobor szent-Mihály Czobor Erzsébethez* (Budapest: Athenaum, 1876).

33. For a brief survey of the tumultuous era of the Fifteen Years' War and the revolt of Stephen Bocskay see: Geza Lencz, *Der Aufstand Bocskays und der Wiener Friede. Eine kirchenhistorische Studie* (Debreczen: Hegedüs and Sandor, 1917; Lászlo Nagy, *Bocskai szabadságharc katonai története* (Budapest: Akadémiai Kiadó, 1961) and David P. Daniel, "The Fifteen Years' War and the Protestant Response to Habsburg Absolutism in Hungary," *East Central Europe / L'Europe du Centre-est* 8 (1981):38–51.

34. This is the general argument of Katalin's *A csejtei várúrno: Báthory Erzsét* (Budapest: Helikon Kiadó, 1985).

MILAGROS ORTEGA COSTA

Spanish Women in the Reformation

From the early medieval times to the beginning of the modern age, Spanish women[1] enjoyed an equality with men not found in other European countries in economic matters, jobs, and their sexual life.[2] Documents show not only that women bought, sold, donated, or traded in their own names but also that women inherited from their parents under the rule of absolute equality established in the *Liber Judicorum*.[3] Further, when a couple sold property it was a frequent practice to stipulate in the documents whose property it was and, if it belonged to the wife, her name would appear before that of her husband's. Also the dowry (*dote*) which at that time was a present from the parents of the groom to the bride, remained her exclusive property unless, widowed, she married again.[4]

Women founded and funded monasteries, convents, and hospitals and often wrote the charters by which the life within was regulated; women paid the same taxes as men, and in Madrid, for instance, the property census of buildings and dwellings show female participation in the production and services; women even taught at the university at least in a couple of known cases; and since 1581 women acted in the theatre.[5]

As for their sexual freedom, there are many scandalized accounts by foreign travelers in Spain who could not understand why men paid so much attention to women. They were further scandalized by their excess of makeup, their mellifluous songs, and the brightness and richness of the clothes they wore.[6] Even in the last years of the "Sad King," Philip II, Pope Clement VIII's legate was not taken by the women at the Spanish court and described them as impudent.[7]

With the advent of mercantilism in the sixteenth century, however, the status of Spanish women deteriorated. Job opportunities for women became increasingly scarce in the cities, and women's salaries—in relation to men's for equivalent work—were losing ground fast.[8] Matters did not look much better with regard to sexual equality when the *Nueva Recopilación* of 1569 recognized the husband's right to kill his wife when she was found in the act of adultery, providing the lover was killed at the same time.[9] Nor do women fare much better in the two sixteenth-century printed guides for the perfect woman written by great Spanish men of letters.

Juan Luis Vives, in his *De institutione foemina christiana*, begins by saying that nothing can be more essential for humanity than attending to the good upbringing of Christian women from the cradle because "one can say, without error, that women are the source of all bad and good deeds in this world."[10] To this effect little girls—how early he does not know—should learn virtuous acts and, at the same time, everything related to the good governance of the household. A young woman should never be idle (*mano sobre mano*) or go to dances and festivities where only vices can be learned. Women should be educated—history proves that learned women do not fall—but they should never show how much they know, nor should they be teachers or have schools. They should abstain from playing chess and dice because there is no more repugnant sight than a woman entertained at such vile exercises. As for makeup, Vives sees only three reasons that women would want to use it, all of them bad: "if she wants to please herself, she is vain; if God, she is mad; if men, she is bad." The greatest virtue in a woman is chastity, and to ensure her purity she should not play, from infancy, with brothers or male cousins, nor overdress or laugh, nor look back at men who are looking at her. Women should be silent—he reminds the reader how Saint Suzanne was delivered from accusations by silence—because though they may think they are well spoken, their words are only garrulity and chatter. Considering that women are, "by nature, sick animals," Vives concluded that "much more important than having learned and well-spoken women is having good and honest ones."

In *La perfecta casada,* written about sixty years later, Fray Luis de León advises a young married woman, María Varela Osorio, on how to be a perfect wife. The author's method, as he explains in the prologue, is to let the Holy Spirit talk while he merely clarifies the concepts, just as an art connoisseur points out the artistic effects of a painting and thereby makes it alive for its viewers. His portrait of the perfect wife becomes, by this method, a carbon copy of the biblical one. Women are created as an afterthought of God, as only a helper and comfort to men, and are loaded with the constant need to atone since "from women came the beginning of sin, and by her we all die."[11]

With headings such as "She seeketh wool, and flax, and worketh willingly with her hands" or "She will do him good and not evil all days of her life." Fray Luis de León directs the newly married María Varela Osorio toward a life of thrift, of working with her hands, and of always providing a source of cheer and rest for her husband. And while the world is the open field for her husband, she, by making profit of useless or forgotten things to procure for herself wool and flax "and other suchlike materials," so using "the weapons and fields of battle on which the good wife gives evidence of her prowess."[12]

No less illuminating is Fray Luis de León's explanation of why a good woman is so much admired and treasured:

> When a woman succeeds in distinguishing herself in something praiseworthy, she wins a victory over any number of men who have given themselves over the same endeavor. For so insignificant a thing as this which we call woman never undertakes or succeeds in carrying out anything essentially worthwhile unless

she be drawn to it, and stimulated, and encouraged by some force of incredible resoluteness which either God, or some singular gift of God, has placed within her soul . . . Of course, for a man to be good, an average degree of perfection suffices; but for a woman, goodness is a matter of very many and very costly degrees of perfection.[13]

With these ideal models in mind, let us look now at a number of Spanish women that I have selected because of their direct involvement with the Reformation. Some are unique: Isabella of Castile, Saint Teresa of Avila, for example. Some can be taken as representatives of their kind—the nun, the *beata*,[14] the housewife. All, however, witness to women's presence, participation, and, at times, leadership, in all major attempts for religious reform from the end of the fifteenth century to the beginning of the seventeenth.

At the dawn of the Reformation—and I use the term broadly to encompass both the Protestant and Catholic reforms—we must begin with a woman who changed the society in which she lived in all respects, not least, the religious one. One cannot emphasize enough Isabella of Castile's role as a complete reformer: in government, finance, church, justice, family life, the arts and language, she ruled.[15] She was everywhere, traveling on horseback all the year round, soothing, scolding, punishing, mending the country as if it were her family.

She insisted on education (she herself learned Latin when near forty).[16] Priests must be more educated; only specialists and professionals (*letrados*) could be in charge of affairs. She insisted to the pope that Spaniards resident in the country be appointed as bishops and canons in place of foreigners, absentee strangers to local troubles who milked the parishes and sees.[17] Although the popes never granted her this right absolutely except in Granada and the Canary Islands, she did get a de facto veto on such appointments.[18] Internally, she accelerated the reformation of the Augustinian, Benedictine, Franciscan, and Dominican orders in favor of the observants, who rejected the relaxed norms of the conventuals and wanted to return to their founders' original rules.[19]

In all her attempts—political, social, religious—her purpose was to create unity and independence in Spain. To achieve this aim she did whatever was necessary.

At the death of Isabella in 1504, Cardinal Ximenes, her faithful adviser in the latter part of her life, gave the Reformation a new impetus. Ximenes, who eventually became a friar, an observant Franciscan, not only continued and enlarged what Isabella had started, but also gave it a particular flavor. Under him, the Franciscan ideals that had been sought by the few became an aspiration of the many.[20]

Ximenes' influence, helped considerably by his vulgarization of mystical works which provided everybody with a means of communicating directly with God, combined with the historic changes the Western World was undergoing to lead to a new religious fervency that sprung up everywhere in

Spain at the beginning of the sixteenth century.[21] From this evangelical wave, filled with all kinds of optimistic religious expectancies and supernatural signs—prophecies, ecstasies, raptures—many women emerged, even within the least contemplative religious order, the Dominicans.

Just as the other orders had been struggling with their reformation, the Dominican province of Spain had, at the end of the fifteenth century, almost settled the long battle. By the beginning of the following century, however, the fragile unity of the order was again in danger. This time the dissenting force came from the convent of Piedrahita around which a movement akin to Savonarola's Congregation of St. Mark was gathering momentum.[22]

At the heart of this pietistic and revolutionary movement we find Sor María de Santo Domingo, known as the *beata* of Piedrahita.[23] Her raptures, prophecies, and many other supernatural signs were a source of inspiration for her followers and an object of contempt for her detractors. Because the stakes were so high in that Dominican battle, the *beata* suffered several interrogations culminating in the so-called Trial of Valladolid under the authority of Rulfo, the pope's legate, in 1509–10.[24]

In order to push forward his reforming aims, Cardinal Ximenes did everything he could to help the Piedrahita movement. He was able, with the help of King Ferdinand, to have the *beata* come out the trial untarnished and free to go back to the convent the duke of Alba had erected for her in Aldeanueva, among the 240 nuns that soon would populate it. Furthermore, in the following year, 1511, Ximenes ordered the translation and publication of Savonarola's "Exposition of the Psalm 'Miserere mei Deus' " and the *Life of St. Catherine of Siena* written by Raymond of Capua and translated by father Antonio de la Peña, one of the most fervent admirers of Sor María de Santo Domingo and her defender at Valladolid. Finally, Ximenes, who had commented on meeting Sor María that he had never seen such living doctrine (*doctrina viva*)[25] requested the *beata's* confessor to write down what she said while in rapture to better diffuse her doctrine; thus originated her *Libro de la oración*.

The tone of her loving raptures with God is lyrical, sometimes naive, sometimes torn by His absence. Her language is filled with images and analogies taken from the perceptible world and pleonasms: "What a dead death," "of blind blindness," and so on. Of particular interest to us is the question about the New World. The theologians asked her if in the islands newly discovered by Columbus the Word of God had been preached before. Sor María answered in the person of God:

> Since I was the creator of all things, it was appropriate that everything I created heard the news of my arrival and felt the pain of my death and thus, all creatures felt it. But because not everywhere were they capable of virtue, even though it had been divulged to all, in some parts it passed by and was not received . . . Creatures were, in those parts filled with the malignancy of sin; as brutes and wild animals in which there is no place for virtue.[26]

Around the same time that Sor María de Santo Domingo's words gained notoriety, a Franciscan tertiary from Guadalajara, Isabel de la Cruz, was starting to be noticed within her order because of her disobedience to her superiors. She was also, probably, beginning to develop her particular doctrine that would be known as *dexamiento* or abandonment of one's will to God.[27]

Little is known about Isabel de la Cruz, but what we do know leads us to believe she was the teacher (*maestra*) of the heretical sect known as the illuminati (*alumbrados*).[28] Isabel de la Cruz and Pedro Ruiz de Alcaraz, her most important disciple and immediate collaborator, formed conventicles in the provinces of Guadalajara and Toledo where they met and taught their new doctrine to friars, clerics, and the laity. In their teachings they opposed the spirit to the letter, mental prayer to vocal prayer. They rejected scholars and attacked overtly church ceremonies as well as the supernatural excesses of the current pseudomystics.[29]

The *alumbrados* had started, in accordance with their times, with the revolutionary cry of Scripture alone. The Bible, mostly the New Testament and a few Psalms, was the only way of knowing God. Soon, however, Isabel developed her doctrine that there should be nothing whatsoever between men and God, not even the Bible or the humanity of Christ. For those already initiated, the only thing to do was to abandon their will to God; while in this abandonment (*dexamiento*) they could not err.[30]

In 1519 their meetings were brought to the attention of the Inquisition. The episcopal visitors that were sent to investigate either did not consider the matter serious or did not collect enough information against them, for the *alumbrados* were left undisturbed to continue preaching and gathering adepts.[31] Another accusation in 1524 prompted quite a different response: Isabel de la Cruz and Pedro de Alcaraz were arrested, tried by the Inquisition, and were flogged through the streets after public sentence at the Toledo auto-da-fé in 1529.[32]

Between these two dates, however, important political and religious changes, both at home and abroad, had occurred, which may account for the different outcome of the two investigations. Abroad, Luther had been excommunicated and the schism that would have irreparable effects for the church and the empire was beginning to take place. At home, the *comuneros*—supporters of traditional town rights and charters—had raised their banner against some of the policies of Charles I, their "foreign" king, and after a long year had been defeated. Toledo alone, following the defeat at Villalar (April 23, 1521), continued the rebellion for nine more months, led by the widow of the executed leader Juan de Padilla.[33]

María de Pacheco, daughter of the count of Tendilla, was, in a sense, a female version of the Renaissance ideal of the well-rounded man, well versed in the use of the pen and the sword.[34] Her strength and cunning, like Isabella of Castile's, allowed her to sustain her rebellion and, when everything was lost, to escape to Portugal and avoid the exemplary punishment the king had in store for her.[35]

What María could not prevent was the scorn of some of her male contemporaries and their unflattering remarks. Even the mild Juan Luis Vives blamed her for her husband's rebellion and pointed out that Juan de Padilla was punished by the king because she had not been punished by her husband.[36] Pedro Mártir de Anglería, in a letter to María de Pacheco's brother, the marquis of Mondéjar, referred to the rumor circulating that María was the "husband of her husband." In another letter, Pedro Mártir wrote that "she was so sunk that there was no hope she could ever emerge"—a prediction that did not come true since María de Pacheco lived peacefully in Portugal, dedicated to her studies until her death. Mártir added that it was known, through one of María's chambermaids, that she was possessed by the demons with whom she consulted in private.[37] In a recent study, however, the actions of María de Pacheco are seen in a different light: her rebellion appears as almost a last stand to defend women's jobs, very much in danger then with the rapidly declining wool industry.[38]

Despite the unrest and destruction brought about by the *comuneros'* uprising, we gather from many Inquisition records and the writings of theologians that people still felt a great sense of religious freedom. True and false *beatas* and *beatos* continued flourishing everywhere.[39] Many people—rich, poor, men, women, nobles, clerics, peasants—were trying the various and easy ways of reaching salvation. Books were written about the sayings of many of these women or were written by the women themselves.[40] Others, like María de Cazalla, preached and wrote letters explaining the new ways of practicing the old doctrine, letters that, in her case, circulated bound like a book among her faithful.[41]

María de Cazalla, like Isabel de la Cruz from Guadalajara and of the same milieu, the "court" of the duke del Infantado,[42] had been, at one point, close to the *alumbrados*. In her case we are not dealing with a nun or a *beata* but with a married woman who was the wife of Lope de Rueda, a small landowner, and mother of several children. She had no formal education, it seems, but she was nevertheless a well-read woman and was in contact, through her brother, Bishop Cazalla, with the intellectual life of the University of Alcalá and with its many recent publications. She was well versed in the works of Erasmus, of whom she was a true admirer, and it is quite possible she had read some of Luther's works since close friends of hers had.[43]

María de Cazalla, typically, had been touched by the religious fever of her time and had followed several paths toward reaching a perfected religious life. She had tried the traditional one: the frequenting of churches, the practice of virtues, and abstinence to the point of denying her husband his marital rights. This nearly led to tragedy, as we learn in her trial. Her husband, tired of coming home and not finding his meals ready nor his wife in attendance, busy as she was praying in her little chapel at home or talking on spiritual matters with her brother and his friends or with Mari Núñez, her mentor at the time, began scolding his wife. Argument followed argument until Lope de Rueda ran to his room to get his weapons ready to kill anyone who would interfere with him. A relative of the duke del Infantado, Alonso de la Cerda, happened to pass by and tried to pacify Rueda. As don Alonso described it on the witness stand, he knocked at the door where María's husband had blockaded himself. Rueda did not want to open the door, but when he did, he came out with the sword in his hand shouting: "death, death to the Jews who come to kill me in my house!" The witness tried to separate the adversaries but found himself in the midst of swordplay and was stabbed in the hand. Soon, however, more people came in and peace was restored.[44]

As a result of this incident, Lope de Rueda took his family from their house in the city of Guadalajara to his property in Horche, a small town nearby. The move did not prevent María from continuing her spiritual explorations or from learning new spiritual discoveries from Isabel de la Cruz and Pedro Ruiz de Alcaraz. For one thing, she was liberated from her wifely reluctance as she learned from them that in the "sexual act with her husband she was as close to God as if she were in prayer."[45] From them, too, she learned not to be "tied" (*atada*) and to rejoice in the highest freedom (*altísima libertad*) thus obtained.[46]

Soon María developed her own doctrine, a mixture of the *dexamiento* (abandonment) of the *alumbrados* and Erasmus' "philosophy of Christ." With Erasmus, she was against the pharisaic ceremonies of the Church and believed marriage more meritorious than virginity;[47] with the *alumbrados* she participated in the doctrine of pure love. For María, as for Isabel de la Cruz and Alcaraz, doing good works to earn eternal life was not true love of God. One had to love Him for the sake of that love, without conditions, ties, or self-interest. Those who sought their own spiritual good were *atados* (tied) and imperfect. Quoting St. Paul, María also used to ridicule those looking for God in churches made of stone, and not inside of themselves, who were living temples.[48]

In the years before her trial, María de Cazalla had gathered a group of devotees among the intellectuals of Alcalá, the Mendoza family, and the surrounding common people.[49] In the record of her trial, we see María sitting in the kitchen of some friends in Pastrana surrounded by men and women, some standing outside the kitchen for lack of space, while she reads and comments on one of Saint Paul's epistles, a psalm, or advises them in how to go to paradise. We see her advising country women on spiritual matters in Horche, or talking to clerics, such as the Maestro Diego Hernández, who came to visit her by recommendation of her Alcalá friends, unaware, it seems, of the danger growing around her.[50]

Why María de Cazalla was not tried with the *alumbrados* is somewhat a mystery considering that accusations against her had been filed since 1519. Perhaps the Inquisition did not want to offend her brother, Bishop Cazalla, who had been very close to Cardinal Ximenes or feared an irate confrontation with the Church hierarchy. After the death of Bishop Cazalla (c. 1528), that trouble was removed, but the gathering of incriminating materials continued in the so-called secret phase of the Inquisition trial for four more years.[51] Finally, the order for María's arrest was signed on April 22, 1532, and from that day to December 20, 1534, she was a prisoner in the secret prison (cárcel secreta) of Toledo.[52]

Her release she owed to her unbending courage. She not only endured, without confessing or admitting any wrongdoing, torture, the last step of an Inquisition trial, but she also shamed the attending inquisitors who forced her, a woman, to disrobe in their presence to her underclothes. Her courage seemed to be admired even by the notary, who had been taking down everything she said, including her cries of pain. As she was leaving the torture chamber he quoted her as saying: "better crippled than defamed."[53] Her penance, in addition to the long two and a half years that she spent in prison, included a fine of 100 ducats for the expenses of the Holy Office and the obligation to attend Mass one Sunday at her parish, standing at the foot of the altar holding a lit candle in her hand while the priest read aloud her sentence.

The arrest of María de Cazalla came during the second wave of arrests in Toledo: the investigation of 1524 of the alumbrados now turned against the Erasmists and the intellectuals and humanists of Alcalá and Toledo. The cataclysm engulfing many serious scholars was set off by another beata from Salamanca, Francisca Hernández. Francisca had grown up in Salamanca in the region where Sor María de Santo Domingo had been influential and may have been encouraged to imitate her successes. Francisca was close to the Franciscan order, though not (as was Isabel de la Cruz) a tertiary in it. In Salamanca she came under the suspicion of the Inquisition for possible sexual relations with some of the clerics and moved to Valladolid, where she continued her teachings to many who came from great distances to learn from this woman whom numbers of enlightened men thought touched by the spirit of God.[54]

Fray Francisco Ortiz, known in his day as "the preacher of preachers," became one of her most ardent admirers. He believed completely in her, insisting that she had worked spiritual wonders for him. When he learned minutes before mounting the pulpit on a day of thanksgiving for rain that the Inquisition had arrested his "angel," Ortiz spoke extemporaneously of Francisca's saintliness and the error of the Inquisition in arresting her. In spite of his usual persuasive sermonizing, it was not surprising that he was arrested as he descended from the pulpit.[55] Meanwhile, in prison, Francisca Hernández herself seized the opportunity to denounce as heretical everyone whom she had met and disliked.

In spite of Francisco Ortiz's angelic vision of Francisca, accepted even in the last century,[56] a study of the original documents shows her attraction was more sexual than angelic for most of her male followers. Nevertheless her spiritual message was not meaningless, and for a time she had a deep influence on a number of members of the Franciscan order and caused much unrest within it.

In Valladolid, Francisca Hernández had charmed some relatives of María de Cazalla, Pedro de Cazalla, and his wife Leonor de Vibero, in whose house Francisca had lived for a number of years. Leonor, though, was soon disenchanted when she realized how many hours her husband spent with Francisca, sometimes well into the night.[57] Interestingly enough, it was at this very house and under the auspices of Leonor de Vibero, still innovative in religious questions, that the Lutherans of Valladolid met some thirty years later.

In this Castilian, so-called Lutheran outbreak no woman is considered the initiator. Until more is known, however, we cannot discount the possibility that Leonor the Vibero, the mother of six of the convicted in the Valladolid trials, played an important role. Her daughter Beatriz was also very active, and her teachings implicated many nuns from the convent of Belén in Valladolid. Quite probably Beatriz was among those who tried to interest in their cause some devout ladies from Avila including a Teresa Ahumada, later Saint Teresa.[58] But initiators or not, there is no doubt that women were very involved indeed, judging by the opinion of one historian who stated that the young and beautiful convicted nuns were "not happy in just being Lutheran, but they had become dogmatizers of that hateful doctrine,"[59] and by the incontrovertible fact that slightly more than half of the Lutherans brought to trial and punished in the resulting Valladolid autos-da-fé were women.[60]

Women were, according to two different traditions, the persons who uncovered the Valladolid Lutheran cells. One story concerns Catalina de Cardona, known as the "good woman" (*buena mujer*) who had been a governess of Juan de Austria. Cardona was a pious woman who spent three years as a hermit, dressed in a man's habit. In the 1550s she was serving the princess of Salerno, who visited the Cazallas of Valladolid often. Soon Catalina not only realized that Agustín Cazalla, one of Leonor's sons, erred in religious matters, but she also saw "fire and smoke, smelling like sulphur, coming out of his mouth." The other, more plausible story, still believed in Valladolid, involves the wife of the silversmith Juan García. Curious to know what was going on when she realized that her husband often went out after retiring for the night, she decided to follow him in disguise. When she saw her husband entering the Cazalla's house and others going inside as well, she followed them and found herself among the Lutherans. After trying in vain to get her confessor to denounce them, she went to the inquisitor general herself.[61]

Ideologically, the Valladolid Lutheran movement is difficult to trace for two main reasons. One is that many important Inquisition documents are missing. The second reason is that the official object of eradicating Lutheranism also hid the intent of crushing once and for all the aspirations to a "universal call to perfection" that since the times of Cardinal Ximenes had

had continuous and worthy proponents, an intent that was not totally realized despite the fall of Archbishop Carranza.[62]

By 1560 the danger of any kind of heterodox Reformation in Spain had come to an end. The Inquisition, following the Roman policy of extreme rigor, was particularly stern and so was Philip II. The punishment had to be exemplary, thus the severity of the sentences and the grandiosity of the autos-da-fé.[63] Some theologians saw in the benign treatment of the religious innovators such as *alumbrados* and Erasmists earlier in the century, the cause for the current heresy.[64] The days in which Ximenes praised and asked advice from women like Sor María la Pobre—the poor—were gone. The *Index,* just published, included not only heretical works, but also all orthodox books in the vernacular that tended to the interiorization of the faith.[65]

A comparison of the behavior of María de Cazalla and that of a relative of Saint Teresa, Cristóbal de Balmeseda, toward their daughters a generation later is illustrative of the effects of these changes in people's attitudes. María encouraged her daughters to read Erasmus and other novelties; Señor Balmeseda refused to allow his to learn how to read and write. While both these parents were against their daughters entering religious life, their reasons differed radically. María saw the convents as lax, vain places where no true religion was practiced; Señor Balmeseda hated convents because "those nefarious people [*alumbrados* and Lutherans] had done so much harm in them."[66] Thus, the lack of zeal that María de Cazalla complained about had not only been corrected, but its excess, thirty years later, reeked of heresy.

A similar contrast is found comparing what Brianda de Mendoza expected, in 1534, of the nuns in the new convent of Nuestra Señora de la Piedad—to know how to read or be read the Bible and other good books—and Saint Teresa's prompt reaction to a young woman who wanted to become a Carmelite novice. Full of enthusiasm, the young novice-to-be explained that she was ready to join, that she had come well prepared with the Bible in her pocket. "Did you bring a Bible? Do not come here, we do not need you or your Bible; we are ignorant women who only know how to spin and do what we are told." By then, the reading of the Bible was becoming suspicious.[67]

In "those rough times," to use one of her expressions, Teresa de Jesús, a Carmelite nun at the Convent de la Encarnación in Avila, not only experienced physically and spiritually the most awesome effects—sicknesses, ecstasies, levitations, "transverberations"[68]—but accomplished what no man could.

The Pope, the General of the Carmelites, the Spanish King wanted desperately a reformation of the Order that would bring back the pristine Christian spirit. Many had tried and failed. Teresa took in her hands such a difficult enterprise and went forth without stumbling even once, helping on the contrary those who fell. Being a frail woman, Teresa not only succeeded in reforming women but brought forth the best reformation for men; those men who had not been able to be reformed by men.[69]

Before she could undertake this reform, though, and before she became, according to the pope's legate Sega, "a restless, wanderer, disobedient, and stubborn *femina* who, under the title of devotion, invented bad doctrines, moving outside the cloister against the rules of the Council of Trent and her prelates; teaching as a master against Saint Paul's orders that women should not teach,"[70] she had to spend almost twenty years externally inactive at her convent in Avila.

But if her physical life remained inactive, that was not the case with her spiritual life, whose external signs were alarming the mother superior, sister nuns, and confessors. The possibility existed that those signs were devil's work (*cosas del diablo*) or, worse, heretical. To make sure, her successive confessors made her put into words her most intimate experiences and her search for her own path to prayer. From these early requests, her *Vida*, one of the jewels of Spanish literature, would evolve.[71]

The concern of the confessors was not unreasonable; fresh in the memory of all spiritual fathers was the fall of Magdalena de la Cruz, abbess of Santa Clara nunnery of Córdoba, one of the most renowned among the fake *beatas.*

> For thirty-eight years she had enjoyed a universal reputation. Her predictions went from mouth to mouth . . . Her confessors asked her to write the wonderful mercies she was receiving from God. In the pulpits she was raised to sainthood. The empress had sent her the blankets of Philip II [just born] for blessing. The inquisitor general, Alonso Manrique, honored her with his own veneration.

Suddenly, the Inquisition arrested her on January 1, 1544. Her confession on May 3, 1546, was staggering: since she was seven years old, induced by a demon, she had feigned all of her saintly signs.[72] And that people thought of Magdalena de la Cruz in relation to Teresa's supernatural manifestations is clearly manifested in this dialogue between a nobleman from Avila and Teresa herself: "Do not forget Magdalena de la Cruz, Spain thought she was a saint and she was a slave of the devil," said the nobleman. Teresa's reply was: "I never remember her without trembling."[73]

On the other hand, Teresa's confessors were well aware that the Inquisition was persecuting at that time, under the *alumbrado* and Lutheran danger, even the works of the most refined spirituals. What they could not anticipate was that the almost palpable fear of the Inquisition probes would bring forth a new literary genre. We are no longer dealing with a confessor transcribing what a nun or a *beata* was saying while in rapture or a nun writing what God dictated to her, as had Mechthilde of Magdeburg, for instance, or confessions such as Saint Augustine's. What we find is a nun who had to write, ordered by her confessor, the most intimate and hidden experiences of her mind so that they could be judged, weighed, and appraised. That this process involved not only sharp introspection and careful analysis of nontransferable experiences, but also clarity in expressing ineffable matters cannot be emphasized enough. And the result was a new literary form that more than autobiography should be called "autoanimography," as Saint Teresa under-stood well.[74]

In a recent study, Teresa's literary vocation is presented so convincingly that the idea of the saint writing against her will, always under the strain of obedience due to her confessors, has been put to rest for good.[75] The fact remains, however, that Teresa's *Vida* originated in her confessors' requests of her to explain in writing her experiences, as so many other spiritually un-conventional "daughters" would be requested to do by their spiritual fathers for many years to come.[76] As for Teresa's *Vida* in the final and polished form, divided in forty chapters that she sent to Saint Juan de Avila, it was a work of love and not of obligation, the work of an author well aware of her merits and, as such, wanting to see her thoughts spread in print.[77]

Another woman who failed to see herself in print is Isabel Ortiz. Her book of devotions—meditations on the *pater noster*—could have been pub-lished, providing she relinquished her authorship. Dr. Majuelo, one of the censors, had approved her work on the condition that it did not carry a woman's name as author, a condition unacceptable to Isabel who felt that, if the book had been written by a woman, the author should get the credit.[78]

Isabel Ortiz, from a family of silversmiths, had been a maid in the ser-vice of Isabel de Aragón, wife of the fourth duke del Infantado, for six years before she was married at age fifteen, by arrangement of the duchess, to Gonzalo Hernández de Plazaola, another silversmith. The marriage did not last long. Her husband abandoned her and their two daughters.[79] The young Isabel, though, by embroidering and sewing and ingratiating herself with the duchess and others was not only able to take care of herself and her daughter—the other died young—but also found time to instruct herself and to avidly read spiritual works, meanwhile enlarging her circle of friends. Slowly the fame of her good grasp of spiritual matters spread all over Guadalajara.[80]

After so much reading, it was only natural that she felt the urge to write her own book of devotions, which she did. No sooner had she finished it than Isabel began distributing handwritten copies of her work among friends and protectors while asking a relative in Alcalá to enquire about the possibilities of its publication. The duchess del Infantado was so touched by Isabel's work that she adopted it as her nightly prayer book until her death. Before she died, when she was too sick and could not read, she asked a maid to read it to her aloud.[81]

We learn of Isabel Ortiz in Alcalá in 1564, just arrested by the visiting inquisitor for having encouraged Leonor de Toledo, marquise of Távara, and other society ladies, to abandon oral prayer in favor of mental prayer. The arrest was prompted by the marquise's lengthy testimony to the inquisitor, following the advice of her husband and of her confessor, about the strange conversation she had had with Isabel Ortiz.[82] What had alarmed the mar-quise was that Isabel, whom she knew mostly by reputation, had asked for a private visit, and when alone, explained that she had been troubled to see the marquise praying overly much at the church of San Juan de la Peña during

Holy Week. Isabel was certain, she told the marquise, that that lady was ready for a more immediate way of prayer if she wanted to become a better servant of God, and that, though Isabel had directed many souls in this method of prayer before, she had not dared to offer it to the marquise prior to this occasion. Isabel suggested that the marquise should consult the fathers of the Company of Jesus, who would help her in this form of prayer. To the answer that the marquise would first consult with her confessor Isabel expressed her doubt that such a cleric would understand, because talking to an unspiritual person about spiritual matters would be like talking Chinese.[83]

While they were engaged in this conversation, the marquise's confessor happened to come by and Isabel Ortiz retired to another room. So unsettled was Doña Leonor that she immediately communicated her concern to her confessor Fray Alonso de Hontiveros, who at once pronounced that the woman was mad or, worse, a Lutheran or on her way to becoming one. After he had seen Isabel at a distance, the Dominican decided that her appearance was not that of a spiritual person; rather, she looked like a washerwoman. He further said that certainly the woman could not be a saint because she showed so much self-esteem and saintly people were never proud.

On hearing the marquise's long report, Inquisitor Soto sent the information to Toledo, where, after being studied, the arrest of Isabel Ortiz was voted on by the other inquisitor and the Holy Office consultants. They also recommended that the investigation proceed in order to ascertain whether she was one of the original *alumbrados* of Guadalajara.[84] To complicate matters further, in the ensuing testimonies of various witnesses, the news of Isabel Ortiz's book came out.

It is fascinating to examine not only how the inquisitorial mechanism begins to gather more information, but particularly how the news of Isabel's arrest immediately generated waves of its own. We see first a group of silversmiths and other merchants chatting in the main street of Alcalá on the evening of her arrest. They all wondered what the causes might be until one of them, Juan Husillo, an employee of an uncle of Isabel Ortiz, mentioned that he had seen a book written by her and had looked at it enough to decide that there was nothing good in it. Then he said that at home they called her the "doctoress" as a joke.

The next morning one of the men who had attended that gathering felt compelled to go to the inquisitor; a woman writing a book, even if he knew nothing about her or it, was suspicious enough to prompt him to clear his conscience. Juan Husillo was called to depose, and he repeated the same story, adding that the book in question had been shown to Dr. Majuelo of the University of Alcalá about seven years before and the doctor had said that he did not see any need to publish any book written by a woman.[85]

Next, Dr. Alonso de Balboa, vicar general of the Alcalá bishopric, that same morning presented a written statement to the inquisitor to explain what he knew of this matter—always through the worried marquise de

Távara—and how he had advised her ladyship to talk to the inquisitor since everything she said about Isabel Ortiz sounded suspicious to him and, he added, the sooner those things were uncovered the better because, "in these times those were dangerous endeavors where many little women (*mugercillas*) had fallen." Dr. Balboa went back to the inquisitor the following day, May 30, with a second statement. This time he informed him that the previous evening—just twenty-four hours after Isabel's arrest—the lawyer Diego Martínez had come to visit him to inquire whether he knew why Isabel had been arrested. The lawyer had mentioned Isabel's book and also that she was an avid reader. Dr. Balboa had replied that women should not know anything beyond spinning, embroidering, and other household duties.[86]

The ripple effects of Isabel's arrest are further evident in the testimony of the lawyer Martínez, who was called as soon as the inquisitor heard about his visit to Dr. Balboa. Martínez, when asked if he knew why he had been called, replied that he presumed it was in connection with Isabel Ortiz and her book. He said that he had seen the book but he could not remember a word of it nor did he think it was any good when he saw it. When asked with whom he had discussed Isabel's detention, he answered that early in the morning of May 29, the notary Ordóñez, in whose house Isabel had been staying, and the silversmith Juan Francisco had come to the witness's house to inquire about it and they both thought the arrest was the result of her book. Also the licenciate Salcedo, the governor, had visited him the previous day for the same reason.

In other words, the men of Alcalá who had come in contact with Isabel Ortiz, from the civil and ecclesiastical authorities to the professionals to commoners, were scurrying about, afraid of being somehow implicated in her fall. And that is not all. The following day, May 31, the inquisitor received another written statement, this time from Dr. Majuelo, canon of St. Yuste, administrator of the University of Alcalá, and commissary of the Holy Office, the very same censor who seven years before had approved Isabel's book for publication on condition that it did not carry a woman's name for its author.

His statement, a masterpiece of evasion, is filled with "to the best of my recollection" clauses in which he minimizes his involvement in the matter, even to the point of doubting that he had done anything at all with the manuscript beyond seeing it when an assistant to the vicar had brought it to his attention. At the end of his statement, he gives the name of that assistant, currently in Madrid, who may know what happened to the confounded manuscript.[87]

Turning to the women in Guadalajara, we find that Isabel Ortiz was not any more charitably regarded. The deceased duchess's duenas, maids, and dwarf all agreed that Isabel was a conceited person who talked only about herself and about her musician daughter;[88] that her alleged book was not of her doing, rather that she had borrowed all of it from a bishop just to be different and to boast of being highly spiritual; that the embroideries Isabel said were of her invention had been copied; that Isabel was vain and only talked of vanities; that she received too many male musicians in her house who, Isabel said, were teaching music to her daughter. Even the countess de Coruña, who, according to one of the maids, had liked Isabel's work and had praised the author's subtlety and wisdom, when asked by Inquisitor Soto about it, answered that she had not read it because it was written "in a despicable handwriting, as of a woman." Furthermore, the countess claimed that she then had some eye trouble and, anyhow, she was not fond "of obscure doctrines."[89]

Despite the ironic comments of the men who were afraid of having compromised their freedom by having befriended this unique woman, and those of women who, in most cases, were simply envious of her strength and self-confidence, Isabel endured and carried herself extremely well throughout the long interrogations at the Holy Office in Toledo. By sheer determination she was able, by appealing to the *Consejo,* the Holy Office Council, to avoid torture and go free. She still had the last word when she asked to have a copy of the verdict so that she could again carry her head high.[90]

In 1576, back in Avila, a fifteen-year-old girl entered the Bernardine convent of St. Ana as a novice. The girl, María Vela y Cueto, was born of a noble family. She was the grand-niece, on her mother's side, of the first viceroy of Perú, Blasco Núñez de Vela. From her mother she had received the good education that corresponded to her social class and had learned not only embroidery and music, but also Latin and the Scriptures.[91]

When María entered the convent there were seventy "solemn and majestic 'lady nuns' with their wide hoods and endless trains." Her aunt, Doña Isabel de Cueto, was the abbess. The house was big and manorial, as was fitting for the residing noblewomen. Each nun had an airy and sunny cell, some of which consisted of seven rooms: a hall to receive visitors, a bedroom, an oratory, a kitchen, a washing and dressing room, and a room for her personal maid. Their fundamental communal obligation was, at the sound of the bell at 3 A.M., to convene for Matins and sing the psalms, responsories, and hymns. Within this framework it was possible to lead a fully individual life on the side. Each of the nuns took care of her own sustenance and was free to attend to her own taste in comfort, food, and dress.[92]

Into this not very austere life, then, young María Vela entered, with Saint Catherine of Siena as her spiritual model. She followed Saint Catherine's example in detail and refused to go to bed until midnight, as Saint Catherine used to do. María would also discipline herself three times a day, sleep on a cork mattress, eat grass, and so on.[93]

From the beginning, however, her obedience was severely tried. After making a general confession the year she entered the novitiate, she was assigned a confessor, Gaspar de Avila, who helped her in her wishes for mortification by putting her under the immediate commands of her aunt, the abbess. The result was hardly satisfactory during the six years that her novitiate lasted: she could only take communion when her aunt allowed it, once every two weeks. As for penance and prayer, matters were even worse. As María said: "the time for prayer was very rationed, hardly an hour a day and there were times when it was only a quarter of an hour."[94]

All of these restrictions only aggravated her overpowering desire for freedom to pray and contemplate. Her aunt, always vigilant, invented "entertainments" for María every time Doña Isabel saw in her niece signs of contemplation: counting the tiles of the roof, changing stones from one side of the garden to the other, sweeping—anything to prevent the appearance of the supernatural signs that her aunt saw as inevitable, given her niece's trancelike meditation.[95] Doña Isabel knew that any nun who began this spiritual path would be immediately associated with those heretics, the *alumbrados* and Lutherans, and the interest of the Inquisition could not be far behind. That she wanted to avoid at any cost.

The feared spiritual signs—the devil's? God's?—in María's case, jawlocking, faintings, tears, voices, and raptures, did not take long to appear. Her second confessor, Fray Salcedo—nephew of Teresa's confessor, Baltasar de Alvárez—was, like others, unsure of his own expertise to guide such a wondrous conscience. He asked her to write her experiences down so that he could consult with an expert. Later she would be given Saint Teresa's *Vida* as a model.

Salcedo, not satisfied with the positive review given by José de Acosta, rector of the Jesuit School in Salamanca, continued consulting everyone, with disastrous consequences for his own tranquility and more so for María Vela's. So many opinions could never coincide, and soon there were two antagonistic views: Jesuits pro, Dominicans con.[96] Laymen were also divided, as were theologians. As a result, María had to suffer many humiliations: being called a "girl" and "silly" in the pulpits, exorcisms, and, finally, being brought to the attention of the Inquisition.[97]

Years later the priest Julian de Avila,[98] who had been her confessor for a while, seemed to touch the trouble exactly when he said to Dr. Vaquero, María Vela's last confessor: "Look, Father, that she is a saint there is no doubt, but her way is very intricate." And because it was so intricate she was never able to be the "new nun" she wanted to be, or carry on a reformation within her convent or live in peaceful contemplation in the service of God.[99]

On a less saintly level, María Vela was a very accomplished woman. She not only played in the church services the music of her contemporary father Vitoria and sang beautifully, but also made with her skillful hands beautiful artificial flowers and embroideries for the altar. She imparted her knowledge of the Scriptures and hagiographic works—which she read in Latin—when she was elected teacher of the novices in 1601. After her death in 1617, her sister nuns cut her hair and removed her clothes and scapular to keep as relics; the people of Avila, pounding at the doors of the convent, demanded to see the body of their "saint."

In order to do justice to the hundreds of Spanish women who were touched by the religious ferment of the sixteenth century, I wish, with Saint Teresa, "that I might write with many hands so that one or another could not overlook any [of them]."[100] But since I have only two hands, I shall finish this gallery of Spanish women with the Venerable Luisa de Carvajal y Mendoza (1566–1614),[101] whose life is quite extraordinary since she chose neither of the two alternatives open to women: marriage or convent.

Born of an old and noble family, Luisa grew up in an extremely pious environment. Orphaned at six, she spent her next four years with her aunt, María Chacón, who took her to visit the sick in hospitals and feed the poor.[102] Her own governess, Isabel de Ayllón, trained her in the most rigorous modesty. But her true religious training came under the direction of her uncle, Francisco Hurtado de Mendoza, count de Monteagudo and marquis de Almazán, with whom she lived from 1576 until his death in 1592.

In Pamplona, where they moved when Luisa was about fourteen, her uncle, as her "spiritual director," led her in the path of perfection with a "somewhat extraordinary method," as the young woman herself recognized:

There was in the house a woman dedicated to God and sufficiently spirited who was, under pledge of the greatest secrecy, given the task of teaching me humility by the use of penances and punishments; and I was ordered to obey her in whatever she commanded, receiving all such things as health-giving purges, for the enlarging and strengthening of my soul. . . . There was a chapel which was handy and private . . . where she ordered me to go many times and wait for her. When she came in and the doors were locked, she, with a severe or at least serious expression, would command me to bare my shoulders. . . . She would bring some guitar strings . . . and would discipline me for however long seemed good to her, with blows so well placed that at times I could hardly bear them, and to give no outward sign of pain I had to squeeze my hands together with all my strength or else compress my fists as hard as possible.[103]

Humility, thus learned, would help her in the future to endure the hardships she chose for herself. Meanwhile, her life continued. She followed her uncle to Madrid, Almazán, back to Madrid, always devoted to pious works and readings and daily mental prayer. Soon these were not enough. She wanted a life of rigorous poverty and total dedication. Her uncle, who wanted Luisa to marry, would not allow her to leave his house for such an unconventional life. His only concession was to permit Luisa to move to the floor above their living quarters in his house in Madrid and live there, with some pious young women and some male servants, as retired a life as she wanted.

When her uncle died, Luisa de Carvajal, having refused marriage and having interpreted a rebellion of her spirit every time she considered entering a convent as a wish of God that she not become a nun, set up a humble house with some young women who, like her, wanted to live a virtuous life. The nobility was shocked by her ragged appearance, so contrary to her social standing. Luisa, on her part, suffered happily all the humiliations she had to endure. Dressed as a beggar she visited hospitals and brothels, consoling the suffering and trying to bring fallen women to the good path. On one occasion she brought to her house a prostitute with advanced syphilis and attended with her own hands the disgusting pustules of the sick woman.

Still not satisfied with this life of sacrifice, she made successive vows to herself: of poverty in 1593, of obedience in 1595, and of martyrdom in 1598. This last vow probably matured following the martyrdom of Edmund Campion in England in 1581. By then, Luisa had already been close to the Jesuits for years but her ties to them became closer as she moved to Valladolid and lived next to the English School of "San Albano" and the chapel of "Nuestra Señora la *Vulnerata.*"[104] There she met many English Jesuits and seminarists and, though it is not clear when England became her spiritual Mecca, these contacts were probably decisive.

Having finally decided on her true mission, she did not stop until she obtained the necessary permissions from her confessors and ecclesiastical authorities. But still she had to wait. She had bequeathed all her possessions to the Jesuits for the founding of an English mission novitiate in Louvain, but the Jesuits did not allow her to leave until she had cleared legally the matter of her estate with the trustees. Inés de la Asunción, one of the companions who had followed Luisa in all these difficult negotiations, gave a vivid image of Luisa's embarrassments, which, to her, did not make sense:

> "How is it possible, M'am, that your Ladyship undergoes such hard trials for something you will not eat or enjoy, going to talk with the magistrates walking under the feet of the horses and lackeys in the street, that a person like your Ladyship should be making yourself the scorn of the world and a living picture of death? Stop it! For the love of God!". . . But she answered me with the sweetness of an angel: "Inés, don't you see I am so commanded by Holy Obedience, and that it is only right that what I am going to give to God should cost me so much?"[105]

Finally she was able to settle her estate, and, without further ado, she started her long dreamed-of voyage on January 27, 1604, when she was approaching her fortieth birthday.

> I left and the Lord gave me strength to do so with joy and without shedding a single tear, though leaving so good a country. And, despite the fact that I had never ridden before, I got on a mule (for the sake of economy) which turned out to be the most comfortable way for the rough and roadless region of Vizcaya, where I was kept for three days, giving me a chance to visit the house of the blessed Father Ignacio, and thence through harsh times of snow, wind and water, almost to Paris. . . . In general, I was respected in France: they thought I was going to found a nunnery, such as the Discalced Carmelites had done shortly before. I hadn't the slightest wish to stop and see the various relics.[106]

When she arrived in England she stayed first in an underground house with a chapel where Father Garnet, the head of the English Jesuit mission, lived and held services for the Catholics hidden there, about ten miles north of London. Luisa described it as a peaceful paradise within a jungle. Apparently this group had lived undetected there for three years. But no more than a month and a half after her arrival, rumors came to the effect the house had been discovered, and the inhabitants all fled in different directions: some through the fields, some by the river. Doña Luisa fled to London with the owners of the house. There she was left alone, hardly able to stand on her feet—she had been sick for the last two weeks—and "without a place to rest them, like Noah's little dove."[107] Although she found another sanctuary, after the discovery of the Guy Fawkes Plot this family felt that lodging a Catholic—and a Spaniard at that—was far too risky. For her safety her friends encouraged her to go to the Spanish embassy.[108]

One difficulty Luisa had not anticipated, or so it seems, in all the years she spent planning her apostolic trip to England, was the language barrier. Soon she realized that "when the tongue prevents, the heart is in chains," and so, at the beginning, she could do little more than small acts of Catholic affirmation such as buying caricatures of the pope depicting him as "vomiting Jesuits, first with two horns and then with four" and cheerfully destroying them in front of the congregating public. Some would call her "papist"; in broken English she would reply that she had never seen such strange people who drew such bad pictures or she would kneel and pray at a cross that had been left standing in Cheapside Street, to the amazement and fury of the passers-by who again would call her "papist."[109]

When she learned some English—like a child, she said—she began visiting imprisoned Catholics in Newgate, the closest prison to the Spanish embassy, and soon she was visiting them in all the prisons of London. Then came another severe blow for the English Catholics: the Fidelity Oath. Prisons began filling with resisting male Catholics and, after 1611, with women as well. The dividing force of such an oath and its consequences among the already scared Catholics did not escape Doña Luisa, who had followed with sorrow the compliance of such important figures as the archpriest Blackwell.

As soon as she learned that her old friend Frey Robert Drury was imprisoned, she went to visit him. Drury had been a Jesuit seminarist in Valladolid when Doña Luisa lived there too. Now a Benedictine, Drury was ambivalent on the matter of the oath, ambivalence which was washed away after long conversations with his Spanish friend. As a result, Frey Drury refused to take the oath and was sentenced to death. Soon it would be the turn of Father Roberts and Father Somers, and Luisa would be there to assist them as she could:

I helped them, as best I could, before their deaths. When they were taken to hear their sentences, Father Roberts trembled so that he almost couldn't tie the sashes or the buttons of his doublet's sleeves; and he said to me: "Look how I'm trembling!" And I responded that I remembered how even the *Gran Capitán* used to shake when arming himself and would remark that his flesh owned his heart. He laughed heartily at this and bowed in thanks for my words.

When they came back from hearing the sentence, they were taken to the place where the heretics, murderers, and thieves were. And, to console myself and them as well—for it is hard to look death in the face—I got, for I forget how many coins, the jailer to let me go to them. He did that, and even one more favor, and that was to let me take them where the others [the religious prisoners] were held, rather late at night through a little secret door at the top of the tower.[110]

Doña Luisa not only helped them to die; she also made sure that their headless bodies were buried according to the Catholic rite, even though it meant stealing their bodies in the deep of the night. According to Luisa, the Catholics were easy to recognize—they were the only ones quartered and buried at the very bottom of the ditch. She tells of a night when, engaged in this macabre endeavor, two Catholic groups, unaware of each other, almost began firing at each other, thinking the others were the guards coming to arrest them.[111]

If Luisa de Carvajal did not suffer the martyrdom she had hoped for in the long waiting years in Spain, she at least was arrested and sent to prison twice. In each case she was imprisoned for only a few days, thanks to the Spanish Ambassador the first time, and again with his help and that of the Flemish ambassador the second. When she was arrested the second time, she was living with other women who had joined her in a semimonastic life under a rule that she had written in a house at Spitalsfield.[112]

Once she was released, her compatriots insisted that she return to Spain. She refused; her mission was in England, and in England she died shortly thereafter in the odor of sanctity. On her death bed she was glad to have again next to her Father Walpole, her English confessor for so many years. For us, Walpole's presence was fortunate too: Doña Luisa with her characteristic modesty had tied in a package all her writings with the clear command to turn them over to Father Walpole if he was there or to burn them immediately after her death if he was not.

Luisa de Carvajal's apostolic work in England is considered quite extraordinary. Not only did she convert non-Catholics, some of whom gave witness in her canonization process,[113] but, by her own example, she also reconverted Catholics and gave strength to those too afraid to stand up for their beliefs. Interestingly, Luisa pointed out that being a female, instead of a hindrance as she probably expected, was an asset. The English simply did not suspect women could be missionaries, which allowed Luisa de Carvajal to reach people freely.[114]

What conclusions can be drawn from the lives of the women we have reviewed? It is evident that some among them were able to fulfill their self-actualization, despite stern male opposition and even scorn. The women who succeeded did so by consciously ignoring the established restrictions imposed on their sex by the Church, society, and long-standing custom. It never entered the mind of Isabella of Castile, for instance, that granting justice or assuming many other "unwomanly" obligations were forbidden to her sex. Reading Saint Teresa we find that, despite her vow of obedience and her often amused and always vigilant lip-service to the conventions, she did not believe in or accept them. When she wrote to "her daughters" about the difficult path to mental prayer and told them how to practice it, she emphasized that from the beginning one had to have "a determined determination" to reach it, even if it meant dying on the way. In her advice Teresa anticipated all the topics used by men in their opposition to women's spirituality: "it is dangerous"; "women will get lost in this path"; "this kind of prayer is not for women because it begets illusions"; "it is better for women to spin"; and so on. She urged her nuns not to pay any attention to the gossipers, even if the world collapsed around them.[115] And, although it is true that Teresa complained constantly about her obligation to write books because, by so doing, she was kept away from the spindle and her womanly chores, these complaints were rhetorical, something expected from her, and not a reflection of her, and women's in general, fundamental role in this world.[116]

It could be argued that the queen and the saint are exemplars and not representatives of the average women or that their concept of women's role in society was not the standard one for their female contemporaries, but we have seen that within their social context, María de Pacheco and Luisa de Carvajal, noblewomen, María de Cazalla, bourgeoise, and Isabel Ortiz, of the merchant class, behaved according to principles similar to those of Isabella and Teresa.

There is no doubt that María de Cazalla felt equal to her brother, Bishop Cazalla, and to her male friends and that she did not have any qualms about her "preachings." Nor did she, when she was in the torture chamber, fear to shame the inquisitors about their iniquity in forcing her to undress. In addition, María made sure that her daughters were as well educated as possible, even though she did not go as far as Isabel Ortiz, who on her own effort gave her daughter a career. Isabel Ortiz, a self-made woman, earned her living in a womanly fashion, by sewing and embroidering, but she had enough independence of mind to instruct herself, to write books of devotion, and to ascertain her rights, both as an author and as a prisoner of the Inquisition, when that time came. Isabel had to protect herself and her daughter because she had no male who would do it for her. On the contrary, when the going became rough, all her male friends tried, as well as they could, to disengage themselves from that "wanton" female. María de Pacheco, "the husband of her husband," carried the defense of Toledo against the king's authority as long as possible and then spent the rest of her life away from the spindle and dedicated to her studies and writings, unconcerned about the scorn of her male contemporaries. Luisa de Carvajal set for herself her way to salvation and her own missionary task. That being a woman, at that moment, helped her, takes nothing away from her incredible faith in herself or from her independent conception of her role in life.

It is also evident that women such as Isabel de la Cruz, bourgeoise, and María Vela y Cueto, noblewoman, never reached total self-actualization because they were unable to break away from the molds that constrained them as females. Despite their achievements they seem to have begrudgingly accepted their confining roles. Isabel de la Cruz, notwithstanding her large male following and her invention of the *dexamiento*, felt that being a woman she could not manifest personally God's grace, and she did not dare to have the book she was writing seen during her lifetime. Once in prison, Isabel recanted many of her beliefs and seemed to accept punishment as just retribution for her act of pride. María Vela's mild attempt at reforming her convent ended up mocked, as were many of her other "novelties."

But what about the average women of the sixteenth century? Much has to be learned. Yet there are clues that indicate a widespread dissatisfaction that manifested itself in role changing, for example, Catalina de Cardona, or that other Catalina, the famous *monja alférez,* who came to America and fought like a brave soldier,[117] or in the writings of despairing young women forced into marriages they did not want or forced into convents to satisfy their parents' desires. Or consider young María Aguirre, who—having fallen in love with Jerónimo de Branchifort, count de Camarata, knight of the Order of Alcántara—was banned from the city of Madrid. When she resumed her liaison she was interned behind the walls of the convent and school for girls of St. Catalina de Siena, where she continued to meet with her lover through a secret door until discovered by the prioress. When all was lost, in her anguish she assured another young woman that the count would send a key, and, lacking a key, "she would leave by the walls even if they were bastions."[118]

Finally, though there is not yet enough information to judge accurately how much the lives of women changed with the Reformation, one thing is certain: the society in which the women I have presented lived did not remain the same. After Isabella, Saint Teresa, María de Cazalla, Isabel Ortiz, to mention a few, no one could say that women had, by nature, an inferior mind or lacked the ability to manage large affairs, to think about important religious truths, or to become missionaries. No one could say that they did not fight as courageously as men or that they had not earned a place of their own in history.

NOTES

1. All of the women I am about to present lived in the Castilian-Leonese region.

2. J. Gentil da Silva, "La mujer en España en la época mercantil: de la igualdad al aislamiento," in *La mujer en la Historia de España (siglos XVI-XIX)* (Madrid: Universidad Autónoma, 1984), p. 13.

3. *The Book of Judges,* put together in 634, contained a common law for all the peninsular peoples. It was known later as the *Fuero Juzgo.*

4. Isabel Pérez de Tudela y Velasco, *La mujer castellano-leonesa durante la Alta Edad Media,* Fundación Juan March, Serie Universitaria 200 (Madrid, n.d.), pp. 35–37.

5. In Brianda de Mendoza's *Constituciones y Ordenanzas* for her convent of Nra. Sra. de la Piedad (1534) the reading of the Gospels and other pious books in transla-

tion is recommended; flagellations and other corporal penances are discouraged, A.H.N., sec. Osuna, Leg. 1763, n. 5 and Francisco Layna Serrano, *Los convento antiguos de Guadalajara* (Madrid: CSIC, 1943); for women's jobs, Gentil da Silva, p. 16; a daughter of Nebrija taught eloquence at the University of Alcalá and María Medrano, Latin at the University of Salamanca, Luis Fernández de Retama, *Cisneros y su siglo,* II (Madrid: el Perpétuo Socorro, 1930), I, 496; women in France did not act until the 1620s, in England until after the Restoration, in Germany later than 1717, Américo Castro and Hugo Rennert, *Vida de Lope de Vega* (Salamanca: Anaya, 1968), p. 120.

6. Gentil da Silva, pp. 14–15; J. de M. Carriazo, "Amor y moralidad bajo los Reyes Católicos," *RABM,* LX, 1 (1954), 53–76; Sverker Arnoldson, *La leyenda negra: estudio sobre sus orígenes,* Acta Universitatis Gothoburgensis Göteborgs Universitets Arskrift, LXVI, 3 (1960); J. García Mercadal, *Viajes de extrajeros por España y Portugal* (Madrid: Aguilar, 1952).

7. P. W. Bomli, *La femme dans l'Espagne du Siècle d'Or* (The Hague: Martins Nijhoff, 1950), p. 24.

8. Gentil da Silva, p. 17.

9. Arnold Rothe, "Padre y familia en el Siglo de Oro," *Ibero-romania,* 7 (1978), p. 127.

10. *Instrucción de la mujer cristiana,* Austral (Buenos Aires: Espasa-Calpe, 1940), p. 9. The text is a composite of Vives' points from pages: 10, 11, 13, 14, 19, 26, 27, 53, 84, 99, 101, 147. Vives wrote this book at the request of Catherine of Aragon, the unhappy wife of Henri VIII. The first Spanish translation was printed in Valencia in 1528.

11. *The Perfect Wife,* trans., intr., and notes by Alice Philena Hubbard (Denton, Tex.: The College Press, 1943). A. Rothe points out that, despite the conservative tone of León's work, it represented a reevaluation of women in that a serious work was exclusively dedicated to them, p. 132.

12. The headings from chapters IV and III. This limitation of her "field of battle" brings to mind what Rothe says about honor and the sexes: "in women honor was limited to her sexual behavior and the most she could do was to preserve her honor, never to increase it," p. 129.

13. León, p. 14.

14. Any pious retired women devoted to prayer and good works, generally living alone, was called a *beata.*

15. The *Isabelino* architectonic style; her notarial reform, Francisco Gómez de Mercado, *Isabel I. reina de España* (Granada: Prieto, 1943); her institution of lawyers for the poor, F. de Retama, *Cisneros,* II, 117; her aesthetic norm, *el buen gusto,* good taste, so successful in Spain and Italy, R. Menéndez Pidal, *La lengua de Cristóbal Colón,* Austral (Buenos Aires: Espasa, 1947), for instance.

16. Vives and Erasmus praised the education of Isabella's four daughters, especially Catherine of Aragón's. On educated women in Isabella's time, María Dolores Gómez Malleda, "La cultura femenina en la época de Isabel la Católica," *RABM,* LXI (1955), pp. 137–95; on Isabella's personal library, Fernández de Retama, *Isabel la Católica, fundadora de la unidad nacional,* II (Madrid: El Perpétuo Socorro, 1947).

17. Excluding the few bishops that Isabella always wanted to have in her council, she insisted on this obligation for all others. No wonder that it would be the Spanish participation at the Council of Trent, some fifty years later, that would render bishops' residency obligatory.

18. Tarsicio de Azcona, *La elección y la reforma del episcopado en tiempos de los Reyes Católicos* (Madrid: CSIC, 1960).

19. Tarsicio de Azcona, *Isabel la Católica* (Madrid: BAC, 1964), p. xvi.

20. F. de Retama, *Cisneros;* Alvar Gómez de Castro, *De rebus gestis a Francisco*

Ximenio Cisnerio (Alcalá: Andrés de Angulo, 1569); Pedro de Quintanilla, *Archetypo de virtudes . . . Fr. Francisco Ximénez de Cisneros* (Palermo: Nicolás Bua, 1633).

21. Lucien Febvre, *Au coeur religieux du XVI*ᵉ *siècle* (Paris: Sevpen, 1957); Marcel Bataillon, *Erasmo y España,* 2nd Spanish ed. (Mexico City: Fondo de Cultura, 1966).

22. Beltrán de Heredia, *Historia de la Reforma de la Provincia de España* (Roma: Ad Sabinae, 1939), *Las corrientes de la espiritualidad entre los dominicos de Castilla durante la primera mitad del siglo XVI,* Biblioteca teólogos Españoles, 7 (Salamanca, 1945), "Introducción a los orígenes de la observancia en España; las reformas en los siglos XIV y XV," *Archivo Ibero-Americano,* XVII, 65–68; Marcel Bataillon, "Un itinéraire cistercien à travers l'Espagne et le Portugal au XVIᵉ siècle," *Melanges le Gentil* (1949); Fr. Michel Ange, "La vie franciscaine en Espagne entre les deux couronnements de Charles V," *RABM,* XXVI–XXXII (1912–15).

23. She was born ca. 1486 in Aldeanueva (Salamanca). Her parents were peasants and "old Christians." From childhood she distinguished herself by her continuous and hard penance. At eighteen she became a Dominican tertiary at the convent of Piedrahita. She was sent later to the convent of St. Catalina de Avila. In 1507 she left it because she said she was persecuted. By then, her raptures and wonders were common knowledge.

24. It was not a "true" trial since it was in the hands of her friends and there was no official prosecutor. The question of her intimacy with confessors and followers, however, came up. In two written defenses by Antonio de la Peña everything was explained: the intimacy was because of her many ailments and the need she had for somebody to console her; the red skirt, jewels, and French little hats (*sombreretes*) she wore, seemingly unfitting for a spiritual, were lent to her by people who thought the clothing would acquire some sort of virtue after she had worn it; her dancing and playing chess, vain pastimes, were not so in her case because she was always thinking of saintly things as was demonstrated by her frequent raptures while thus engaged. Bernardino Llorca, "La beata de Piedrahita ¿fué o no fué alumbrada?" *Manresa,* XIV, 50 (1942), 46–62 and XVI, 60 (1944), 275–85; Beltrán de Heredia, "La beata de Piedrahita no fué alumbrada," *Ciencia Tomista,* 63 (1942), 249–311; Pedro Mártir de Anglería comments on this investigation in his letters 428, 431, 489, *Documentos inéditos para la historia de España,* 10–11 (Madrid: Imprenta Góngora, 1955–57).

25. Ximenes was not alone. Father Castillejo, professor of theology at Valladolid, said "that he did not know why men learned anything else than serving God since that frail woman knew more than all scholars of the kingdom because her science came from the Holy Spirit," Beltrán Heredia, *Reforma,* p. 107.

26. *Libro de la oración de Sor María de Santo Domingo,* ed. José Manuel Blecua (Madrid: Hauser y Manet, 1948), p. d, ij. This work, found by Blecua, was dedicated to Adrian of Utrecht, cardinal of Tortosa and general inquisitor. It contains a brief account of the *beata's* virtuous life; some of her sayings when she was in a trance; answers to the questions theologians asked her while she was entranced; a copy of one of her many letters.

27. A decree signed by Francisco de Quiñones, presiding over the general chapter of the observant Franciscans (May 22, 1524), shows that this doctrine had penetrated several convents of the province and that it was a spiritual way, recently invented, with the *dexamiento* and interior illumination as its most characteristic traits. The decree imposed immediate incarceration to any friar who practiced it, Melquíades Andrés Martín, *El misterio de los alumbrados de Toledo, desvelado por sus contemporáneos (1523–60)* (Burgos: Imprenta de Aldecoa, 1977), pp. 15–16.

28. Her trial is lost. Information is available only from other trials, particularly Alcaraz's, in which, in addition to the *Sumario*—a precis of the accusations against her—many of Isabel's confessions are found. In one of these we learn of her dissatisfaction that being a woman she was deprived of manifesting the graces she had received from God, *Proceso de Pedro Ruiz de Alcaraz,* A.H.N., sec. Inquisición, leg. 106,

n. 5, fols. 113–17; John Longhurst, "La beata Ysabel de la Cruz ante la Inquisición," *Cuadernos de Historia de España*, XXV–XXVI (1957), 279–303 and *Luther's Ghost in Spain* (Lawrence: Coronado Press, 1969); Antonio Márquez, *Los alumbrados: orígenes y filosofía*, 2nd ed. (Madrid: Taurus, 1980); Ralph J. Tapis, *The Alumbrados of Toledo: A Study in Sixteenth-Century Spanish Spirituality* (Park Falls, Wisc.: Weber and Sons, 1975).

29. For example, when Alonso de la Palomera, a weaver from Pastrana, went to visit Isabel de la Cruz talking about his spiritual signs—fainting, crying in church, shaking—Isabel said not to use them for his own advantage, not to turn into property (*propiedad*) the gifts of God, *Proceso de Beteta*, A.H.N., sec. Inquisición, leg. 102, n. 3, fol. 8. Alcaraz went to Valladolid, Pastrana, and so on, exclusively to try to get Francisca Hernández and her followers and the Pastrana group away from their excesses and self-important airs, *Alcaraz*, fols. 277–87.

30. Alcaraz explained: "The *dexamiento* to the love of God that I was looking for was such that the *dexados* were led to the pinnacle of perfection such as the glorious Saint Dionysius put it in his purgative, illuminative, and unitive ways," *Alcaraz*, fol. 176. For the *alumbrados*, then, the *dexamiento* was their mystical way to God as contemplation was for other spirituals. Isabel de la Cruz's "discovery," what made the *alumbrados* free, was her finding a way of "contemplating" while leading a normal life since the *dexamiento* could be practiced in the square, at home, or conducting business.

31. The informer was Mari Núñez—also known to her detractors as Mala (bad) Núñez or Mari Nueces (nuts)—an escaped nun, it seems, from a Carmona convent, who went to Guadalajara at the beginning of the sixteenth century. She lived in the house of some relatives of the duke del Infantado. For a while she had the reputation of being very spiritual, even though she had a number of affairs with priests and laymen. She had been friendly with Isabel de la Cruz and Alcaraz and with María de Cazalla and her brother. She was turbulent and by 1519 she had quarreled with everybody. After her accusation against Isabel de la Cruz, the people of Guadalajara and the Franciscans were angry and she left the city in disgrace, *Alcaraz*, fols. 51, 263, 299, and so on.

32. To emphasize the punishment of the *alumbrados* the Holy Office Council sent specific instructions to the Toledo inquisitors to postpone for a day the execution of the public flogging to anyone not related to the matter of the *alumbrados*, *Alcaraz*, fol. 2.

33. Antonio Ferrer del Río, "Historia del levantamiento de las Comunidades de Castilla," *Decadencia de España*, 1ª parte (Madrid: Mellado, 1850); Joseph Pérez, *La révolution des "Comunidades" de Castille (1520–21)*, Bibliothèque de l'École des Hautes Études Hispaniques, Fasc. XLIII (Bordeaux, 1970); Pedro Mártir, *Epistolario*. After the defeat of Villalar, Padilla's widow took command of the Toledo "Comunidad" with dictatorial authority. From the Alcázar, she appointed the municipal authorities, levied taxes, and alone decided and commanded. Until February 3, 1522, she was the absolute ruler of the city, J. Pérez, p. 365.

34. This woman, though less interested in religious matters than in literary, political, and economical ones, represents another important facet of the Spanish female. Furthermore, she tried hard, in vain, to manipulate the ecclesiastical authorities in order to get her brother elected archbishop of Toledo.

35. By then she was not only accused of witchcraft with a black woman, but also of treason since her letters to the French general who was attacking Navarra and had Pamplona under siege, had been intercepted. Disguised as a peasant, she fled and did not leave the authorities any other revenge than to order her house razed.

36. Pérez, p. 344.

37. Pedro Mártir, *Letters*, 711 and 727.

38. Gentil da Silva, p. 16.

39. The Franciscan Luis de Maluenda who seems the formulator of the antimystic, notoriously antifeminist, current in Spain identified this flowering as "little plaster saints, saintly witches, secret witches, half brutes, proud and fake devout persons, teachers of swindling devotions, false saints, walking idols of flesh . . . persons of new sainthood and doctrines, preachers of new noncanonized saints. . . ." Andrés Martín, p. 25.

40. We know that the sayings of la Texeda—a woman from Guadalajara who prophesied and had other spiritual signs about 1519—were collected by the cleric Pedro de Rueda the younger, *Alcaraz*, fols. 209, 270, and bachiller Medrano the sayings of Francisca Hernández, *Proceso de Antonio de Medrano*, A.H.N., sec. Inquisición, leg. 104, n. 15, fol. 126; Isabel de la Cruz was writing a book on her new doctrine, a book not to be seen, though, until after her death, *Alcaraz*, fols. 41, 44, 106; María Arias was writing a book with Bishop Cazalla, Milagros Ortega Costa, *Proceso de la Inquisición contra María de Cazalla* (Madrid: Fundación Universitaria Española, 1978), p. 82.

41. One of the persons carrying them around was Cueto, a professor of logic and metaphysics at the University of Alcalá in 1523, Ortega Costa, *Cazalla*, p. 73.

42. The Mendozas were one of the most powerful and richest families in Spain. The palace of the dukes in Guadalajara, built around 1484 in the Isabelino style, was a center of culture until the dukes moved to Madrid in the seventeenth century. Francis I of France stayed there in luxurious captivity after his defeat at the battle of Pavia (1525), Francisco Layna Serrano, *Historia de Guadalajara y sus Mendozas en los siglos XV y XVI*, IV (Madrid: CSIC, 1942) and *Los conventos;* Fray Hernando Pecha, *Historia de Guadalajara* (Guadalajara: Marqués de Santillana, 1977), first edition of Pecha's 1632 manuscript.

43. Bernardino de Tovar, among others. She was accused of saying that Luther was a good man who was right to raise questions against the abuses in the Church, Ortega Costa, *Cazalla*, p. 171. As for Erasmus, she was supposed to have ordered some of his *Coloquia* translated into Spanish to give them to the countess de Saldaña and to have said that Erasmus should be canonized.

44. Ortega Costa, *Cazalla*, pp. 351–53.

45. This was the twenty-fifth heretical proposition of the *alumbrados* in the 1525 Edict, Milagros Ortega Costa, "La proposiciones del Edicto de los alumbrados: autores y calificadores," *Cuadernos de Investigación Histórica*, 1 (Madrid, 1977), 23–36.

46. The humanist Juan de Maldonado in *De foelicitate* said about the *alumbrados* that "they affirmed they were the bearers of Christian freedom and that they were liberating the people of many loads," Andrés Martín, pp. 27–28; Márquez, "El tema de la libertad" in *Los alumbrados*.

47. According to Diego Hernández, however, María de Cazalla said that there was no God anymore in marriage, that women were loved for their money and beauty: "I do not see a single Christian man to whom I can give my daughter, because it seems to me that marriage now is no better than putting her in a whorehouse," Ortega Costa, *Cazalla*, p. 81.

48. Ortega Costa, *Cazalla*, p. 219.

49. Alcaraz, interrogated about María, said he had a bad opinion of her because she talked about the Holy Scriptures, which was wrong for a woman. When he was asked what she taught, he replied that he did not remember, that they were complex things and well above the understanding of simple people, Ortega Costa, *Cazalla*, pp. 188–89.

50. According to Luis de Maluenda the *alumbrados y dejados* were born of reading Saint Paul's Epistles and not understanding them. Considering how difficult they are for wise men to understand, "how can a little female (*mujercilla*) who forgets the spindle for boasting of reading St. Paul? . . . What has a *mujercilla*, no matter how saintly she is, to do with St. Paul? And what about clerics and friars learning with

mujercillas in the lessons of St. Paul?" *Excelencias de la Fe,* quoted by Andrés Martín, pp. 26–27.

51. Readers accustomed to Anglo-Saxon law will best understand a *Proceso*—trial—(an offshoot of Roman law) if they think of it as our "inquest" (from the same root word as inquisition) or a grand jury proceeding. The purpose was to say if a crime (heresy) had indeed been committed, two accusations were enough to open it, and the process might be reopened any time new evidence was presented. As in our proceedings, the possible criminal was not legally represented.

52. The secret prison was secret only in the sense that, once inside, one could not communicate with the outside world and once released, not divulge anything at all; thus, a swearing to secrecy was the last act before going free or being transferred to a perpetual prison.

53. Ortega Costa, *Cazalla,* pp. 649–72.

54. Francisco de Quiñones, the new general of the Franciscans, went to see her because Fray Francisco Ortiz had praised her so much. Quiñones was fascinated—he had never met anyone of such perfection—and advised the young Ortiz to visit her daily. Quiñones himself went to consult her before his trip to Italy, Fr. Michel Ange, XXVIII, pp. 216–17.

55. Angela Selke, *El Santo Oficio de la Inquisición, proceso de Fr. Francisco Ortiz* (Madrid: Guadarrama, 1968) and "El caso del bachiller Medrano, iluminado epicúreo del siglo XVI," *Bulletin Hispanique,* LVIII (1956), 393–420.

56. Edward Boehmer, *Francisca Hernández und fray Francisco Ortiz* (Leipzig: Hoessel, 1865).

57. The first trial against Francisca had taken place when Adrian of Utrecht was general inquisitor. Later he explained that if he had not let her go completely free—she had been forbidden to continue her close association with clerics such as Medrano, Tovar, and so on—it was not because her doctrine was in error but because she had "laughing eyes; that so much gayety did not belong to a servant of God," Boehmer, p. 112.

58. *Santa Teresa de Jesús, Obras completas,* Efrén de la Madre de Dios and Otilio del Niño Jesús, eds. (Madrid: BAC, 1961), p. 493, n. 16.

59. Gonzalo de Illescas, *Historia Pontifical y Católica* quoted by Marcelino Menéndez Pelayo, *Historia de los heterodoxos españoles,* 2nd ed. (Madrid: CSIC, 1965), III, 437.

60. On May 21, 1559, punished for Lutheranism were fifteen men and twelve women, of which nine men and six women were relaxed to the secular arm; on October 8, six men and ten women, of which six men and six women were relaxed. Leonor de Vibero died shortly before four of her children died at the stake and two others were condemned to *sanbenito* and lifetime imprisonment. Leonor's own remains were exhumed and burned and her house was razed.

61. The Holy Office was proceeding using some witnesses who had come forward as *agents provocateurs.* The intent was to entrap as many as possible, particularly, Archbishop Carranza. All this caution was blown by the bishop of Zamora, who, after having read an edict in his churches, found that there were so many heretics around that he ordered some of them incarcerated. At the first sign of danger many of them fled or tried to flee, L. P. Gachard, *Retraite et mort de Charles Quint . . . lettres inedites* (Bruxelles: C. Muquard, 1855), II, 419–25; José Ignacio Tellechea Idígoras, *El arzobispo Carranza y su tiempo,* II (Madrid: Guadarrama, 1968) and his edition of Carranza's trial published by the Real Academia de la Historia.

62. As a background to the Lutheran repression the deep crisis that had been brewing among the Dominicans in the 1550s has to be taken into account: Melchor Cano, Domingo Cuevas, and others were adamant against "the universal call to perfection, including married men and women; meditation open to all; theological and pious books in translation" that Bartolomé de Carranza, fray Luis de Granada, and

many others promulgated. For women, the fall of Carranza was of great conse-
quence: the antimystics, like Melchor Cano, were openly antifeminists, as we have
seen, Andrés Martín, pp. 31–33.

63. The two Valladolid autos-da-fé of 1559 were more imposing, more solemn,
and more public than ever before in order to emphasize the gravity of the crime.
While the autos da-fé were in progress, no one was allowed to ride a horse or carry
arms. Thousands of people from far away congregated in Valladolid. As one eyewitness put it: "it looked like the world general congregation . . . the very portrait of
Judgement," Menéndez Pelayo, III, 419–23. For the history of Lutheranism in Spain,
Ernst Schäfer, *Beiträge zur Geschichte des spanischen Protestantismus und der Inquisitionen
im 16. Jahrhundert* (Gütersloh: Bertelsmann, 1902–3); Agustín Redondo, "Luther et
l'Espagne de 1520 à 1536), *Mélanges de la casa de Velázquez,* I, extrait (Paris: Boccard,
1965).

64. Antonio Márquez, "Origen y naturaleza del iluminismo según un parecer de
Melchor Cano," *Revista de Occidente,* 63 (1968), 320–33.

65. Antonio Márquez, *Literatura e Inquisición en España* (Madrid: Taurus, 1980);
Bataillon, *Erasmo.*

66. Manuel Serrano y Sanz, *Biblioteca de escritoras españolas,* II (Madrid: Sucesores
de Rivadenayra, 1903), II, 282–84.

67. See n. 5. How suspicious, Teresa knew well. But one cannot avoid noticing
Teresa's tongue in cheek when she uses all the official clichés about women's role and
behavior.

68. *Obras completas de Santa Teresa de Jesús,* intr. and notes by Efrén de la Madre de
Dios and Otger Stegging (Madrid: BAC, 1967), *Vida,* 35, 5. Teresa's works, when
from this edition, will be listed simply by title, chapter, and paragraph. For Bernini's
representation of Saint Teresa transverberation, Robert T. Petersson, *The Art of Ec-
stasy: Teresa, Bernini, and Crashaw* (London: Routledge, 1970).

69. Alberto Risco, *Santa Teresa de Jesús,* 4th ed. (Bilbao: "El mensajero del
Corazón de Jesús," 1944), pp. 311–12.

70. Ludovico Saggi, "Vetera et nova' nella biografía di S. Teresa," *Carmelus*
(1971), p. 148.

71. Víctor G. de la Concha, *El arte literario de Santa Teresa* (Barcelona: Ariel,
1978); Francisco Márquez Villanueva, "La vocación literaria de Santa Teresa,"
NRFH, 32, 2 (1983), 355–79.

72. Efrén de la Madre de Dios, *Santa Teresa,* p. 466; Jesús Imirizaldu, *Monjas y
beatas embaucadoras* (Madrid: Editor Nacional, 1978).

73. Petersson, p. 71.

74. After completing the final version of her *Vida,* Saint Teresa began referring to
it as *alma* (soul) instead of *vida, Carta* 10, 3.

75. Márquez Villanueva, aware that he may scandalize some of Teresa's hagiog-
raphers, reaches the conclusion that the enjoyment Saint Teresa drew from writing
was like an addiction, pp. 358–59.

76. Not all confessors approved of this practice. Julian de Avila was adamantly
against women writing their revelations. For him, the worst thing that a confessor
could do was to command his spiritual daughters to write. According to Dr. Vaquero, Avila had advised Teresa not to write her *Vida* or any other work; her retort:
"Do not say so, Father, what I am writing may be very profitable for God's
Church," Miguel González de Vaquero, *Obras completas,* p. 101. As for this new "literary genre," it may be the only one written exclusively by women.

77. Márquez Villanueva, p. 368, indicated how much Saint Teresa longed to see
herself in print all her life and how cruel fate was with her dream since, by only a
few months, she failed to have in her hands a printed copy of her *Camino de perfección*
published in Evora.

78. As a trophy, Isabel Ortiz kept the censors' decree authorizing the printing of

her work, on condition. It was found among her papers when her possessions were impounded as she was imprisoned, *Proceso contra Isabel Ortiz,* A.H.N., sec. Inquisición, leg. 104, n. 5, fol. 61. To my knowledge, this is the first published study of Isabel Ortiz.

79. It is not clear why her husband left her eighteen years earlier. One may presume that Isabel was too independent and outspoken for the taste of a typical husband of his time.

80. Ginesa de Villalobos, a witness, said that in Guadalajara there was no one Isabel did not know or a place where she was not known or talked about, fol. 26.

81. Ana Terreros, the duchess's dwarf, when asked about Isabel's book, explained that the maid María de Avila knew it by heart and prayed from it with the duchess every night. Ana herself had been asked to do it a few times, but she had never been able to memorize it, fol. 46.

82. Francisco de Soto Salazar, the inquisitor listening to the marquise's testimony, is the same Inquisitor Soto who a short time before had recommended Saint Teresa to obtain Saint Juan de Avila's opinion of her *Vida*.

83. Fray Alonso de Hontiveros, rector of the Dominican school in Alcalá, was another antimystic Dominican, which explains why Isabel thought that he would not understand spiritual matters.

84. No wonder the name Ortiz rang a bell to the inquisitor and consultants in relation to the *alumbrados:* the fall of fray Francisco Ortiz—nn. 55 and 56—still echoed in a religious milieu more than thirty years later.

85.In a folio included in this trial without date or any other reference, except with Isabel's name as a heading, we find an evaluation of some works of devotion, presumably Isabel's, signed by an Alonso Muñoz, *presentatus*. The reasons Muñoz gives for having the works burned are illuminating: they should be burned not because they contain any errors of faith, but because the cold and poor style, of no benefit to a wise man, could easily harm a *mujercilla,* who, as soon as she understands two words of anything, becomes arrogant and less devout to the preaching of the parish priest.

86. Fols. 12–14.

87. Fol. 19.

88. Isabel de Plazaola, Isabel's daughter, was about twenty-two years old. She was a good singer and player of plucked instruments who used to be invited to sing and play at many of the noble houses. Shortly before her mother was arrested, Plazaola had been hired as a house musician to the wife of the duke de Albuquerque, newly appointed governor of Milan. When Plazaola reached Barcelona to embark for Italy, the governor cancelled her position saying that the king did not approve of having a young woman just to sing and play on a military expedition, and Plazaola was sent back to Alcalá, fols. 81–82.

89. Fols. 27–46. What the countess calls "obscure doctrines" was as clear as water to Isabel: when asked by the inquisitor to explain how she felt about vocal and mental prayer, she answered "there is good and there is better" or, more graphically, "their difference in value is such as straw and gold." fols. 71–73.

90. The not-guilty verdict was received in Toledo on February 22, 1565, and that same day Isabel was informed and released. On March 2 of the same year, Isabel requested from the inquisitor a copy of the absolving sentence, considering she had an unmarried daughter whose name she wanted to keep untarnished. The petition was duly granted by the inquisitor Soto.

91. When Francis Parkinson Keyes, preparing a book on Isabella of Castile, went to visit the convent of St. Ana of Avila where the young Isabella had received a large part of her education, she learned about the Venerable María Vela and of her unpublished works. She was shown the uncorrupted body of the Venerable—a title given by public acclaim—and some altar frontals that she had embroidered almost four

hundred years ago, *The Third Mystic of Avila: The Self Revelation of María Vela, a Sixteenth-Century Spanish Nun* (New York: Farrar, 1960). Thus, the *editio princeps* of this work came to light in Keyes' English translation. The following year appeared the first Spanish edition, *Autobiografía y Libro de las mercedes de Doña María Vela y Cueto,* intr. and notes by Olegario González Sánchez (Barcelona: Juan Flors, 1961). I shall refer to this edition [Hereafter, *Autobiografía*].

92. *Autobiografía,* p. 14.

93. Ibid., p. 315.

94. Ibid., pp. 307–8.

95. Ibid., pp. 308–9.

96. This controversy continued after her death, and many accusations were made against María's last confessor's book. At one point it seemed it was going to be seized; even in Italy there was opposition, Miguel González Vaquero, *La mujer fuerte / por otro título / la Vida de Doña María Vela / monja de San Bernardo en el convento de Santa Ana . . .* (Madrid: Vda. de Alonso Martín, 1618). Despite the opposition, it was one of the most widely read books in the seventeenth century, not only in Catholic Europe but also in Latin America.

97. *Autobiografía,* pp. 314, 352–53.

98. Julian de Avila was a very important personality in the religious life of the city of Avila at that time. For an interesting insight of Avila at this time around another famous *beata,* Mari Díaz, Jodi Bilinkoff, "The Holy Woman and the Urban Community in Sixteenth-Century Avila," *Women and the Structure of Society* (Durham, N.C.: Duke University Press, 1984), pp. 74–80.

99. Her attempt to go back to primitive rule was received with scorn one feast of Saint Francis when she appeared at the refectory dressed in an *aljuba*—the simple habit of rough material the Discalced had adopted—and shoeless. When a few days later this was followed by several other nuns and the abbess herself, the whole convent reacted immediately: they called the rector of the Dominicans to put order in the house. The prelate ordered to put an end to such singularities and told the abbess that she was committing a mortal sin by consenting to them, p. 349.

100. *Camino de perfección,* p. 34, 4.

101. Most of her writings and the *Información sumaria* (brief) about her virtuous life, gathered between 1625 and 1627 to be sent to the Congregation of Rites as a first step toward canonization, are in the archive of the Encarnación Convent in Madrid. Her incorrupt body rests there too. Luisa de Carvajal y Mendoza, *Epistolario y poesías* in *Biblioteca de Autores Españoles,* 179 (1965); Luis Muñoz, *Vida y virtudes de la Venerable virgen Doña Luisa de Carvajal y Mendoza* (Madrid: n.p., 1632); *Vble. Doña Luisa . . . : escritos autobiográficos,* intr. and notes by Camilo María Abad (Barcelona: Juan Flors, 1966) [hereafter *Escritos*], *Una misionera española en la Inglaterra del siglo XVII: Doña Luisa . . . ,* "D. Rodrigo Calderón a la luz de una correspondencia inédita [Dña. Luisa's]," *Boletín de la Real Academia de la Historia,* 153 (1963), 247–93.

102. María Chacón, mother of cardinal archbishop of Toledo Sandoval y Rojas, was the governess of Isabel Clara Eugenia and Catalina Micaela, daughters of Philip II. She was living then next to the Descalzas Reales monastery. Luisa recalls how she played with the *infantas* in the cloisters "making more noise than the nuns could wish for," *Escritos,* pp. 138–41.

103. Despite what one may think of these methods, Luisa wrote very kindly about her uncle and his good-heartedness, how easily he forgave his enemies, and how knowledgeable he was in spiritual matters.

104. For her vows, *Escritos,* pp. 239–45. This image of Our Lady was so named because it had been mutilated by the British and Dutch who, under the command of Admiral Howard and the count of Essex, had entered and sacked the city of Cádiz in the summer of 1596.

105. *Canonization brief,* p. 37.

106. *Escritos*, pp. 225–26.

107. *Escritos*, p. 49. The Blessed Thomas Garnet, a priest who became a Jesuit in Valladolid, and later was condemned to death and executed at Tyburn in 1608.

108. Pedro de Zúñiga, the Spanish ambassador, had arrived about three months later than Luisa. He had heard about her but had not been able to find her. It was after the Guy Fawkes Plot was discovered that somebody approached the ambassador's confessor in the hope that he would know of a small and safe place for Luisa. At Zúñiga's insistence Luisa accepted to stay in the embassy for a while.

109. *Escritos*, pp. 59–60.

110. In a letter to the former Spanish ambassador (April 16, 1611), Luisa explains in detail the deaths of the latest martyrs and reminds Zúñiga that Father Thomas Somers (alias Wilson) was the one who helped his English servants, *Escritos*, pp. 81–83.

111. In a letter to D. Rodrigo Calderón where she explains the execution of the priest Moulineux, *Escritos*, p. 101.

112. Apart from the normal rules applying to any order of nuns (for example, chastity, poverty, obedience, prayer, and manual work), the "Company of Our Sovereign Lady, the Virgin Mary" had special rules made necessary by the anti-Catholic laws of England in those days: clothing worn in the streets should be discretely ordinary so as not to attract attention and denunciation by the authorities and so endanger the lives of the other members of the company. To help the return of the country to Catholicism there was a special vow of obedience to the pope and a place of honor made for the Virgin Mary over the altar in the oratory and at all functions of the company, be they prayer or manual labor.

113. Among them were Richard Brouch, an English Puritan who, as a carpenter, had worked for her in her house at Bishopsgate and a Calvinist preacher who, when asked by the priest why had he been more moved by a woman than by many learned men available, had answered: "he had found in her words an irresistible force," *Escritos*, p. 66.

114. *Escritos*, pp. 64–65.

115. *Fundaciones*, p. 35, 2.

116. Márquez Villanueva, p. 362.

117. For Catalina de Cardona, see p. 16. *Historia de la "Monja Alférez," Doña Catalina de Erauso, escrita por ella misma* (Barcelona: José Tauló, 1838); O. P. Gilbert, *Women in Men's Guise*, trans. by Lewis May (London: John Lane, 1932), pp. 146–70.

118. Milagros Ortega Costa, "Una carta del Siglo de Oro," *Anales de la Fundación Joaquín Costa*, 2 (Madrid, 1985), pp. 45–50; *Proceso contra Hierónimo Branchifort, Cavallero de la Orden de Alcántara*, A.H.N., sec. Ordenes Militares—Tribunal Judicial de Toledo—leg. 27783.

SHERRIN MARSHALL

Protestant, Catholic, and Jewish Women in the Early Modern Netherlands

The coming of the Reformation, the wars of religion that were interwoven with the gaining of political independence for the north Netherlands in the sixteenth and seventeenth centuries, the attainment of religious compromise and toleration for which the seventeenth-century Netherlands was re-nowned—all of these brought lasting change to the northern Netherlands. These great events have been thoroughly studied from a number of different viewpoints. Until recently, however, such studies tended to focus on major political and religious leaders; only within the past few decades have some historians concentrated on the ordinary people of this era.

This essay examines women in the sixteenth- and seventeenth-century Netherlands. They are rarely leaders of political and religious change, al-though in such extraordinary times there are examples of remarkable behav-ior by both sexes. More often, women lived out their lives as did the majority of men, in anonymity. How did the monumental upheavals of church and state alter patterns of life for women—if at all? Along with the changes that occurred, what patterns of continuity can be seen over the span of nearly two centuries? What concerns remained unchanged for women? In what ways do we see women involved in activities that have an identifiably religious dimension? Finally, what differences can be observed among Prot-estant, Catholic, and Jewish women, and what similarities can be traced?

To be sure, there were important doctrinal distinctions between Protes-tants, Catholics, and Jews. There were important social differences within and without religious groups. For example, the most comprehensive archival records exist for the Portuguese Sephardim who emigrated to Amsterdam at the end of the sixteenth century. We know much less of the Ashkenazim who came from Germany and Eastern Europe to the Netherlands. Catholics by the end of the sixteenth century were nearly invisible. Although we can find some information on the fate of the religious orders and convents, for example, the role of "ordinary" Catholics during this period is more prob-lematic to trace. The Protestants cannot be grouped together, either, for their social and self-identification was bound up in whether they were actu-ally members of a church and which church they attended—there was a world of difference between the situation of Reformed and Anabaptist. Finally, for all of these religious groups, differences in social status must be taken into account. The experiences of a shipbuilder's widow in Amsterdam and a farmer's wife in Gelderland were so different that valid comparison of them is impossible.[1]

One factor does remain constant for women, however, and cuts with force across religious lines and social boundaries. That was the role of the family, and women within and without it.[2] Because all religious groups shared at least to some extent in a common ethical and scriptural tradition, norms and values affected the family whatever the religious affiliation. There were several important results of this common heritage and shared values. First, whenever the family was threatened, for any reason, the various components of the body social rallied around to give support. This support frequently knew no religious boundaries, or at least failed to recognize religious boundaries. Second, activity sanctioned by the family, again for any one of a variety of reasons, allowed women a wide range of options and behavioral patterns. The legal rights and privileges enjoyed by Dutch women allowed them to have considerable freedom and autonomy—when their actions were in accord with familial goals, which they themselves might help define. Additionally, as widows, women had well-defined authority which they enjoyed to such an extent that they did not remarry as frequently as widows did (or were perhaps pressured to do) in other European societies.[3] As will become evident, however, when Dutch women sought self-actualization in ways threatening to the family, their options became rapidly restricted.

Models of women in sixteenth- and seventeenth-century Holland reveal both social approbation and condemnation. One important historical image—visual, verbal, textual—is that of Kenau Hasselaar Simonsdr, allegedly a heroine of the siege of Haarlem in 1573. A modern commentator on the nineteenth-century Romantic painting portraying Kenau leading a company of three hundred Haarlem women against the Spanish focuses on the probably erroneous image of aristocratic and burgher women fighting side by side. The aristocratic woman bearing the standard at Kenau's side, identified by the modern art historian as the "young lady Geertruida van Brederode" fails to appear in genealogies of the Brederode family. Therefore, he continues, these women of different social classes could not have fought together. Further, he emphasizes that "the picture of Kenau as heroine of Haarlem, as commander of a multitude of fighting women who stood by the side of the men in the battle, seems untenable. She was simply one of the many women who worked at the time of the siege to strengthen and improve the [town] walls, probably also kept the watch, and perhaps also participated in some skirmishes. The information with regard to mutual combat, as well as [that] pertaining to women pouring pitch or cooking oil from the battlements, originates in very unreliable sources."[4] Contemporary accounts of sixteenth-century diarists offer another view. One German mercenary wrote that Kenau herself carried a loaded pistol and a short spike or javelin, that she brought bullets as the walls of Haarlem were stormed, and that she treated the soldiers in the thick of the fight to a jug of beer. Another account described her as a "very manlike Woman, by name Kenu . . . who supported the common weal with funds (for she was extremely well-to-do), with labor, weapons and rifle . . . and had above all else a manly heart in her life."[5]

A number of conclusions can be drawn from the images of the heroic Kenau fighting alongside the men, with or without her band of women. The nineteenth-century artist expresses the ideal of solidarity from the time of the Revolt of the Netherlands, when patriotism superseded class affiliations. Moreover, the expressed ideal was not only of all classes engaged in mutual combat against a mutual enemy, but also of both sexes fighting that same foe. Kenau certainly lived and fought, perhaps not as a leader, but not as a bit player in a skirmish either. The message was that women as well as men could and did stand up to be counted.[6]

Similarly, the Utrecht burgher Trijn (Catharina) van Leemputte—significantly from the same social milieu as Kenau Hasselaar of Haarlem—supposedly lead the storming of the fortress Vredenburg.[7] During the Revolt of the Netherlands, women such as Trijn van Leemputte and Kenau Hasselaar assumed the traditionally masculine image and role of warrior. Although the historical reality of their experience was romanticized and embellished, such roles were for a time socially acceptable during this period of upheaval, when the role of patriot was at least temporarily not limited by gender distinctions.

Trijn van Leemputte and Kenau Hasselaar have been identified as Protestants. Their religious affiliation may have legitimized their activities, at least for others of their religious persuasion. It is also highly significant that the actions of both were sanctioned within their families, particularly their families of birth. Both women came of families with strong civic involvement, and this commitment was at least as important as the religious identification. Finally, Kenau was a middle-aged widow at the time, related by marriage as well as birth to many members of the town elite.

If patriotism superseded gender, it could also on occasion supersede religious affiliation. Magdalena Moons was a Catholic whose father had been a councilor of the emperor Charles V; her brother filled a number of bureaucratic positions under Philip II. In 1574, she supposedly threatened to refuse to marry her sweetheart, the Spanish commander Valdez, if he carried out the siege of Leiden. According to the contemporary account, he wavered for one day, during which time the wind turned the salt water into the dikes which had been breached near Leiden; with the rising water, the Spanish troops fled, and Leiden was saved. Again, despite some doubt about what really happened, Magdalena Moons actually lived, and the expressed ideal of a Catholic woman supporting the cause of the revolt was important.[8]

Other heroines of this period have a more specifically religious affiliation. The women in the martyrologies of John Fox and Thielemann van Braght often stepped out of traditional feminine roles. Instead of being chaste and silent—and female martyrs were surely not the latter—they became heroines for their religious witness, which often resulted in their death.[9]

Not only Protestants achieved heroism in the cause of religion. Jewish women were similarly revered for professing their religious beliefs during a time of persecution, again sharing a tradition with men. Maria Nunes, who emigrated to Amsterdam from Portugal in 1597 or 1598, allegedly endured extraordinary vicissitudes in search of religious freedom. Caron, the Dutch representative to London, wrote to the States-General in April 1597, mentioning a ship from Vlissingen that had been captured by the Spanish not far from Calais. On board were four Portuguese merchants and a Portuguese girl dressed in men's clothing. All were fleeing to Amsterdam, and the girl—described as a young aristocratic woman—was to be wed there. Her parents, Caron's letter continued, had been imprisoned in Portugal by the Inquisition. Legend had it that Maria's beauty was so great that when she reached England, an English duke proposed to her. Nevertheless, she continued on the proper course to Amsterdam, where the historical, as opposed to the legendary, Maria was wed to the scion of a prominent Portuguese Sephardic family in exile.[10]

As we have seen, Kenau Hasselaar and Trijn van Leemputte fought alongside men. The contemporary chronicles that survive portray them as decidedly unfeminine women. Trijn carries an axe over her shoulder and wears an expression of grim determination on her face. Kenau brandishes a sword in one near-contemporary image of her. Magdalena Moons's behavior was more traditionally feminine. So, too, was that of Maria Nunes, who fled dressed as a man to disguise her feminine beauty, as the account of her activities states. In part her aim was to preserve her prized virginity. In other words, certain situations enabled women to engage in activities which were not ordinarily acceptable for those of their sex. In such circumstances, their behavior became legitimized. In three of the above instances, those of Kenau Hasselaar, Trijn van Leemputte, and Maria Nunes, we have enough information to ascertain that their activities were also sanctioned by their families, for a variety of reasons. Women who assumed masculine roles or cross-dressed in more ordinary situations, however, were regarded as deviants and subjected to punishment.

Two examples of Dutch women whose activities went beyond established limits appear in the criminal records. Maeyken Joosten was brought before the civil authorities in Leiden in 1606. It was alleged that she had deserted her husband the previous year, leaving him with the two surviving children of the four she had borne. She then corresponded with a certain Bertelmina Wale, "a young maiden of this town," representing herself as a youth named Pieter Verburch. Maeyken had herself baptized as "Abraham Joosten" and promised to marry Bertelmina with solemn religious vows, all the while dressing in men's clothing. Once this occurred, continued the sentence, "the result of these evil events provoked God's divine wrath on the country and cities with inexcusable sodomy (*sodomie*), which following God's law and all civil right is forbidden on pain of grave punishment." Maeyken's actual sentence seemed less severe than this seemed to threaten, however: she was exiled.[11]

Barbara Adriaens van Brouwershaven, whose case was brought before the court in Amsterdam in 1632, transgressed for somewhat different reasons. The twenty-one year-old Barbara stated that she had begun to cross-dress three years earlier, "having sold her women's clothes and purchased men's clothing in their stead." After cutting her hair, Barbara approached a soldier and asked if he knew where she could join the service; accompanying him to Heusden she joined the State's army. The intervening period was spent in military service, at which time she made the acquaintance of Hilletje Jans. Barbara testified that the two decided to marry, but she never told Hilletje that she was a woman. Barbara's testimony further states that she believed she could keep this a secret. Hilletje, however, had other ideas, and although Barbara kept her physical distance by telling Hilletje that she had smallpox, Hilletje complained to her sister that her new husband had not fulfilled his husbandly obligations (*mansplict*). Shortly thereafter, Barbara began to abuse Hilletje. Barbara's testimony also revealed that she was probably an alcoholic and had already been incarcerated in the *Spinhuis* (prison) for two years at the age of thirteen. She stated that she had never had carnal knowledge of any man and further never desired or lusted for men. Her sentence—banishment for twenty-four years under pain of the *Spinhuis*—emphasized the following transgressions: transvestism, military service, openly marrying Hilletje Jans in a religious ceremony.[12]

Neither Maeyken Joosten nor Barbara Adriaens could conform to feminine roles and norms psychologically, emotionally, or socially. Their behavior included transvestism and representation of themselves as men so that they might formalize conjugal relationships with other women. Each had the need, perhaps personal as well as social, to marry her lover in a religious ceremony. In both situations, the protagonist's behavior was held to be against Scripture and civil law. This conduct was illegal because it threatened the traditional norms of the family and society. Maeyken's marriage had clearly failed. She had abandoned her husband and children. Barbara, on the other hand, had apparently never attempted to find self-actualization through traditional feminine roles, but rather focused her identity in military activity as a soldier, behaving as she felt men were entitled to behave. It seems probable that her social background and upbringing had given her no other model of masculine behavior with which to identify. Further, it might be postulated that she believed by "becoming a man" and conducting herself as if she were male, she could rid herself of her feelings of powerlessness. These women had failed as women in the terms of their society by flaunting familial and social norms. By sentencing them to banishment, the civil authorities attempted to render them invisible.

The strong, competent, "unfeminine" Dutch woman was thus not always regarded with approbation. She was at best viewed with ambivalence and at worst treated as a threat. The deviants were an exception to the established norms, but Dutch women often led riots, which had many causes in the early modern period. In the mid-sixteenth century, they took part in iconoclastic outbursts along with men and boys. It was widely recognized that women were less liable to be arrested than men and, if arrested, less liable to be punished. There were therefore practical reasons why they felt encouraged to take a prominent role in riots, and women were occasionally manipulated by men into initiating riots precisely because they were less legally vulnerable. At the same time, women's actions and language reveal them to be independent in identity.[13] One series of riots with religious overtones were those between remonstrants and contra-remonstrants in the seventeenth century. An eyewitness account of a riot of remonstrants in Rotterdam does not emphasize this religious dimension, however, but, rather, states that "many women ran through the streets and hollered in an unseemly fashion that 'women could do no wrong.' "[14] Their language was not always "seemly," either. In one women's riot in 1614 in Oudkarspel, Holland, when the sheriff tried to restore order by stating that he had come on behalf of the county (*grafelijkheid*), one woman answered, "Yes, on behalf of the shitliness," (*strontelijkheid*).[15]

Male contemporaries were critical of the fact that women were less severely punished for their criminal behavior. One popular seventeenth-century author wrote that: "Through neglect of a meaningful operation of justice . . . it is thus that one much more frequently excuses guilty women . . . Of these cursed viragos (*hellevegen*), we recollect that so few who really deserve to hang are actually punished, although they themselves are most proficient at murder and arson; otherwise, they should at least be branded or flogged." This writer was angered by the fact that women seemed to evade responsibility for criminal actions because of their gender. Although the approved roles for women were articulated within the social context, women's behavior often explicitly challenged and threatened such norms.[16]

To what extent, if at all, did the religious changes that occurred affect roles of women? During the period of Protestant and Catholic Reformations and the age of religious wars, the lives of women were touched by the currents of religious change. They responded to religious issues that had a bearing on their lives. By the mid-sixteenth century, the Protestant reform had already affected religious patterns significantly in the Netherlands. The Roman Catholic Church was still the state church and its wealth and prestige still omnipresent. Women shared in the wealth of the church and were members of the religious establishment. There were nearly ten thousand female religious in the mid-sixteenth century Netherlands, about three times as many women as men. Numbers alone, however, provide no indication of true vocation, and the reforms that followed the Council of Trent were badly needed. Many, if not most, of the people attended church sporadically. Their commitment was more to individual, familial, or communal participation in rituals, holidays and religious celebrations, and pilgrimages. They had little identification with the church hierarchy. In fact, personal religious faith was often coupled with a cynicism regarding that hierarchy, and some responded to abuses within the Church with a strident anticlericalism.[17]

Implicit as well as explicit criticism of the Church was thus widespread; by the middle of the century, at least a partial break with the Church had been accomplished. What was clear at that time was that traditional religious forms were questioned and in flux; less clear was what would appear in their stead. Early dissent had been expressed by those individuals loosely termed "sacramentarians" in the Netherlands; by the end of the 1530s they and various Anabaptist sects had been suppressed. In Gouda, a certain Jannichgen expounded anticlerical beliefs which have been linked with those of the Lollards in England.[18]

The activities of many Anabaptists chronologically followed the sacramentarians and reveals a similarly unsophisticated ideology. Anabaptism, it has been shown, was attractive to many women in its simplicity, as sacramentarianism had been. Women were executed for their beliefs as were men, although beyond the fact of trial and execution we often know little of their lives. In the early phases of Anabaptism, Dutch women were public participants in a number of eccentric activities. These included the pilgrimage of many to Münster, as well as the famous outburst at Amsterdam in February, 1535. In this most notorious public example, a group of Anabaptists—seven men and five women—threw their clothes into the fireplace and ran naked through the streets. As a near-contemporary reported, no more ghastly spectacle was imaginable. When apprehended by members of the civil militia, who undoubtedly found their ardor warm for mid-winter, the Anabaptists responded that the truth had to appear naked. The Amsterdam Anabaptists also attempted to seize control of the town as at Münster. As was the case at Münster, the failure of events in Amsterdam ushered in ongoing repression and a growing emphasis on the pacific Anabaptism espoused by Menno Simons.[19]

The second half of the century witnessed the gradual spread of the Reformed faith, which also had its extremist aspects. Participants in the iconoclastic outbursts that swept the Netherlands in 1566 included women as well as men. One iconoclast, Neel Spaens, was sentenced to death in Utrecht for her activities, which included providing tools to break open the church doors and smash images. Although Neel was imprisoned, she negotiated a dramatic escape and fled into exile. Women and youths were important participants in the image breakings. We have already seen that there was official reluctance to bring women to trial for acts of malfeasance. It seems clear that Neel used traditional feminine roles to her own advantage.[20]

By the time of the "Twelve Years' Truce" of 1609, which effectively created the Dutch Republic, a number of religious changes had been achieved. The political changes that occurred appear on the surface to be radical, but one perceptive historian has labeled them "new wine in old bottles."[21] Similarly, the religious changes that appear so dramatic at an institutional level may well have affected women and the family less than is often asserted.

Catholic and Protestant teaching with regard to marriage and the family, for example, have been distinguished as clearly different. Prior to the Reformation, the parish priest had primary responsibility for encouraging high moral standards, familial responsibilities, proper upbringing of children, and for functioning as mediator between the individual and the religious hierarchy.[22] The unmarried state was preferable, in terms of theological thinking. Some have argued that Protestants regarded marriage and the family from another point of view. With the loss of power and influence for parish authorities and the affirmation by Protestants that marriage was no longer a sacrament, secular authorities assumed responsibility for legal and juridical aspects of marital matters. By advocating that the clergy marry, the Protestants created both a new social group and a new social norm—one wherein marriage rather than celibacy was the preferred state. Marriage was seen as part of the natural order. The equality between man and wife was at least theoretically advanced by Calvin, although interpretations of this doctrine vary.[23]

One possible reason for the appeal of Calvin's teachings in the Netherlands was that they meshed well with the existing social and legal philosophy. If marriage was seen as part of the natural order, what was crucially important to Netherlanders within that order was a life of balance and harmony. Theology taught that the husband was above the wife in the order of things and that the wife was subject to her husband. Dutch writings, however, practical as well as theoretical, tempered that emphasis on hierarchy with an affirmation of reciprocity, or balance.[24] A ceremonial plate commemorating the marriage of Pieter van Harinxma and Susanna van Burmania in 1648 reveals a number of important familial values that were widely shared throughout the Netherlands. The plate features the clasped hands of man and wife, coats-of-arms of both gentry families, two doves, and two entwined hearts. Below the hands, the inscription reads: "A twin-heart, that glows aflame; two hands, grown into one; two doves, that hover over the pair; two cords, that cannot be untwined; the true-wedded picture of van Harinxma and of his bride. Grant, o Lord, that this, their marriage, will here, on Earth, a Heaven build." The affirmation of family and lineage was an important bond in this marriage; equally important was the notion of marriage as partnership.[25]

On the other hand, it was important for women to know where they fit in this scheme of things. The Protestant moralist Jacob Cats, writing on marriage, illuminated more traditional sentiments on roles within the family: "There is a strange custom of many wedded folk . . . to wit, that the wife, also in the marriage bond, stands above her man, stands on the right side. This is not right, young woman, and not merited by the past. To appear to be as the Head, is beyond all reason. It contradicts the nature of God's ancient law, that put you beside your husband, not above him." Cats did not state that the wife was below or beneath her husband but, rather, beside him. It is true that he also mentions the "right side," for it was an artistic convention that always placed men at the right, considered the "better" place. But Cats is also addressing what he considered to be inappropriate behavior in women, a sure sign that such behavior was widespread—especially inasmuch as he himself refers to it as the "custom of many wedded folk."[26] How greatly the Protestant and Catholic reforms altered behavior between man and wife is far from evident.

The practical, as opposed to theoretical, dimensions of change can be regarded somewhat differently. One institutional change had monumental effect on the immediate situation of women: the convents and cloisters were closed. In Amsterdam, sixteen cloisters and a *Beguinehof* (courtyard) existed in the mid-sixteenth century.[27] The so-called Alteration of 1578 replaced Catholicism with the Reformed faith, removed the religious sisters from their houses, and liquidated the convents' holdings. The dowries with which the nuns had entered religious life were returned to them, along with a pension. Amsterdam's regents provided eight buildings where groups of nuns could live together and assumed responsibility for the upkeep of the houses. Although one group, the Poor Clares, refused to vacate their cloister, and as late as 1591 Mass was still being said there, the numbers in religious orders greatly diminished in the second half of the sixteenth century. This was true throughout the Netherlands.[28]

In Utrecht, the fate of the convents parallels that of Amsterdam. Utrecht, a bishopric, was an important center of religious activity from the early Middle Ages. The convents figured in that activity, as was the case in Amsterdam, when the convents were closed the nuns were pensioned off. They either returned home or continued to live together in small groups. This second practice may have led naturally to the arrangement whereby the so-named *kloppen* (the same word provides the definition for Beguine in modern Dutch), who avowed the Catholic faith, continued to live together throughout the northern Netherlands in unrecognized, informal groups. Obviously, this new activity resulted at least partially from the closing of convents and cloisters. It also was a typical sort of response to a state-supported religion that many people could not or would not support.[29]

Even prior to the coming of the Reformation, a wide range of religious establishments coexisted quite peacefully in the northern Netherlands. Not all women chose, or had chosen for them, the lifelong commitment of a professed nun. Many lived as Beguines, for example, or as Sisters of the Common Life following the spread of the Modern Devotion in the fourteenth century. As was the case with many professed nuns, the houses of the Beguines were closed in the second half of the sixteenth century, and the Beguines were sent packing. As was true of the nuns, often their numbers dwindled to such an extent that their houses were uninhabited: in Rotterdam, when the *Beguinehof* stood empty, the regents turned it over to the nuns of the Carmelite cloister of St. Anna, whose house had been confiscated but who continued to stay together.[30]

In her study of Beguines Florence Koorn concludes that at least on occasion they were better treated after the coming of the Reformation than had they been professed nuns. Conceivably, because they were not linked so closely with the Church establishment, they appeared less threatening and less identified with anticlerical sentiments. Since many Beguines came of wealthy patriciate families, it is perhaps not surprising that they were sometimes able to effectively reverse the termination of their community. In Haarlem, after the Beguines were forced to evacuate their *beguinehof*—Beguine houses were often centered around a common yard or park. One group purchased a whole street of houses, one by one.[31]

The expansion of these informal groups after the end of the sixteenth century is difficult to trace. It is apparent, however, that the numbers of *kloppen* or *geestelijke maagden* grew during the seventeenth century and that their activities expanded. Since the formal activities of the Catholic church had been banned, the unrecognized activities of the *kloppen* were necessarily clandestine. Inasmuch as there were only about five hundred priests in the entire northern Netherlands by the mid-seventeenth century, the *kloppen* took their place on numerous occasions. One study of the *kloppen* suggests that the women engaged in these clandestine activities assumed authority that had previously been within the realm of men within the Church. As a result, they were disparaged within the Church (which had rejected the model of more open religious orders for women espoused by Mary Ward) and without it, by those who regarded them as too independent, too free, and not under male authority as they should be.[32] It seems to me, rather, that their activities were strongly supported by the family. Many of the *kloppen* in Utrecht were also members of wealthy patriciate families which were brought only very slowly, if at all in the first half of the seventeenth century, into the Reformed church. Their daughters could no longer be nuns, but they could become, as they are recorded in one genealogy after another, *geestelijke maagden*, "holy maidens." Behavior that might appear intimidating or presumptuous to some within the Catholic church establishment, or to the reformed population, did not appear threatening to the families of these women. And they were the ones who mattered most in this setting.[33]

The fate of the convents' physical facilities was more apparent. Although the Provincial States of Utrecht were charged with their upkeep, in many instances these buildings were not recycled as they were in Amsterdam. By the mid-seventeenth century most had fallen into disrepair. The *Wittevrouwen* ("White Ladies," so called because of the distinctive habit worn by the nuns) convent was in such a state of "ruin" that the consideration in a *Memorie* to the nobility of the States of Utrecht of September 1645, was whether it could be salvaged at all.[34] Earlier, it had been suggested that both the *Wittevrouwen* and St. Servaes convents be converted into housing. Apparently, this had failed to happen, for by 1645, it was estimated that repairs to the woodwork alone in the former would cost 800 guilders. The labor would add another 200 guilders, while the cloister buildings themselves might be renovated for no less than 2500 guilders. Clearly, little interest had been taken in the buildings' maintenance.[35]

The nobles had no desire to finance these costly repairs in 1645 either. They did, however, have an ongoing interest in collecting the incomes which continued, albeit at a much diminished rate, to accrue well into the seventeenth century. One such income was provided by prebends. By this time, the members of the Utrecht nobility who sat in the provincial States had become members of the reformed church. Such membership was necessary to hold political office in the United Provinces. Although their daughters no longer entered convents, the prebends were still used to fund incomes for the young noblewomen. The gentlemen drew lots to establish which incomes would fall to whose daughters:

> On June 11, 1634, as well as April 23, 1640 . . . for the purpose of conferring by lottery the *Jouffrouw* prebends of the Convents of St. Servaes, and of the *Vrouw-enclooster* [that is, *Wittevrouwen*] . . . at the time that these respective prebends would become vacant . . . notes with lots were drawn up, placed in a hat, shaken, and drawn by each nobleman.

Each then had the right to nominate a candidate to fill each vacant prebend, typically a family member and usually a daughter. Nominees would receive a "yearly income . . . of six hundred guilders until her death or marriage."[36] The principle of providing economically for unmarried daughters thus continued even after the functional value of the prebends in religious terms had disappeared. Because their families had endowed these prebends hundreds of years before, the nobles had no intention of relinquishing the incomes.

These funds were also used to provide for needy relatives, evidenced by a revealing correspondence between Catharina van Reede tot Nederhorst, a widow, and Adam van Lockhorst, Lord of Zuylen. Catharina wrote to Lockhorst on July 4, 1648, ostensibly to invite him to her husband's funeral, but in reality to pave the way for her request for financial assistance.[37] Lockhorst did loan her money; Catharina wrote in 1655 to acknowledge her debt of 350 Carolus guilders, which she had incurred between 1650 and 1652.[38] But that was not all.

By 1652, Lockhorst had exchanged letters with two of Catharina's sons over the prospect of a "juffer prebend" for "juffer Uyttenhove," their sister.[39] In fact, Emerentia van Reede tot Nederhorst wrote to Lockhorst in 1654 to request the prebend "for one of my children; insofar as that is possible for my lord to do so . . . if my child can receive the benefice we shall be grateful as long as we live and remain always your obedient servant, Emmerens van Reede." Her daughter appears to have received the prebend.[40] Although the convents had ceased to exist, the nobility considered these emoluments to be familial property. The purpose continued to be to provide for unmarried young women within the family, regardless of the ways in which religious forms had been altered beyond recognition.

Religious organizations often emulated familial functions for those less well endowed financially. After the Reformation, private or state-funded charitable works replaced those earlier ministered by convents, although the charitable function of the convent continued throughout the sixteenth century. The Abbey of Rynsburg fed more than 3,000 victims of the famine of 1557; the Abbey of Leeuwenhorst pursued similar activities. During the plague of July 1573, the St. Clara cloister at Delft carried out at least three hundred dead for burial. Throughout the vicissitudes of the Revolt of the Netherlands in the second half of the sixteenth century, convents aided those who had nowhere to turn.[41]

The continuity of these charitable activities appears throughout the period of religious change. "In terms of the official policy for care of the poor," notes one historian, discussing the situation of Catholics in Amsterdam after the Alteration of 1578, "in the orphanages, at least, there are no signs of discrimination on grounds of religion."[42] Despite religious overtones, orphanages filled a quasi-familial function, one that made their religious identification acceptable during a period of religious upheaval. Funds for the continued support of the so-called *Maagdenhuis* (maidens' home) came from the 1573 testament of Laurens Spieghel, which stated that: "from hence legated and reviewed to the benefit of the poor girls' home established by his (*sic*) daughters Marie Laurens and Aelken Pieters, a yearly annuity of fifty guilders. . . ." Marie Laurens Spieghel and Aeltje Pieter Fopsdr, as well as the latter's sister Meynau, had initiated this project by bringing homeless girls into their own homes as well as to a house rented for the purpose in which they themselves lived with the girls. The Fop daughters pledged fifty guilders a year to the support of the enterprise, Marie Laurens Spieghel one hundred, as well as the additional amount allocated by her father's will.[43]

Following the Alteration of 1578, and concomitantly the closing of Amsterdam's convents, a group of nuns from the St. Margaret's cloister approached Aeltje Pieter Fopsdr and Jan Micheielsz Loeff and contracted with them at the end of 1578 or beginning of 1579 to serve "as caretakers for poor girls."[44] Although the Amsterdam regents considered this attempt to found a new convent illegal, a notarial act dated May 2, 1582, shows that "Aeltgen and Meynau Pieter Fopszns daughters, sisters, burghers and citizens (*poorteressen*) of the city of Amsterdam . . . by irrevocable gift, . . . offered, ceded, transported to this the poor girls' house, funded by the said Aeltgen Pieters, in the said city of Amsterdam, to the behalf and for the upkeep of it, and of the poor orphans."[45]

The difficulties incurred by several relocations brought the Spieghel family back into the picture. Despite their Catholicism, they were highly regarded, influential citizens of Amsterdam. The regents that were ultimately chosen to oversee the orphanage in 1590 were both identified as Catholic. As the plans of Marie Spieghel and Aeltje Pieters became a reality, men, who considered themselves more politically astute, were placed in charge. After Aeltje became estranged from the project, it proved difficult to find other women willing to become involved. Their presence was missed. As Loeff wrote in 1591: "This administration must on the whole be women's work." The role of the women's families had not ended; Marie Spieghel willed 100 guilders yearly to the orphanage in 1614. And Meynau Pieter Fopsdr, mentioned with her sister in the notarial act of 1582, became regent in 1610.[46]

The orphanage's Roman Catholic identification continued, and by the seventeenth century the institution incorporated a sewing school for girls who were not orphans but rather came of families who could pay the fees. This helped subsidize the others. On the orphanage's oldest extant name list, dated 1668, seventy-six names from the ages of six to sixty-six appear. The youngest were placed with families rather than in the home.[47] Funded and administered by Catholics, the home was left to organize its works of charity within a tradition that continued to live, despite its officially legislated death.

Jews were also outsiders to the official world of church and state in the seventeenth-century Netherlands. Although Ashkenazim, Jews from Germany and Eastern Europe, traveled in and out of the Netherlands in the Middle Ages, the Sephardim who arrived in Amsterdam as exiles from Spain and Portugal had a more readily identifiable community and more comprehensive records are extant. The charitable organizations administered by the Portuguese Jews in Amsterdam incorporated—as did those of the Catholics—elements in keeping with the outcast community's own religious traditions and with an ideal of replicating family life and ties for those whose families had been lost.

Daniel Swetschinski, writing on the Amsterdam Sephardim, sees the "foundation of the Santa Companhia de Dotar Orfans e Donzelas Pobres," or "Dotar," as representative of the "use of kinship for purposes of social solidification." The company's regulations were drawn up in 1615. In it, the society stated that it would dedicate itself to:

> marry orphans and poor maidens of the Portuguese and Castilian nation, residing between Saint-Jean-de-Luz and Danzig, whether in France or in Flanders, England, and Germany. All those wishing to support such a pious work who are of our Hebrew nation, whether Portuguese or Castilian, or their descendents in masculine or feminine line, residing anywhere in the world, can become members of the society, if they contribute at least 20 Flemish pounds in Amsterdam money.[48]

Clearly, Dotar was a charitable organization that functioned effectively for the purposes for which it had been established—marriage broker, financial support for preferred candidates, religious support for a beleaguered faith. Equally clearly, it provided a religious focus for social problems. Dotar existed to aid the marriage of young Jewish women, and not all young women were eligible. The drawings by lot of Dotar were restricted to:

> orphans and maidens . . . who are poor and need support for their marriage; (who are) of the Portuguese or Spanish nation; Hebrews who confess the unity of the Lord of the World and the truth of His Most Sacred Law; (who are) of

good conduct and manners, honest and honorable, without any taint of vileness; who live and dwell, during the year in which they are admitted, in the area designated in the preamble to the *haskamoth*.[49]

Just as a few prominent Catholic women were among the key supporters of the Amsterdam *Maagdenhuis,* a few Jewish women were among the prominent supporters of Dotar. Of the sixty-eight names on the 1618 membership list, three were those of women; in 1619, with a membership list of seventy-four, four were women; in 1620, the membership list of seventy-eight included three women.[50] Jewish women played less of a role as financial supporters and, unlike the Catholic women, do not appear to have been the initiators or founders. Although the "entrance requirements," as well as the ways in which Dotar regarded some preferentially were not directly paralleled by the Roman Catholic *Maagdenhuis* in Amsterdam, the latter's specifically Catholic identification, with its emphasis on catechism and the teachings of the Church, effectively prevented those of other religions from entering.

Further, there was no need. The Protestants created charitable organizations of their own. Each religious community looked out for its own, while the municipal authorities dispensed charity for citizens. Those who were not members of a church or burghers of a town were the ones who fell between the cracks. The poor could beg or protest, as they did on a number of occasions. The above discussion might convey an erroneous impression that there was little or no interaction between the various religious groups. Nothing could be further from the truth, at least in an urban environment such as Amsterdam. Notarial records show the accommodations that Jew and Christian made with one another and with the secular world.

One such *modus vivendi* pertained to marriage. Christians read their marriage banns in church on the Sunday preceding the nuptials. Following the Reformation, marriages were then registered with the civil authorities. If there were objections to the religious practice, the intent to marry could be declared from the *pui* or steps in front of the Town Hall. The Portuguese Sephardim initially registered few marriages with the civil authorities; they considered their own religious ceremony as the only ceremony of import. The Jews did not wish to draw attention to themselves or to matrimonial practices which they considered lawful but the state did not. These included uncles marrying the offspring of one of their own siblings; widowers, the sisters of their deceased wives; and men, the widows of their deceased brothers. Such marriages were not only permissible under Judaism but even encouraged by the close-knit Sephardic community, which had only recently found sanctuary in Amsterdam. Unfortunately for the Jews, marriages between blood relatives of this degree were expressly forbidden by the States of Holland and West Frisia in 1580. As practiced as the Portuguese exiles were in evading civil interference in their religious practices, the civil authorities frequently found them out.[51]

The situation of David Abudiente, also known as Duarte Gomes, reveals multiple layers of complicity and duplicity between Jew and Christian in seventeenth-century Amsterdam. On January 8, 1618, the sheriff of Amsterdam notified David that he was liable for a second fine of 100 guilders, inasmuch as he had continued to live with his sister's daughter despite his fine of six weeks previous. David protested that he had registered his marriage to Branca at the Town Hall on December 14; when the Commission for Matrimonial Affairs finally closed its books on their investigation, it was noted that David had misunderstood the difference between *neef* and *cousijn* (nephew and cousin), which could be used interchangeably in Dutch, although not in Portuguese. Finally the marriage was permitted to stand legally. Another view of David Abudiente's marriage, however, comes from the contemporary records of an Amsterdam notary. David had been accused of impregnating Beletgen Pelgroms, an Amsterdam Christian, in 1615. When her family initiated legal proceedings against him, David's relatives decided he should contract a marriage as soon as possible. Branca was indeed David's niece, but the motives for this hastily arranged marriage appear somewhat mixed.[52]

Sexual matters, inter- and intrafaith, were the subject of intense social and legal scrutiny. It appears that the goal of the States was once again to support familial values rather than to legislate against the Jews in particular. As of November 8, 1616, Amsterdam Jews were forbidden to have "fleshly conversation" or sexual intercourse with Christian women, even prostitutes. But this prohibition was lifted for those who agreed to convert: Jan de Pontremo agreed in 1619 to convert to Lutheranism to legitimize his relationship with Grietgen Christians. The authorities had no objection, provided Jan would not "converse" with Grietgen until after his religious conversion.[53]

It was customary for servants to be called as legal support and character witnesses. They were also particularly vulnerable with regard to their own sexual conduct. If female servants became pregnant while employed in a household with Jewish males, it was important for them to testify as to how they had become pregnant unless the men of the household were guilty. When Marritgen Jansdr, a servant in the employ of the nineteen-year-old Manuel Cardoso, became pregnant in May 1619, for example, Manuel's father procured a deposition from Marritgen. This stated that she had had an affair "some thirteen or fourteen months ago with a certain Pieter from Rotterdam who has (since) left for Guinea, and that she is pregnant by him. She declares that she had no other affair during that period."[54]

Marritgen Jansdr was a free agent and could testify in court as such. Breach of contract cases also offer insight into the rights of women in early modern Holland. In 1636 Margaretha Pauw, daughter of a prominent regent and patriciate family, apparently brought suit in the provincial Court of Utrecht against Jonkheer Adriaen Ram for breach of contract. Had Ram in fact contracted a "clandestine or secret marriage" (*matrimonia clandestina*) with Margaretha Pauw? Both were over twenty-five years old; the document gives the clear impression that they were both legally empowered to make their own decisions in this matter. Margaretha's case argued that Adriaen Ram had promised marriage so that she might engage in "fleshly conversation" with him. Adriaen promised not to leave her, she said, but also implied that he would end their relationship if she refused to trust him, saying that he would not serve a suspicious woman. During this courtship, he was able to lure her into sin. "Her honor was his, her shame was his, or so he said, but above all else he openly professed before her friends and kin that he was satisfied and wished to marry her; that he also had a soul to save; and that he hoped a son or daughter might result through their copulation."[55]

Breach of contract cases that had set legal precedent were cited in addition to Margaretha Pauw's recollections. The appeal court of Amsterdam had heard the case of Elbert Ooms of Amsterdam against Geertruyt Scheepels, of the same locale, earlier in 1636. Geertruyt brought the case because of her defloration by Elbert. She then became pregnant. As proof of marital intent, Geertruyt said she had given Elbert an armlet and he had given her a gold coin, a *roosenobel*. Geertruyt argued that these were in token of marital gifts, and indeed the exchange of presents was always held to be a tangible sign of matrimonial intent or reality. More important to the court, Elbert and Geertruyt were of the same social group—*goede middelen*—and thus represented well enough equals, or *egale partijen*.[56]

Adriaen Ram made this conclusion regarding social parity the crux of his argument. Margaretha Pauw was of much lesser quality in terms of her background and lineage (*geslachte ende affcompste*), he argued, and as a result of this great disparity, Adriaen declared that his intention had never been to marry Margaretha.[57] The record breaks off at this point, and although it appears that Margaretha's case carried the day, Adriaen was relying on a legal argument that was generally victorious: social disparity.

Geertruyt Scheepels, Marritgen Jansdr, and Margaretha Pauw probably represented three different social strata, but all three are represented as acting on their own behalf. In other words, other family members did not bring the court case for the women. On other occasions, the family provided advocacy, succor, and support when women appeared to stand alone or when familial interests were challenged. In 1619, Gracia Henriques, her father, Antonio, and her "brother and proxy Diogo" pressed charges of desertion against Gracia's estranged husband, Simao Gomes Dias with the object of reclaiming her dowry. The Portuguese Jewish emigrants functioned well within Holland's legal system and learned quickly how to use it. Women recognized the ways in which law protected them and supported their rights both as individuals and within the family. Branca Nunes, widow of Simao Rodrigues, protested that her husband's will, which had been drawn up in February 1618, did not grant her the half of his estate that Dutch law entitled her to receive: she claimed that half later the same year. The deposition which followed in her name authorized the collection of monies due her.[58]

Familial values provided an underpinning for communal values. In 1621, Marritje Harmens testified before the notary at the request of Francisco de

Caceres. Although Marritje was identified as the thirty-four-year-old wife of Coenraet Hillebrant, she was probably in Caceres's employ, for her statement noted that she had been standing at the door of her room in Caceres's house when she witnessed the following events. She had seen, Marritje said, the son of the boxmaker's widow, who lives in the neighborhood, hit Caceres's wife in the back with his fist because she would not allow him and his friends to climb on her roof. Caceres's wife was badly frightened, took to her bed, and suffered a miscarriage. Her testimony was confirmed by Aeltje Evert, possibly a friend visiting Marritje at the time.[59]

What seems significant about this case is that the Christian servant, herself a mature, married woman, appeared to give testimony in support of familial values. It was less relevant that her employers were Jewish and her testimony was on their behalf. Caceres's wife had been maltreated while she was pregnant, and had apparently miscarried as a result. Familial and communal values were a joint social buttress. Similarly, although the religious identification of Dotar and the *Maagdenhuis* differed, the purpose was to fill familial roles and functions and support familial values when no family existed to do so. Religious identification provided a basis for financial support, but shared familial values provided the basis for social support.

Religious changes created a milieu in which women could emerge in strong and independent positions. Because of the political and social unrest, women were able to become leaders, even if only for a short period of time. Although religious institutions changed extensively during this period, functional change did not necessarily occur. It is arguable that this functional continuity represented deep-rooted social values that crossed the lines of religious identification. What religion meant in the daily lives of ordinary people and the ways in which common values affirmed social norms remained surprisingly constant.

NOTES

Research for this essay was funded by the American Philosophical Society and the National Endowment for the Humanities. The author also wishes to express her appreciation to the Baroness van Hardenbroek-Snoek Hurgronje for the use of unpublished archival documents from the Archive van Hardenbroek, Utrecht, and to Miriam Usher Chrisman, who commented on the manuscript. All translations are my own.

1. Few published sources exist for Jewish women in the early modern Netherlands. *Die Mij niet Gemaakt heeft tot Man,* ed. Rachel van Emden, (Kampen: J. H. Kok, 1986), deals in the Introduction and Background with a bit of their history. General works consider the Jewish woman within the family, for example, H. Brugmans and A. Frank, eds., *Geschiedenis der Joden in Nederland,* vol. 1 (Amsterdam: Van Holkema & Warendolf, 1940). The listing of documents in the Amsterdam notarial archives by W. Ch. Pieterse and E. M. Koen is a boon to the historian; installments appear in *Studia Rosenthaliana* at regular intervals under the headings of "Amsterdam Notarial Deeds Pertaining to the Portuguese Jews up to 1639," later renamed "Notarial Records Relating to the Portuguese Jews in Amsterdam up to 1639." Although

specific topics have been investigated with regard to Catholic women, no work deals with them systematically or comprehensively. A. Th. van Deursen, *Het kopergeld van de Gouden Eeuw,* esp. II (*volkskultuur*) and IV (*hel en hemel*) (Assen: Van Gorcum, 1978, 1980) includes a great deal of useful information on religious groups (other than Jews).

2. For recent works that consider the Dutch family, see: Sherrin Marshall, *The Dutch Gentry 1500–1650: Family, Faith, and Fortune* (Westport, Conn.: Greenwood, 1987), Donald Haks, *Huwelijk en gezin in Holland in de 17de en 18de eeuw* (Utrecht: Hes, 1985), and H. F. K. van Nierop, *Van ridders tot regenten* (Amsterdam: De Bataafsche Leeuw, 1984).

3. Marshall, *Dutch Gentry,* pp. 31–68.

4. The commentary is on "Kenau Hasselaar op de wallen van Haarlem," dated 1854, *Het Vaderlandsch Gevoel,* catalogue from the Rijksmuseum, Amsterdam's exhibit (Zutphen: Nauta, 1978), p. 91.

5. J. W. Wijn, *Het Beleg van Haarlem* (Amsterdam: P. N. van Kampen & Zn., 1943), p. 52.

6. For other sources on Kenau, see Sherrin Marshall Wyntjes, "Women and Religious Choices in the Sixteenth Century Netherlands," *Archive for Reformation History* 75 (1984), 283, n. 25. A different interpretation of Kenau and the symbolism of her life appears in Fia Dieteren, Els Kloek, and Antoinette Visser, *Naar Eva's beeld* (Amsterdam: Elsevier, 1987), p. 102.

7. J. G. Riphaagen, "Een standbeeld voor Trijn van Leemput," *Jaarboek Oud-Utrecht* (1977), 85–109.

8. In *Vaderlandsch Gevoel,* commentary on: "Magdalena Moons bij Valdez," dated ca. 1848, p. 105.

9. Wyntjes, "Women and Religious Choices," p. 284.

10. J. d'Ancona, "Komst der Marranen in Noord-Nederland de Portugese Gemeenten te Amsterdam tot de Vereniging (1639)," in H. Brugmans and A. Frank, pp. 204–205.

11. The criminal record appears in an appendix of Rudolf Dekker and Lotte van de Pol, *Daar was laatst een meisje loos* (Baarn: Amboboeken, 1981), pp. 135–36.

12. Ibid, pp. 137–39.

13. Rudolf Dekker, *Holland in beroering* (Baarn: Amboboeken, 1982), pp. 51–60.

14. Ibid, p. 57.

15. Ibid, p. 54.

16. The quote from the writer Simon de Vries appears to Dekker, p. 58; Natalie Zemon Davis, "Women on Top," in *Society and Culture in Early Modern France* (Stanford: Stanford University Press, 1975), pp. 124–51, showed the ways in which such tensions could be exploited both positively and negatively.

17. R. R. Post, *Kerkelijke verhoudingen in Nederland voor de Reformatie van +/-1500 tot +/-1580* (Utrecht, 1954); "De Roeping tot het Kloosterleven in de 16de eeuw," *Mededelingen der Koninklijke Nederlandse Akademie van Wetenschappen* 13 (1950), 31–76.

18. Alastair Duke, "Dissident Voices in a Conformist Town: The Early Reformation at Gouda," S. Groenveld, M. E. H. N. Mout, I. Schoffer, eds., *Bestuurders en Geleerden* (Amsterdam: De Bataafsche Leeuw, 1985), pp. 27–28.

19. Albert Mellink, *Amsterdam en de Wederdopers in de zestiende eeuw* (Nijmegen: SUN, 1978), pp. 46–48; Cornelius Krahn, *Dutch Anabaptism* (The Hague, 1968).

20. Wyntjes, "Women and Religious Choices," p. 285.

21. S. Groenveld, *De kogel door de kerk?* (Zutphen: De Walburg Pers, 1983), pp. 182–84.

22. Haks, *Huwelijk en gezin,* pp. 9–11.

23. Jane Dempsey Douglas, *Women, Freedom, and Calvin* (Philadelphia: Westminster Press, 1985), esp. pp. 34–36, chaps. 3 and 5; Sherrin Marshall Wyntjes, "Women in

the Reformation Era," R. Bridenthal and C. Koonz, eds., *Becoming Visible* (Boston: Houghton Mifflin, 1977), pp. 172–81.

24. Marshall, *Dutch Gentry*, pp. 31–44, 163–65.

25. The plate appears in E. De Jongh, *Portretten van echt en trouw* (Zwolle: Waanders, 1986), 52.

26. Ibid, pp. 36–37, 40.

27. I. H. van Eeghen, *Vrouwenkloosters en Begijnhof in Amsterdam van de 14e tot het eind der 16de eeuw* (Amsterdam: H. J. Paris, 1941), p. 12.

28. H. C. de Wolf, *De kerk en het Maagdenhuis* (Utrecht: Het Spectrum, 1970), pp. 52–64.

29. Elisja Schulte van Kessel, "Vis noch vlees," *Jaarboek voor vrouwengeschiedenis* (Nijmegen: SUN, 1981), pp. 167–92; Wyntjes, "Women and Religious Choices," pp. 285–87, 288.

30. F. W. J. Koorn, *Begijnhoven in Holland en Zeeland gedurende de middeleeuwen* (Assen: Van Gorcum, 1981), pp. 34–35.

31. Ibid.

32. Schulte van Kessel, "Vis noch vlees," pp. 171–92.

33. Marshall, *Dutch Gentry*, chap. 5.

34. Archief van Hardenbroek (Cothen, Utr.), fol. 443/5, no pagination.

35. Ibid.

36. Ibid., fol. 443/1, no pagination; fol. 443/5.

37. Ibid., fol. 1532.

38. Ibid., fol. 1444.

39. Ibid., fos. 1539, 1540.

40. Ibid., fol. 1544. Although undated, the lists of recipients of prebends in the mid-seventeenth century (prior to the first dated lists of 1665) include "Joff Anna Elisabeth van Reede," possibly the same as the "Elisabeth van Reede," who follows her with the notation of *nupsit*: Archief van Hardenbroek, fol. 443/7, no pagination.

41. Moquette, *Maatschappelijk Leven*, pp. 32–33; I. H. van Eeghen, ed., *Dagboek van Broeder Wouter Jacobsz* (Gualtherus Jacobi Masius), I (Groningen: J. B. Wolters, 1959), includes a large number of examples demonstrating this point.

42. De Wolf, *De Kerk*, p. 69.

43. Ibid., pp. 268–69. Unfortunately, the relevant documents have at least temporarily disappeared from the Gemeente Archief (GA), Amsterdam.

44. Ibid., p. 271.

45. Ibid., p. 272.

46. Ibid., pp. 274–280.

47. Ibid., pp. 281–283.

48. Daniel M. Swetschinski, "Kinship and Commerce: The Foundations of Portuguese Jewish Life in Seventeenth-Century Holland," *Studia Rosenthaliana* 15, no. 1 (1981), 67.

49. Ibid., p. 68.

50. E. M. Koen, "The Earliest Sources Relating to the Portuguese Jews in the Municipal Archives of Amsterdam up to 1620," *Studia Rosenthaliana* IV (1970), 35.

51. Ibid., pp. 30–33.

52. Ibid., pp. 32–33; I. H. van Eeghen, "Mr. Daniel Mostart en de 'Huwelijkse Zaken'," *Studia Rosenthaliana* XVII (1983), pp. 17–18; GA Amsterdam, Not. Arch. 280, fol. 28.

53. Koen, p. 34.

54. GA Amsterdam, Not. Arch. 546B, fol. 130.

55. Archief van Hardenbroek, fol. 1699, no pagination, is a large portfolio record of all the documentation in the case.

56. Ibid.

57. Ibid.

58. Koen, "Notarial Records Relating to the Portuguese Jews in Amsterdam up to 1639," *Studia Rosenthaliana* XVI (1982), 62. Quoted from GA Amsterdam, Not. Arch. 382, fol. 133 (in Portuguese).

59. GA Amsterdam, Not. Arch. 645B, fols. 1303–1304.

DIANE WILLEN

Women and Religion in Early
Modern England

Contemporaries in early modern England thought women "inclinable to holiness" and more likely than men to practice the virtue of religious piety.[1] As
if to verify the claim, historians have remarked on the participation of
women, often in disproportionate numbers and influence, in a wide variety
of religious movements from Catholic recusancy to Protestant sectarianism.
Explanations for women's piety and religious involvement sometimes take
into account the special appeal of Protestantism but also focus on the rewards which religion in general offered: escape from passivity in a highly
patriarchal society, the promise of a meaningful life, the satisfaction of emotional catharsis, opportunity for self-expression, spiritual egalitarianism, and
a means to cope emotionally with the perils of childbirth.[2] Whatever the
motive in individual cases, a great many women in all social classes justified
their lives and ordered their daily activities according to their religious
beliefs.

In the extreme, both recusants and sectarians experienced religious fervor
strong enough to defy the law. Yet defiant, radical acts in public should not
obscure the significance of household religion, which demanded the participation of the entire family in daily religious observance within the home.
The Reformation had removed the parish priest and elevated in his stead the
male head of household who was responsible for the oversight of religious
observance and the spiritual instruction of family and friends. Increasingly
important in England during the course of the sixteenth century, such
household religion evoked strong religious commitment and made home and
family the center of religious piety. Not surprisingly, a religious structure
which focused on family, even the patriarchal family of early modern England, depended on and recognized the influence of wife and mother. Within
the confines of household religion, women exerted influence, found enhanced meaning for their lives, and established important personal relationships. Moreover, many of these patterns of behavior crossed Protestant and
Catholic lines since in Reformation England the suppression of Catholicism
confined that faith to secret worship within the household.[3]

This essay begins by weighing one effect of women's religious participation: the involvement of women of all social classes in the process of religious change. Part II considers the role of women in Protestant household
religion and suggests that the historiographical debate over patriarchy has

obscured the actual activities of women. Part III looks specifically at recusant women. Finally, Part IV assesses the implications of household religion and considers those most elusive of women, women of the working poor, beyond the pale of household religion. Throughout the essay, the term Protestant includes all parties who accepted the break with Rome and embraced the principle of justification by faith. A variety of terms distinguish groups among the Protestants, groups that sometimes overlapped one another. Anglicans conformed to the Elizabethan liturgy. Puritans—whether or not they conformed, and the majority did conform—wished to further the process of reformation in England. In the eyes of contemporaries they might appear as zealots, but Puritans saw themselves as godly. Separatists and, in the seventeenth century, sectarians represented the most radical of the Protestants, for they broke from the Anglican church to create their own congregations.

The essay has relatively little to say about the most prominent women in Reformation England—individual women of aristocratic status who usually received the best education available to their sex. The names of Catherine Parr, Mary Fitzroy, Anne Seymour, Catherine Brandon, Anne Boleyn, Jane Seymour, Elizabeth Tudor, the Cooke sisters, and Mary Sidney Herbert come to mind immediately. A great deal of the scholarly literature on English women in the Reformation already focuses on this group, and perhaps too much ink has been spent in debating whether such women enjoyed a Renaissance, benefited from humanist educational theories, or had influence within their society. It is evident that their numbers were exceedingly small; their writings, usually translations rather than original texts, were confined to a religious context; their concern for feminism nonexistent. Nonetheless, they effectively promoted the cause of reformation through their patronage, their pen, and their example. Silence in this essay is not meant to belittle that contribution.[4]

I

Recent scholarship on the English Reformation underscores the role of the laity in resisting, accelerating, ignoring, and accepting religious change. The implications for women's history should be clear. No longer a simple act of state, the Reformation is now seen as "a long and complex process," initially "indecisive," neither inevitable nor irreversible.[5] Along with Protestantization, we now recognize other, contradictory forces: significant and continued resistance to change among the laity; strong geographic variations in religious beliefs; indigenous and spontaneous recusancy; indifference and ignorance of religion among the poor. Yet, even though Protestantism did not triumph until the 1580s, well into the Elizabethan era, the concept of Protestantization retains its validity.[6] The crown failed to impose its views on Reformers no less than conservatives: hence, Protestant agitation during the Henrician Reformation, the subsequent development of Elizabethan Puritanism, the slow growth of separatism, and finally the emergence of radical sectarianism in the seventeenth century.

The prototype for much of women's subsequent participation in radical Protestantism was their involvement in late medieval Lollardy. Often of artisan status, Lollards were followers of Wycliffe, whose doctrines survived into the sixteenth century to become one of several forces influencing the course of the Reformation. Numbers are at best suggestive, but they do indicate significant female participation in the sect, as in the case of Coventry, where one-third of alleged Lollards examined in 1511–12 were women. Moreover, women perpetuated and promoted Lollardy through their role as wife and mother, for the heresy had little alternative if it were to survive but to function as a "family sect."[7] A few examples are instructive and establish themes evident in subsequent household religion. Agnes Grebill, aged sixty, was burned for her Lollard beliefs in Kent in 1511. Among the accusations against her was the charge, by her family, that she had taught her husband and son Lollard principles. Other women at the Kent heresy proceedings also allegedly converted their families to Lollardy. Maternal influence followed children even into their adult lives. John Pykas was an established baker in Colchester when in 1523 his mother Agnes introduced him to Lollard texts and doctrines; John subsequently became one of the local leaders of the sect. Family religion did not confine or isolate women. Several taught Lollardy to neighbors or outsiders, and evidence suggests a female network of sorts as mothers brought their daughters to female teachers. Women also helped organize the distribution of Lollard books, although the extent of their literacy remains unknown.[8]

Lollardy survived and merged with reformed religion as Protestantism developed in England under the influence of the continental Reformation and the Henrician schism.[9] Significantly, many of the women who embraced varieties of early Protestantism continued to act within the context of the family, where they both drew support and exerted influence. When Thomas Hemsted abjured before Bishop Tunstall in May 1528, he claimed his wife had taught him the Pater Noster, Ave Maria, and Credo in English.[10] Fifteen years later, after the Henrician Reformation was well on its way, charges against the Tofteses of Canterbury showed how easily heresy might become a family affair. Margaret Toftes the younger was alleged to have described images in church as devils and idols. Neither she nor any of her household had "crept to the cross on Good Friday, saying openly on that day that it was abominable to see it." Her mother, Margaret Toftes senior, agreed, "adding that she would creep to the Lord in her heart, which was the right creeping." One of their menfolk, John Toftes, helped remove images from the church and read Scriptures in English aloud to his wife and other women.[11]

Although such women as the Toftes challenged the hierarchy of church and state through their religious views, as long as they acted within the context of family religion, they could see themselves as good wives and mothers. No matter how strong their religious radicalism, their social radicalism was thus constrained, for they did not defy the patriarchy on which society rested. Not all women involved with religious change acted within the context of family, however. Some embraced both religious and social radicalism: in defying patriarchal authority in the family, they challenged at its root what has been called the "ideology of gender," societal teaching about the subordination of women.[12] Scriptures provided justification for the prescriptive ideals of obedience, chastity, humility, and silence, all feminine virtues which remain intact throughout the period of Reformation.[13] But religious values extolled to reinforce patriarchy and keep women deferential did not silence the radicals.

Anne Askew is perhaps the most well known of the early Protestants who acted in defiance of family. Well educated and of gentry status, she adopted the reformed faith through her reading of the Bible. According to the propagandist Reformer John Bale, Askew and her Lincolnshire husband, Thomas Kyme, clashed over religion. Once his wife "fell clerelye from all olde superstyons of papystrye," Kyme acted on the advice of local priests and shut her out of the house. Askew in turn departed for London and sought (but never received) a divorce. Bale justified Askew's actions since Scriptures allowed a faithful wife to leave an unbelieving husband.[14] Once in London, Askew joined the circle of Reformers associated with Queen Catherine Parr. Charged in 1545 for her views on the Mass, she abjured before Bishop Bonner and acknowledged the presence of the body of Christ. But brought again before the authorities in 1546, she stood her ground. Despite the use of torture, she refused to implicate any of Parr's circle in heresy and died in defiance for her beliefs.[15]

Askew's case was significant on several grounds. For the crown to torture a woman on the rack was illegal and to torture a woman of gentry status was all the more remarkable.[16] Reformers took pride in her courage and steadfastness. She became a role model for subsequent Protestant martyrs and may have been especially important as an example to the Marian martyrs, one-fifth of whom were female.[17] Bale certainly intended this effect: "An example of stronge sufferaunce myght thys holye martyr be, unto all of them that the lorde shall after lyke manner put forewarde. . . ."[18] But Askew insured her own legend by providing a written account of her two examinations and a description of her torture; Bale fully annotated Askew's accounts and saw to their circulation. Historians have claimed that Askew created "the most significant writings on religion by a Renaissance Englishwoman" and provided "the rarest form of sixteenth-century writing, the self-portrait."[19] Bale put the matter differently: "A gloryouse witnesse of the lorde did thys blessyd woman shewe her self . . . whan she sayd that god was a sprete and no waffer cake. . . ."[20]

Gender remained an inescapable, obtrusive reality for Askew's interrogators, her defenders, and for Askew herself. In her first examination, she answered the charge that women were forbidden to speak or talk of the Word of God by arguing that Paul's prohibition referred only to women who spoke to an entire congregation. Later on, she took on the cloak of weak womanhood to avoid answering questions.[21] In one exchange when Askew wished to qualify her first confession of the faith, Bishop Bonner angrily charged that Askew was a woman and that she would not deceive him. One of her male defenders then asked the Bishop "not to sett . . . weake wommannys wytt, to hys lordshyppes greate wysdome." These and other references to gender reinforce the radicalism of Askew's actions.[22]

Askew's justification was the traditional Protestant defense: "I beleue as the scripture doth teache me."[23] Her familiarity with Scriptures, much praised by Bale, deserves special notice and raises a fundamental issue about women's involvement in the process of the Reformation. Throughout the course of the sixteenth century, no matter the variety of their Protestantism, knowledge of the Bible characterized and underlay strong piety and religious activism of Protestant women just as it did Protestant men. Yet it is not clear how women, as distinct from men, acquired their knowledge of Scriptures. Specifically, did Protestant women below the rank of gentry read the Bible for themselves or were they forced to rely on memorization and the readings of others?

No move in the official Henrician Reformation was more profound than the appearance of the Great Bible in 1539. Its publication and mandated availability in parish churches stimulated the development of Protestant doctrine far beyond the king's intention. Not surprisingly, apprehension grew about the wisdom of an open Bible policy, and, after the fall of Thomas Cromwell, in the midst of a conservative reaction, that policy was reversed. An act of Parliament in 1543 limited access to the Bible according to class and gender. Among the nobility and gentry, men and women alike might read the Bible in private, but only males enjoyed the right to read aloud to their families and households. Moreover, males who were merchants might read in private, a privilege which was denied their wives and daughters and denied all men and women in the lower ranks of society.[24] Gender, like class, was thus recognized in policy: the crown saw danger in allowing women, even in the context of the family, unlimited use of Scriptures. The government could not, however, effectively enforce this legislative prohibition.

Illiteracy rather than legislation limited access to the new bibliocentric religion. Unfortunately, historians are unlikely to uncover the rate of illiteracy for women. Statistics, available primarily for the seventeenth century, suggest high rates of illiteracy: as late as the 1690s, outside London, some 80 percent of the female population could not yet sign their names. Even so, this figure hides important class and local variations. The figure for London—a 52 percent female illiteracy rate—reflects dramatic decline during the seventeenth century.[25] More significant, the general discrepancy between male and female illiteracy in London and East Anglia diminished during the century, from one literate woman for every eight literate men in the years prior to 1640 to one woman for three men by the late century.[26] The ratio refers to all women and therefore suggests a high degree of literacy for women of the gentry and noble rank.

Moreover, all statistics which have been compiled necessarily rest on signatures and therefore exclude those who knew how to read but could not write. The common method of pedagogy in the early modern period—teaching reading first, then writing—meant that many girls would acquire the ability to read and then, for cultural or economic reasons, leave the local petty school without acquiring the ability to write. Writing, more than reading, seems to have been viewed in utilitarian terms, its acquisition tied to occupational use.[27] Hence in the Cambridgeshire village of Orwell, boys learned to read, write, and figure accounts while girls learned to read, sew, knit and spin. Evidence suggests this pattern was typical elsewhere.[28] Moreover, if a young girl learned to write her alphabet as a child, the skill was easily lost without regular use in adult life. In the Henrician period, even Honor Lisle, an aristocrat whose husband served as Lord Deputy of Calais and who herself conducted extensive correspondence and could read handwriting as well as print, never demonstrated that she could write her own letters. Historians agree that a century later, women remained "overwhelmingly" illiterate in terms of writing skills.[29]

Beyond signatures, other forms of evidence—for example, the spread of dameschools, the popularity of chapbooks, a growing market for books addressed to women's issues, and book ownership itself—reinforce the notion that women may well have read without knowing how to write.[30] The traditional wisdom is still applicable: Protestantism and reading undoubtedly reinforced one another. If writing was linked to occupational needs, reading was necessary on grounds of religion. Thus Elizabethan Puritans in the town of Dedham sought to fund a scheme whereby "all yonge children of the towne be taught to reade Englishe."[31] According to the Protestant humanist writer Thomas Becon, parents should provide "wholesome, holy, and godly books" for children to read.[32] The Puritan minister William Gouge advised "When children begin to read, let them read the holy Scripture. . . . Thus will children sucke in religion. . . ."[33] And in 1616 the Protestant mother Dorothy Leigh wrote an advice book to her sons in part "to entreate and desire you, and in some sort to commaund you, that all your chyldren, be they Males or Females, may in their youth learne to read the Bible in their owne mother tongue. . . ."[34] Children generally progressed from hornbook, spelling book, and primer to catechism, psalter, and Bible as they learned to read. At home, at school, or in the parish church, they thus read within a religious context.[35]

Women did not participate in full literacy or in the so-called educational revolution of the Elizabethan and Jacobean period, which rested on the expansion of grammar schools and increased admissions to the universities. But at transient dame or petty schools, in the homes of family, from masters or mistresses, and through self-education, females likely learned to read in greater numbers than can be possibly quantified. Although some radical Protestants depended on memorization of the Bible, the ability to read penetrated to all social classes, including some of the women of those classes. Margaret Spufford suspects that in some families "a tradition of literacy" existed independent of economic factors.[36] The cultural consequences are not clear. Historians like Margaret Hannay and Mary Beth Norton emphasize the passivity involved in reading as opposed to the implicit activism and self-expression of writing. Hannay argues that incomplete literacy was a method of silencing women; Retha Warnicke criticizes Protestants for failing to institutionalize female education and provide adequate schools; Suzanne Hull emphasizes the patriarchal tone of the religious and devotional writings which women did read.[37] Yet the activities of Protestants like Anne Askew demonstrate that the ability to read, rather than silencing women, often led to greater activism.

A continuous tradition linked female Reformers and sectarians throughout the sixteenth and seventeenth centuries.[38] A few examples must serve to make the point. Although less than ten percent of those executed for heresy in Henry VIII's reign were women, by Mary's reign the figure rose to 20 percent. Like most of the Marian martyrs, the fifty-five female victims were predominantly of the lower classes; about half of them were married, one-fifth single, the rest widowed. Some embraced beliefs more radical than the Edwardian settlement of 1552.[39] Other Protestant women who remained in England but escaped persecution were active in the underground congregations of London and Colchester. In Canterbury and in Suffolk gentry women worked to form Protestant cells.[40]

During the Elizabethan period, "hotter" Protestant sorts tended toward Puritanism and, despite their dissatisfaction with aspects of the Elizabethan Settlement, the vast majority remained within the Church. Crossing class lines, Puritans were nevertheless most likely to come from the more substantial groups in society—artisan, yeomen, gentry, and noble families. The "godly women" of such families achieved their influence through the practice of household religion, discussed in section two of this chapter. Some also participated in public acts. At court, the Cooke sisters, especially Lady Anne Bacon and Lady Elizabeth Russell, patronized Puritan clergy or furthered the Protestant cause by their religious translations.[41] At the other end of the social spectrum, women were prominent in London mobs of the 1560s protesting "popish ceremonies," and a delegation of sixty women descended on the bishop of London on behalf of a suspended Puritan lecturer.[42] In 1588, when Puritan families, each with its own Bible, gathered on the Isle of Ely, "men, women, boys, girls, rustics, labourers and idiots" argued Scriptures with one another, or so complained the Jesuit William Weston.[43] Women assisted in the distribution of the Martin Marprelate tracts and as widows served as printers in other Puritan causes. In the seventeenth-century, godly women were well represented among Puritans presented at visitations.[44]

In contrast to Puritanism, Elizabethan separatism appears as a small, un-influential, largely lower-class movement. Women predominated among the separatists in Bridewell in 1568, and some immigrated without their husbands to the Netherlands in the 1580s.[45] By the 1630s, as sectarians gained greater visibility, women still contributed significantly, whether as godly matrons or as religious visionaries and enthusiasts.[46] The consensus is that even the revolutionary turmoil of the Civil War did little to weaken patriarchy, although the activities of sectarian women may have indirectly stimulated seventeenth-century feminist concerns.[47] It is worth noting that contemporaries were well aware of the issue of gender and the social implications of women's participation in religious causes. Thus, when Anne Stubbe, wife of the outspoken writer John, argued with the Puritan cleric John Cartwright about the advisability of separation from the Elizabethan church, Cartwright noted her "fraility as a woman."[48] Gender has recently been offered as a viable explanation for the phenomenon of female prophecy in the seventeenth century. What were seen as the traditional female qualities—passivity, irrationality, and passion—allowed contemporaries to accept women as visionaries while at the same time to deprive them of political power and respectability.[49]

II

The qualities which earned respectability are clear from the sermons preached at the funerals for godly women and the seventeenth-century "lives" compiled by Samuel Clarke. Typical was the gentlewoman Katherine Brettergh, "by nature very humble and lowlie . . . very meeke, and milde. . . ."[50] Mrs. Jane Ratcliffe, wife of the mayor of Chester, was "very sparing of her speech"; strength of character in the face of illness earned Mrs. Margaret Ducke praise for her "Masculine patience."[51] Often these women were said to enjoy affectionate marriages but allegedly always accepted their subordination to their husbands. The Elizabethan Puritan Philip Stubbes explained how his late, young wife Katherine had comforted him: "if he were sad, she was sad . . . if hee were angry, she would quickly please him."[52] Women themselves internalized these values. Writing to her unborn child, Elizabeth Jocelin, herself educated in the humanist tradition, warned that it were better for a daughter to hide her knowledge than "to boast it." Jocelin worried that a daughter would be more vulnerable than a son to the temptations of vanity and pride, for female nature was the weaker.[53] Dorothy Leigh wanted women "aboue all other morall vertues . . . to imbrase chastity, without which we are meere beasts, and no women."[54] Yet a mere catalogue of such passive virtues can be misleading. Clark's exemplary women led active lives, albeit within the confines of household religion. They were pious, which meant they read Scriptures daily, attended sermons, and spent time in private meditation. They were good mothers as well as wives, which meant they provided religious instruction and moral example for children as well as servants. They were charitable, which meant they not only dispensed alms but they also performed charitable acts within the community.

Rather than examine the activities of such Protestant wives and mothers, a good deal of recent historiography focuses on the nature of Protestant marriage in Tudor and Stuart England. Much of it theoretical or dependent on prescriptive sources, the scholarship tends to address two predominant issues: the "spiritualized household" and the patriarchal nature of that household. The Reformation removed priests from private households and de-emphasized the institutionalized church. Hence the phenomenon of the spiritualized household: religious observance and religious education increasingly took place within the confines of the family, which was responsible for its own spiritual care. For a number of historians the chief result of the spiritualized household was the enhanced authority of the father, a phenomenon which reached its height in Puritan families. Lawrence Stone goes so far as to speak in terms of "the despotic authority of husband and father," although he admits that increased authoritarianism cannot be proved.[55] According to Stone, harsh patriarchy was all the more likely given the lack of deep affection in families of the sixteenth and early seventeenth century. According to other historians, however, patriarchy did not exclude a more reciprocal Protestant marriage. The spiritualized household created mutuality and spiritual companionship, and it enhanced both marriage and motherhood, values derived from Christian humanism.[56] Moreover, the presence of strong emotional bonds, romantic love, and parental concern for children mitigated the practice of patriarchy.[57] Eric Richardson even argues that through household religion women exerted "great influence . . . over religious affairs."[58]

Biased toward religious women of the upper classes, literary sources emphasize the faith and devotion of those who practiced household religion. Analysis of women's diaries reveals their emotional involvement with God and their frequent preoccupation with childbirth and the illness or death of a child. But if women sought in religion a path to personal security and a way to give meaning to the haphazard events in their lives, they were in these respects no different from their male counterparts.[59] Like their husbands and sons, they experienced religious doubts and spiritual crisis. On her deathbed in 1601, Katherine Brettergh feared she had not loved God adequately.[60] Others also expressed their own sense of inadequacy. Thus Lady Margaret Hoby, a devout Puritan in the late Elizabethan period, spent her entire Sabbath in a series of prayers, religious discussions, and private meditations; besides her worship at home, she attended church in both the morning and afternoon where she heard two sermons and received catechism. Still she found fault with her own piety and complained in her journal: "this day, as euer, the diuell laboreth to hinder my profittable hearinge of the word. . . ." Not only was the devil a real force in Lady Hoby's personal life, but so too was the Lord, who frequently inflicted bodily punishments—stomachaches, toothaches, and the like—as a form of warning and "iust punishment to corricte my sinnes. . . ."[61]

For devout Protestant women, the importance of Scriptures and therefore the necessity of literacy was central. Writing in 1592, Philip Stubbes claimed that one could have seldom entered his home without finding the Bible "or some other good booke" in his wife's hand.[62] Lady Hoby records reading not only John Foxe but also such Puritan clerics as Thomas Cartwright, William Perkins, and Richard Greenham. Hoby and other godly women took notes on sermons in order to ponder what they had heard and share sermons with household servants.[63] Katherine Brettergh accustomed herself to reading daily eight chapters in the Bible as well as other "godlie books" for her further instruction.[64] Jane Radcliffe allegedly became proficient in religion by attending sermons "and reading good Books, the Bible especially (unto which she was addicted with an incredible desire). . . ." William Gouge praised one of his parishioners, Mrs. Margaret Ducke, on her death in 1646 for reading such books has "made her heart . . . a library of Christ."[65]

In his popular advice book *Of domesticall duties,* Gouge listed religious instruction of young children as a special responsibility of godly matrons. In fact, Christian humanists, both Catholic and Protestant, as well as subsequent Puritan writers consistently emphasized the mother's role in the training of her children. Writing in 1552, Thomas Becon advised parents to begin instruction as early as possible. "From their cradles" children should learn "godly words" and then proceed to sentences which "may kindle in them a love toward virtue." Parents should next teach their youngsters the Lord's Prayer, the Ten Commandments, the articles of faith, the act of saying grace. For Becon and subsequent writers, fathers *and* mothers who did not provide such education were themselves "ungodly." Gouge made a point to distinguish public assemblies, where a woman could not teach, from private families "in which she may and ought to *teach.* . . ."[66]

Historians disagree on how important or fulfilling such a role could be,[67] but evidence strongly suggests that women themselves took seriously their responsibility to provide religious instruction for their children and other members of their household. Rose Hickman, a Marian exile whose father and husband were London merchants, recalled late in her life how in Henrician times her mother had secretly read Protestant books to her and her sisters despite the danger involved.[68] Likewise, Lady Anne Clifford, always a staunch Anglican, recalled in 1674, at age eighty-four, how she was "bourne, bred and educated (in the Church of England) by my blessed mother." Interestingly, Clifford credited not her tutors but rather her mother—Margaret Russell, countess of Cumberland, an Elizabethan Puritan—with her religious education.[69] Grace Mildmay, the wife of a Puritan official at Elizabeth's court, wrote of her concern for the education of her daughter, an only child, and then of her grandchildren. In her journal she argued that parents "who seek not to make theyr children good" could themselves have no virtue.[70] Mildred Cecil and Lady Anne Bacon, two of the Cooke sisters, supervised the religious education of their sons and gave them spiritual advice as adults.[71] Elizabeth Jocelin wrote *The Mothers Legacie to her unborn Child* as a form of religious instruction. She prophetically feared that her own death in childbirth "might prevent me from executing that care I so exceedingly desired, I mean in religious training our Childe."[72] Margaret Hoby had no children of her own but nevertheless provided religious instruction for members of her household. She read to her "workwemen," attended their catechisms, heard one of her maids read from Foxe's *Book of Martyrs,* discussed sermons she had attended, and instructed one "Tomson wiffe in som principles of religion."[73]

Household religion also entailed performing charitable acts for members of the greater community. Gouge considered charity a joint duty: "husbands and wiues in distributing alms may receive good direction from one another." His own wife used her quarterly household allowance to provide relief for strangers, some of whom appealed privately to her.[74] Margaret Hoby's charitable acts included the practice of midwifery and general health care for the poor in her neighborhood.[75] In his exemplary lives, Samuel Clarke praises godly women for both their deeds and their open purses.[76] Such emphasis on charity was not unique to Protestantism, but it is worth noting as an important feature of household religion. Moreover, as W. K. Jordan and others have argued, Protestant philanthropy tended to have its own secular agenda. Jordan documents the philanthropic activities of Protestant women who supported almshouses, schools, loan funds for merchants, and the like. Lady Mildmay went so far as to devise a scheme for her estate reminiscent of poor-relief schemes adopted by various Elizabethan and Jacobean urban communities. According to Mildmay's plans, the able-bodied poor were to be relieved if they worked, poor children were to be maintained as apprentices, and loans given to families in need. Whereas Mildmay focused on the employable poor, Lady Anne Clifford assisted the so-called deserving poor, a category that included large numbers of widows, often elderly, and deserted wives with dependent children. Clifford maintained the almshouse which her mother had established for poor women and in the mid-seventeenth century established another such institution.[77]

The marital relationship was fundamental to the exercise of household religion, but some women relied on other personal relationships for additional or alternative sources of support in their daily activities. A number of godly women developed strong ties, even emotional dependence, on Puritan clergymen. Hoby's diary frequently mentions Richard Rhodes, a spiritual advisor. Rhodes did not reside in the Hoby household but apparently served as family chaplain and sometimes accompanied Lady Hoby on her travels. In 1600 she went to London alone but wrote to Rhodes and received "certaine papers of instruction" from him.[78] Earlier in the century, Mrs. Elizabeth Bowes established a "spiritual and ideological relationship" with John Knox, who became her son-in-law. Though married for some thirty years and mother to fifteen children, Bowes left her husband about 1555 to join Knox and her daughter in exile. Bowes relied on Knox to provide not only religious instruction and guidance but also reassurance for her own sense of inadequacy and sinfulness.[79] Other women, including Rose Hickman and Anne Locke, an important Elizabethan Puritan, were on close terms with Knox. Locke's second husband, the minister Edward Dering, also maintained a female following, among whom was Catherine Killigrew, one of the Cooke sisters.[80]

Undoubtedly, individual women acted on a variety of motives in establishing such relationships. Some—the example of Hoby comes to mind—may have sought to compensate for an unsatisfactory marital relationship, while others wanted no more than spiritual guidance as they confronted complex theological issues. For all of them, friendship with a cleric advisor was the only legitimate relationship permissible between a male companion and a respectable married woman.[81] Patrick Collinson has argued that many women sought spiritual direction because they found the doctrine of election "perplexing." But these women may have sought a mentor not because of their intellectual confusion but rather because of a sense of inadequacy and insecurity bred by a society which preached their inferiority and subordination. They are a long way from confident sectarian women and make Protestant household religion look a bit less innovative. As Collinson notes, at least some godly women "leant on the preachers as a Catholic would lean on his confessor."[82]

Godly women also drew support from one another, most noticeably in the strong bond between generations in mother–daughter relationships.[83] Although parental affection by no means followed lines of gender, strong mother–daughter ties are understandable. More easily than in the case of their sons, mothers remained closely involved in the instruction and training of their daughters even when in other households. As their daughters married and began families of their own, mothers served as figures of authority and offered advice on domestic matters. After Grace Mildmay's death, her daughter Mary collected and copied her mother's books of prescriptions and recommendations.[84] Anne Clifford depended on her mother for a variety of needs. In this unusual case, Anne allied with her widowed mother to contest her father's will. Anne faced opposition from her husband, the earl of Dorset, who harassed her to make a cash settlement, and indeed from the whole of the male establishment, including the king and the archbishop of Canterbury. Yet she and her mother "had much talk about this business," and although the matter was not settled in Margaret's lifetime, the two women never compromised on Anne's rightful inheritance. Anne also relied on her mother for more ordinary matters, writing to her about her own infant daughter and worrying when her mother's letters were late in arriving. As already noted, Anne respected her mother's piety, and at age sixty-three, she attributed her own survival as a child to her mother's "incessant" prayers for her safety.[85] Religion and affection also bound together Margaret Hoby and her mother, for they frequently visited one another and shared in household religious observance. Indeed Hoby's diary gives as strong a sense of the relationship she enjoyed with her mother as that she had with her husband.[86]

Writing in another context, the historian Patricia Crawford has asked if a "female subculture" existed. Crawford demonstrates that women, at times from different social classes, exchanged health cures and discussed menstrual disorders among themselves.[87] Evidence suggests that women also turned to one another for religious support to form a type of female network that could go beyond family and kin. In exile in Antwerp in the 1550s, Rose Hickman relied on a secret congregation of Protestants and through the "helpe of some godly weomen" had her child secretly baptized by a Protestant minister. In the next century, similar practices prevailed among female sectarians.[88] Margaret Hoby, in conversations very distinct from the religious instruction she provided her servants, sometimes discussed religion with other women. When visiting Matthew Hutton, archbishop of York, Hoby "talked with Mrs Huten of relegion." At a cousin's house, she had a "Conferrance with a relegious gentelwoman. . . ." Frequently on the Sabbath she "talked of the sarmon and good thinges" with a Mrs. Ormston. She returned from church on a Sabbath in 1600 to "reed of the bible with some Gentlewemen that were with me. . . ." Such activities make less remarkable the underground network created in the seventeenth century by female sectarians and suggest that some Protestant women, even in the Elizabethan era, overcame the isolation often attributed to household religion.[89]

III

Whatever their disagreements about the sources and inspiration of Elizabethan Catholicism, scholars agree that household religion prevailed among the literate Catholic laity. No matter that the Council of Trent banned Masses in private houses. Given the legal prohibition of Catholicism in England, the household with its surreptitious domestic Mass necessarily replaced the parish. The special circumstances surrounding Catholicism in England therefore made Christian humanism and its concept of the spiritualized household more relevant than Tridentine Catholicism. And women, numerically strong among recusants, found within Catholic household religion the opportunity for influence and action.[90]

Recusants were those Catholics who defied the Act of Uniformity and refused to attend services in the Elizabethan church. They are to be distinguished from Catholics who conformed outwardly in order to escape legal penalties and the stigma of being labeled a papist. Although a small minority of the population, about 2 percent by the mid-seventeenth century, recusants were the object of penal legislation and periodic Puritan agitation.[91] By the late Elizabethan period, they no longer posed the papal threat that was feared, but their commitment was strong enough to insure the survival of Catholicism within England. The high degree of female participation in their ranks is striking. In the city of York in 1576, nineteen out of the thirty-three persons not attending church were female; later that year the figure was fifty-one females out of sixty-nine recusants. Most of the women were married, and most cited grounds of conscience to explain their nonattendance.[92] In York, recusants came from artisan and trading families, but in gentry and noble families too "the staunchest and most zealous recusants were often women." In some cases husbands disapproved of their wives' recusancy. In others, men conformed, kept their legal and public status intact, yet condoned Catholicism at home within their families.[93]

As conforming husbands well understood, authorities faced special problems in proceeding against married recusant women. They could not impose fines, the usual penalty for nonattendance, since, according to common law, wives controlled no property. Imprisonment, the alternative punishment, disrupted families and under the circumstances seemed an unwarranted intrusion into family life. According to prevailing assumptions, as long as the husband himself conformed, he deserved the right to act as religious head of his household. But the dilemma remained: what of husbands who were unable or unwilling to make wives comply? In 1588, local authorities queried the Privy Council what to do about men who themselves went to church but allowed Mass in their homes for their wives. Even more troublesome were the recusant wives of a mayor of York and a mayor of Newcastle-upon-Tyne, public officials who set embarrassing examples and undoubtedly discouraged enforcement of penal legislation in their neighborhoods. The state never effectively solved this dilemma despite legislation in 1593 which allowed a husband to be sued jointly with his recusant wife.[94]

Historians who minimize the influence of women in Protestant household religion are willing to attribute an important role to recusant wives and mothers.[95] According to their argument, a Catholic wife did not have to contend with her husband as religious head of her household; priests, although spiritual authorities, were also dependent figures and only intermittently present in such households. In practice, however, Catholic women functioned in a patriarchal society no less than did their Protestant counterparts. And, as always, patriarchy varied according to circumstances and individual personalities. Margaret Clitherow, one of the few women actually executed for harboring priests, defied her husband with her recusancy, but, if her biographer is believed, she became emotionally dependent on priests, gave them her utmost confidence, and relied absolutely on their advice. "So long as she had with her a ghostly Father to serve God, no time seemed wearisome; for after her household business were despatched, she would once or twice a day serve (him), and no trouble nor sorrow could make her heavy during this time." Although defying her husband's wish that she conform, she enjoyed an affectionate marriage, and at her death she acknowledged her husband as her head.[96]

Strong parallels exist between aspects of Clitherow's daily spiritual regime and that of Protestant godly women. The wife of a butcher, Clitherow learned to read during times of imprisonment. At home she followed a rigorous schedule of religious worship that included an hour of private prayer and meditation both morning and night, an hour of prayer in the afternoon "with her children about her," and, whenever possible, Mass and confession twice a week. Her biographer singles out "her humility, the Foundation of all her virtues." He considers the spiritual comfort she provided others and her harboring of priests as charitable deeds.[97] Lives of other exemplary Catholic women emphasize more traditional feminine acts of charity, including nursing, midwifery, and general care of the poor.[98]

Margaret Clitherow acted in a hostile environment to perpetuate a culture and religion. It was this environment, hostile to the very survival of Catholicism, and not the nature of their households, which separated recusant wives and mothers from their Protestant counterparts. Given their environment, the religious instruction and moral leadership which recusant women provided as alternative models became all the more significant. In this respect, English recusant women resembled French Huguenot women, although they never participated in public policy as did some Huguenot women. Even in the private realm, however, their influence was such that the Elizabethan Privy Council complained "by their example whole families refuse to resort to Church. . . ."[99] Dorothy Lawson, a Yorkshire recusant, provides a good example. Her husband, Sir Ralph Lawson, conformed to the Elizabethan church. But her mother-in-law, a lapsed recusant, together with Ralph's siblings and their families, followed the young Dorothy Lawson's lead and instituted Catholic observance in their households. Even her husband on his deathbed asked for a priest. Her Yorkshire neighbors also felt Lawson's presence, for she provided them opportunity to attend daily Mass and send their children for daily catechisms in her chapel. Likewise Magdalen Browne, Viscountess Montague, encouraged her relatives to return to the Catholic church and in widowhood supervised an important Catholic household of eighty persons.[100]

The influence such women had on their children is remarkable. Dorothy Lawson learned her creed from her own mother, a victim of imprisonment. Lawson in turn sent her children abroad for a Catholic education: one became a Benedictine monk, one a Jesuit, and four became nuns.[101] Margaret Clitherow harbored not only priests but also a schoolmaster who taught her children and others as well. Two of her elder sons she secretly sent abroad to study for the priesthood, a strategy other recusant mothers, including Elizabeth Cary, also followed. Cary, Viscountess Falkland, kept her Catholicism a secret from her husband for over twenty years and on revelation of her religion, she endured his cruelty as well as the disapproval of some of her eleven children. Yet of her eight surviving children, six ultimately joined holy orders, including all four of her daughters. Again evidence suggests the existence of strong mother–daughter relations. Margaret Clitherow, just before her death, sent her hose and shoes to her eldest daughter, Anne, age twelve, as a sign that the daughter should follow the mother in service to God. Subsequently Anne joined a Flemish Augustinian convent. Clitherow is said to have inspired Jane Wiseman, an Essex widow, who hid priests but whose life was spared by Queen Elizabeth and whom James subsequently pardoned. All four of Wiseman's daughters entered nunneries on the continent.[102]

One Catholic mother, Elizabeth Grymeston, provides vivid evidence both of maternal religious instruction and moral example in an advice book addressed to her son, the sole survivor among her eight children. Published in 1604, one year after her death, her treatise closely resembles subsequent advice books written by Protestant mothers Dorothy Leigh and Elizabeth Jocelin, although, significantly, Grymeston omits the Protestant emphasis on Scriptures and literacy. Like her Protestant counterparts, however, Grymeston was motivated to write out of concern for her child's salvation. She wishes her son good fortune in the two most crucial hours of his life: "In the houre of thy marriage, and at the houre of thy death." She shows deep affection: "there is no loue so forcible as the loue of an affectionate mother to hir natural childe." That love is best shown "in aduising hir children, out of her own experience, to eschewe euill. . . ." The Catholic Jocelin thus seems to have agreed with humanists and Puritans on the important role which a mother played within household religion.[103]

IV

Women were involved in the process of Reformation and Counter Reformation through public discourse, patronage, and public example, and to a greater extent through the realm of the family. Restricted to the household, they dealt with options and opportunities significant but undeniably limited. The Elizabethan Puritan classis at Dedham made clear how low a profile women should maintain. When the query was made "whether it were convenient a woman should pray having a better gift than her husband," the issue was tabled and never even addressed.[104] Neither Protestant nor Catholic authorities were comfortable when women assumed a public role. When a host of Elizabethan Puritan women descended on Edmund Grindal, then bishop of London, on behalf of a suspended lecturer, Grindal was aghast. He suggested that he would talk instead with half a dozen of their husbands.[105] When Mary Ward, a nun and Catholic educator, successfully organized an institute of Catholic women who led uncloistered lives on the continent and taught poor girls in free schools, the Catholic hierarchy reacted negatively, suppressed the Rule and closed a number of the institute's houses.[106] Ward's activities—like those of contemporary female Protestant sectarians—make clear that some women rebelled aginst patriarchal restrictions in order to lead a life which they defined as meaningful.

At the same time, it is anachronistic to assume that women who acted solely within the context of household religion necessarily felt themselves oppressed or even relegated to a separate, private sphere. The very existence of two spheres, private and public, at least in the modern sense, remains problematic for Tudor and early Stuart England. By the seventeenth century, contemporaries did recognize a dichotomy between domestic or family business on the one hand and activity outside the home on the other.[107] Nonetheless, in intellectual, political, economic, and religious terms, the early modern English family was integral to society and state.[108] The household served as a productive economic unit, whether or not the wife participated in the public marketplace. In intellectual and political terms, the patriarchal family served as analogy for the hierarchal state. Likewise, in an era when the crown predicated all policy on religious uniformity, contemporaries never doubted an organic relationship between family and state in matters of religion. From the Henrician Reformation until the outbreak of civil war, the men who controlled the machinery of church and state believed religious pluralism threatened political stability. Under such circumstances, religious practice never became a private matter relegated to a separate sphere.

The futility of separating public and private spheres is most apparent in the case of recusant households that harbored Catholic priests, a capital offense punishable by death. It is estimated that hundreds of women, some spinsters and widows, received priests into their homes, although sometimes only for a few hours at a time. Even when both spouses were recusant, the wife usually made the arrangements for the priest's arrival and his secret stay.[109] At first impression, Protestant women would seem to have played a less dramatic role in reinforcing and transferring a religious culture largely sanctioned by the state. But in the long term, the importance which godly women placed on the literacy of all their children had profound cultural implications.

Household religion in Tudor and early Stuart England remained confined to a minority of families, for, whether Catholic or Protestant, it demanded certain material resources and some level of literacy. What then were the religious beliefs and practices of the inarticulate majority of the population? The concept of "popular religion" is usually cited to answer this question. Applied to the majority of the population, popular religion is defined as a set of attitudes, largely devoid of "sound" doctrine, comprised instead of magic, ritual, superstition, and apathy.[110] According to this view, the literacy demanded of Protestantism confined its appeal and made the bibliocentric religion "a disaster in the countryside."[111] Instead of rapid and thorough Reformation, a "folklorised Christianity" prevailed, a syncretic mixture of beliefs, in part irreligious, in part ignorant, in part oppositional to the established church.[112] Some statistics have been cited to show how superficial was the process of Reformation: less than 10 percent of the Elizabethan population in Kent understood basic Christian doctrine; "something like" 20 percent of the Kentish population did not regularly attend church in the late sixteenth century; and excommunicants comprised about 15 percent of the population in scattered parishes in the early seventeenth century.[113] The concept of popular religion is, however, not free from flaws: statistics hide methodological problems, sources contradict one another, and what is one person's superstition may easily function as another's religion. Moreover, the concept of popular religion and its corollary, the existence of two cultures, one religious and respectable, the other plebeian or popular, too easily implies a correlation between religious piety and social class that did not necessarily exist.[114]

In all the debate about the religious views of the humbler classes, little attention has yet been given gender as a category of analysis. The burdens of daily existence confronting women of the lower classes would seem to have been so great as to have left little time or energy for devout religion. When towns like Warwick, Salisbury, Ipswich, and Norwich drew up surveys of their poorer citizens worthy of relief, women were seen as a majority of the indigent. Many of these were elderly women or else abandoned wives with dependent children. Frequently they were already employed, although they could not earn enough to sustain themselves or their dependents.[115] Where households were intact, women also performed a variety of menial tasks for very low wages. Their economic vulnerability, their domestic responsibilities, and the demands of employment left them physically and emotionally exhausted. Added to all the demands on their time, the problem of child care may itself have been decisive in preventing church attendance. In one case, suggesting the danger in making assumptions about household roles, when an Elizabethan husband was presented for absence from communion, he claimed he had small children to tend at home in order that his wife could receive communion. In another episode, a woman brought her small child to church with her, only to be reprimanded when the child disturbed the minister. The mother's resort to "lewd" rather than apologetic speech was perhaps a sign of her own frustration.[116]

Given our current state of knowledge, we cannot say how such women (or their male counterparts) saw religion. Thousands who conformed to the Elizabethan liturgy left no record of their thoughts, and it is impossible to determine whether they acted out of personal commitment, obligation, or habit. Even when evidence does survive, it is often inconclusive and enigmatic. What can the historian conclude in the case of the Canterbury widow who committed suicide, whose property was valued at only £8, but who had in her possession an old Bible?[117]

Whether representative or isolated, individuals of the lower classes occasionally do emerge from the records when, for the sake of religion, they sacrificed their immediate interests and jeopardized their personal safety. One cannot but be impressed, for example, by the likes of Susannah Cooke, who in 1689 defied the board of governors at St. Bartholomew's hospital by refusing communion in the Anglican church. Cooke was employed as the hospital cook, a staff position that brought room and board and a modest annual salary. The board of governors, appointed by the corporation of London, represented the Anglican establishment. Yet so impressed were they by Cooke that they allowed "this upright woman" to retain temporary residence in the hospital.[118] Cooke was either widowed or single; by her stand, she jeopardized and lost both her home and her salary. In a similar episode, three women employed at St. Thomas' Hospital as sisters—a menial position, part nurse and part housekeeper—were discharged during the Commonwealth when, despite a warning, they persisted in their Quaker opinions. In 1699 a widow, who served as sister to the charity ward at St. Bartholomew's was discharged when she acknowledged herself a Roman Catholic and refused communion in the Church of England.[119]

It is futile to debate whether the legacy of the Reformation was a negative or positive influence in the lives of these women. The religious changes of the sixteenth century were linked to a variety of intellectual, social, political, and economic forces, each complex, ambiguous, even contradictory. They affected individual lives in a variety of ways that transcend any single, simple set of criteria. Consider the sisters employed by London hospitals. As nurses they enjoyed little of the dignity and respect given to those godly matrons who voluntarily performed charitable acts among neighbors. The Reformation had brought the secularization of the hospitals and deprived single women of the option of holy orders. Rather than a spiritual avocation, their work had become menial employment. Yet clearly the Reformation had created a pluralistic society which touched these women. In its wake choices and values developed which allowed some, in the midst of both poverty and patriarchy, to create their own meaning to their lives.

NOTES

I wish to thank Sherrin Marshall, Paul Seaver, and Lois Schwoerer for reading earlier versions of this essay and providing me the benefit of their comments and suggestions.

    1. Richard Hooker quoted in Patrick Collinson, *Godly People: Essays on English Protestantism and Puritanism* (London: Hambledon Press, 1983), p. 274; Sara H. Mendelson, "Stuart Women's Diaries and Occasional Memoirs" in *Women in English Society 1500–1800*, ed. Mary Prior (London: Methuen, 1985), p. 185; Nancy L. Roelker, "The Appeal of Calvinism to the French Noblewomen in the Sixteenth Century," *Journal of Interdisciplinary History* 2 (Spring 1972): 391–413.

    2. Among those who comment on this issue, see Keith Thomas, "Women and the Civil War Sects" in *Crisis in Europe 1560–1660*, ed. Trevor Aston (Garden City, N.J.: Doubleday, 1965), pp. 336, 346; Patrick Collinson, *The Religion of Protestants: The Church in English Society 1559–1625* (Oxford: Clarendon Press, 1982), p. 241; Collinson, *Godly People*, pp. 274–76; Richard L. Greaves, ed., *Triumph over Silence: Women in Protestant History* (Westport, Conn.: Greenwood Press, 1985), p. 6; Lawrence Stone, *Crisis of the Aristocracy* (Oxford: Clarendon Press, 1965), pp. 738–39; Ralph A. Houlbrooke, *The English Family 1450–1700* (London: Longman, 1984), p. 113; Dorothy P. Ludlow, "Shaking Patriarchy's Foundations: Sectarian Women in England, 1641–1700" in *Triumph over Silence: Women in Protestant History*, ed. Richard L. Greaves, p. 116; R. C. Richardson, *Puritanism in North-West England: A Regional Study of the Diocese of Chester to 1642* (Manchester: Manchester University Press, 1972), pp. 112–13. For relevant continental studies, see Roelker, "The Appeal of Calvinism to French Noblewomen," pp. 409–11; Natalie Z. Davis, *Society and Culture in Early Modern France* (Stanford, Calif.: Stanford University Press, 1975), pp. 66 ff.; Sherrin Marshall Wyntjes, "Women in the Reformation Era" in *Becoming Visible: Women in European History*, ed. Renate Bridenthal and Claudia Koonz (Boston: Houghton Mifflin, 1977), pp. 171 ff.

3. Cf. Joan Kelly's seminal argument that when family or kinship played a significant role in political structures, women enjoy favorable status and influence; Joan Kelly, *Women, History, and Theory* (Chicago: University of Chicago Press, 1984), pp. 10–14.

4. For recent accounts, see Retha M. Warnicke, *Women of the English Renaissance and Reformation* (Westport, Conn.: Greenwood Press, 1983) and Margaret P. Hannay, *Silent But for the Word: Tudor Women as Patrons, Translators, and Writers of Religious Works* (Kent, Ohio: Kent State University Press, 1985).

5. Christopher Haigh, "The Recent Historiography of the English Reformation," *The Historical Journal* 25 (December 1982): 995–1007.

6. For the now classic interpretation of Protestant advance, see A. G. Dickens, *The English Reformation* (New York: Schocken Books, 1964).

7. Claire Cross, " 'Great Reasoners in Scripture': Women Lollards 1386–1530" in *Medieval Women*, ed. Derek Baker (Oxford: Blackwell, 1978), pp. 359–60, 366, 378–80.

8. Ibid., pp. 364–65, 369–78.

9. On residual Lollardy, see ibid. p. 375; Margaret Bowker, *The Henrician Reformation: The Diocese of Lincoln under John Longland 1521–1547* (Cambridge: Cambridge University Press, 1981), p. 178; John F. Davis, *Heresy and Reformation in the South-East of England, 1520–1559* (London: Royal Historical Society, 1983), pp. 93, 115–16, 149. Davis discusses Joan Bocher, most notorious of the female Lollards who subsequently embraced radical Protestantism; Davis, pp. 91–92, 104–5.

10. John Davis, *Heresy and Reformation in the South-East of England*, p. 63.

11. Ibid, pp. 92–93.

12. Mary Beth Rose, "Making Gender the Question," *Journal of British Studies*, 25 (July 1986): 341.

13. For example, Thomas Becon, *The Catechism of Thomas Becon*, ed. John Ayre, Parker Society, no. 3 (Cambridge, 1844), p. 340; John Lyster, *A rule how to bring vp children* (T. East, 1588), p. 27; Dorothy Leigh, *The Mothers Blessing; Or the godly counsaile of a Gentle-woman not long since deceased* . . . (London: for John Budge, 1616), pp. 33–43; William Gouge, *Of domesticall duties* (J. Haviland for W. Bladen, 1622), p. 259.

14. John Bale in Anne Askew, *The lattre examinacyon of Anne Askewe, latelye martyred in Smithfelde, by the wycked Synagoge of Antichriste, with the Elucydacyon of John Bale* (Wesel: D. Van der Straten, 1547), p. 15.

15. Ibid.; also Anne Askew, *The first examinacyon of Anne Askewe* . . . (Wesel: D. Van der Straten, 1546); Elaine V. Beilin, "Anne Askew's Self-Portrait in the *Examinations*" in *Silent But for the Word: Tudor Women as Patrons, Translators, and Writers of Religious Works*, ed. Margaret Hannay, pp. 77–91.

16. Beilen, "Anne Askew's Self-Portrait in the *Examination*," p. 89.

17. Warnicke, *Women of the English Renaissance and Reformation*, pp. 75–76.

18. Bale in Askew, *The first examinacyon* . . ., p. 10r.

19. Betty Travitsky, *The Paradise of Women: Writings by Englishwomen of the Renaissance* (Westport, Conn.: Greenwood Press, 1981), p. 36; Beilen, "Anne Askew's Self-Portrait in the *Examinations*," p. 78.

20. Bale in Askew, *The lattre examinacyon* . . ., p. 35r.

21. Askew, *The first examinacyon* . . ., pp. 10r, 31v.

22. Ibid., p. 38v. See Beilen, "Anne Askew's Self-Portrait in the *Examinations*" for further discussion of the significance of gender. 23. Askew, *The first examinacyon* . . ., p. 27r.

24. 34 & 35 Hen. VIII, c. 1. J. F. Mozley, *Coverdale and His Bibles* (London: Lutterworth Press, 1953), p. 284.

25. David Cressy, *Literacy and the Social Order: Reading and Writing in Tudor and Stuart England* (Cambridge: Cambridge University Press, 1980), pp. 119–21, 144–45,

147; Rosemary O'Day, *Education and Society, 1500–1800: The Social Foundations of Education in Early Modern Britain* (London: Longman, 1982), p. 191.

26. Lawrence Stone, *The Family, Sex and Marriage in England 1500–1800* (New York: Harper and Row, 1977), p. 353.

27. Jonathan Barry, "Popular Culture in Seventeenth-Century Bristol" in *Popular Culture in Seventeenth-Century England*, ed. Barry Reay (London: Croom Helm, 1985), p. 63.

28. Margaret Spufford, *Contrasting Communities: English Villagers in the Sixteenth and Seventeenth Centuries* (Cambridge: Cambridge University Press, 1974), p. 203. In the late seventeenth century, Christ's Hospital employed female personnel to teach female students the subjects of reading and spinning. William Lempriere, *History of the Girls' School of Christ's Hospital, London, Hoddesdon, and Hertford* (Cambridge: Cambridge University Press, 1924), p. 14; Guildhall Library, MS. 12878/1, fols. 81, 96–99.

29. Muriel Byrne, ed., *The Lisle Letters* (Chicago: University of Chicago Press, 1981), 4:375–76; Mendelson, "Stuart Women's Diaries and Occasional Memoirs," p. 182.

30. William Hudson and John C. Tingey, eds., *The Records of the City of Norwich* (Norwich: Jarrold and Sons, 1910), 2:352–53; Barry, "Popular Culture in Seventeenth-Century Bristol," p. 63; Keith Wrightson, *English Society, 1580–1680* (London: Hutchinson, 1982), pp. 185, 198; Spufford, *Contrasting Communities*, pp. 207–10; Warnicke, *Women of the English Renaissance and Reformation*, p. 153; Suzanne Hull, *Chaste, Silent and Obedient: English Books for Women, 1475–1640* (San Marino, Calif.: Huntingdon Library, 1982); Margaret Spufford, *Small Books and Pleasant Histories: Popular Fiction and Its Readership in Seventeenth-Century England* (Athens: University of Georgia Press, 1981); Peter Clark, "The Ownership of Books in England, 1560–1640"in *Schooling and Society*, ed. Lawrence Stone (Baltimore: Johns Hopkins University Press, 1976), p. 211.

31. Roland Greene Usher, ed., *The Presbyterian movement in the reign of Queen Elizabeth as illustrated by the Minute book of the Dedham classis, 1582–1589* (London: Royal Historical Society, 1905), p. 100.

32. Becon, *The Catechism*, p. 351.

33. Gouge, *Of domesticall duties*, p. 539.

34. Leigh, *The Mothers Blessing*, p. 24.

35. Barry, "Popular Culture in Seventeenth-Century Bristol," p. 64. Philippa Tudor, "Religious Instruction for Children and Adolescents in the Early English Reformation," *Journal of Ecclesiastical History* 35 (July 1984):391–413, does not address the issue of gender.

36. Spufford, *Contrasting Communities*, pp. 203–204. Cross suggests some women educated themselves; Claire Cross, " 'He-Goats before the Flocks': A Note on the Part Played by Women in the Founding of Some Civil War Churches" in *Popular Belief and Practice*, ed. G. J. Cuming and Derek Baker (Cambridge: Cambridge University Press, 1972), p. 201.

37. Margaret P. Hannay, ed., *Silent But for the Word*, pp. 7–8; Mary Beth Norton, "The Evolution of White Women's Experience in Early America," *American Historical Review* 89 (June 1984): 607–8; Warnicke, *Women of the English Renaissance and Reformation*, pp. 154, 177; Hull, *Chaste, Silent and Obedient*, p. 140.

38. Cross, "He-Goats before the Flocks," p. 195.

39. Warnicke, *Women of the English Renaissance and Reformation*, pp. 68, 74; John Davis, *Heresy and Reformation in the South-East of England, 1520–1559*, pp. 143–44. The marital status of six female martyrs is not clear; Warnicke, p. 74.

40. Warnicke, *Women of the English Renaissance and Reformation*, p. 76; Mary Prior, "Reviled and Crucified Marriages: The Position of Tudor Bishops' Wives" in *Women in English Society 1500–1800*, ed. Mary Prior, p. 128; Spufford, *Contrasting*

Communities, p. 247; Peter Clark, *English Provincial Society from the Reformation to the Revolution: Religion, Politics and Society in Kent, 1500–1640* (Hassocks: Harvester, 1977), p. 100.

41. Richard L. Greaves, "Foundation Builders: The Role of Women in Early English Nonconformity" in *Triumph over Silence*, ed. Richard Greaves, pp. 79, 81; Patrick Collinson, *The Elizabethan Puritan Movement* (London: Jonathan Cape, 1967), p. 443; Mary Ellen Lamb, "The Cooke Sisters: Attitudes toward Learned Women in the Renaissance" in *Silent But for the Word*, ed. Margaret Hannay, pp. 107–25.

42. Collinson, *The Elizabethan Puritan Movement*, p. 93; cf. p. 82. Also Collinson, *Godly People*, p. 274.

43. Weston quoted in Spufford, *Contrasting Communities*, p. 263.

44. Warnicke, *Women of the English Renaissance and Reformation*, p. 146; Greaves, "Foundation Builders: The Role of Women in Early English Nonconformity," pp. 86, 83; Collinson, *Godly People*, p. 283; Richardson, *Puritanism in North-West England*, pp. 109–10. Cf. Cross, "He-Goats before the Flocks," p. 198.

45. Greaves, "Foundation Builders: The Role of Women in Early English Nonconformity," p. 76.

46. Cross, "He-Goats before the Flocks," p. 201; Peter Burke, "Popular Culture in Seventeenth-Century London" in *Popular Culture in Seventeenth-Century England*, ed. Barry Reay, p. 42.

47. Cf. Thomas, "Women and the Civil War Sects," pp. 355–56; Ludlow, "Shaking Patriarchy's Foundations," pp. 115–17; Hilda Smith, *Reason's Disciples: Seventeenth-Century English Feminists* (Urbana: University of Illinois Press, 1982); Patricia Crawford, "Women's Published Writings 1600–1700" in *Women in English Society 1500–1800*, ed. Mary Prior, p. 213.

48. Cartwright quoted in Warnicke, *Women of the English Renaissance and Reformation*, p. 146.

49. Phyllis Mack, "Women as Prophets during the English Civil War," *Feminist Studies* 8 (1982): 35.

50. William Harrison and William Leygh, *Deaths Advantage Little Regarded, and the Soules solace against sorrow . . . two funerall Sermons . . . at the buriall of Mistris Katherin Brettergh . . .* (London: Felix Kyngston, 1617), p. 79.

51. Samuel Clarke, *A Collection of the Lives of Ten Eminent Divines* (London: for William Miller, 1662), p. 417, 493.

52. Philip Stubbes, *Cristal Glas for Christian Women* (London: Richard Jhones, 1592), sig. A 3ʳ.

53. Elizabeth Joceline, *The Mothers Legacie to her unborn Child* (London: John Harland, 1624), sig A 3ᵛ and p. 33.

54. Leigh, *The Mothers Blessing*, p. 43.

55. Stone, *The Family, Sex and Marriage in England*, pp. 151–55, 216. For others who comment on Protestantism, patriarchy, and the household, see Christopher Hill, *Society and Puritanism in Pre-Revolutionary England* (New York: Schocken, 1964), pp. 443–81; Thomas, "Women and the Civil War Sects," p. 333; Gordon Schochet, *Patriarchalism in Political Thought: The Authoritarian Family and Political Speculation and Attitudes Especially in Seventeenth-Century England* (Oxford: Basil Blackwell, 1975), pp. 57–58; Ian Maclean, *The Renaissance Notion of Woman: A Study in the Fortunes of Scholasticism and Medical Science in European Intellectual Life* (Cambridge: Cambridge University Press, 1980), pp. 84–85.

56. The literature on this issue is substantial with many variations in interpretation. See Kathleen Davies, "The Sacred Condition of Equality: How Original Were Puritan Doctrines of Marriage?" *Social History* 5 (May 1977):563–80; Margo Todd, *Christian Humanism and the Puritan Social Order* (Cambridge: Cambridge University Press, 1987); Levin Schucking, *The Puritan Family: A Social Study from the Literary Sources*, trans. Brian Battershaw (London: Routledge and Kegan Paul, 1969); Betty

Travitsky, "The New Mother of the English Renaissance (1489–1659): A Descriptive Catalogue," *Bulletin of Research in the Humanities* 82 (Spring 1979):63–89; Natalie Davis, *Society and Culture in Early Modern France*, pp. 79–88. For useful studies which examine godly women in the context of their families, see Jacqueline Levy, *Puritans and Roundheads: The Harleys of Brampton Bryan and the Outbreak of the English Civil War* (Cambridge: Cambridge University Press, forthcoming 1989); Patricia Crawford, "Katharine and Philip Henry and Their Children: A Case Study in Family Ideology," *Transactions of the Historic Society of Lancashire and Cheshire* 134 (1984):39–73; Miriam Chrisman, "Family and Religion in Two Noble Families: French Catholic and English Puritan," *Journal of Family History* 8 (Summer 1983): 190–210.

57. Alan Macfarlane, *The Family Life of Ralph Josselin, A Seventeenth-Century Clergyman* (New York: Norton, 1970), p. 106–109; Mendelson, "Stuart Women's Diaries and Occasional Memoirs, p. 193; Houlbrooke, *The English Family 1450–1700*, p. 119; Steven Ozment, *When Fathers Ruled: Family Life in Reformation Europe* (Cambridge, Mass.: Harvard University Press, 1983); Lois G. Schwoerer, "Seventeenth-Century English Women Engraved in Stone?" *Albion* 16 (Winter 1984): 397 ff.; Paul S. Seaver, *Wallington's World: A Puritan Artisan in Seventeenth-Century London* (Stanford, Calif.: Stanford University Press, 1985), pp. 75 ff., 87–92.

58. Richardson, *Puritanism in North-West England* p. 110.

59. Mendelson, "Stuart Women's Diaries and Occasional Memoirs," pp. 186–87, 197–98. Cf. Macfarlane, *The Family Life of Ralph Josselin*, pp. 171–82 and Seaver, *Wallington's World*, pp. 46–50, 52, 65. See for example, Clarke, *A Collection of the Lives of Ten Eminent Divines*, pp. 415, 420.

60. William Harrison, *A Brief Discovrse of the Christian Life and death of Mistris Katherin Brettergh . . .* (London: Felix Kyngston, 1617), pp. 11 ff.

61. Margaret Hoby, *Diary of Lady Margaret Hoby 1599–1605*, ed. Dorothy M. Meads (Boston: Houghton Mifflin, 1930), pp. 66, 64.

62. Stubbes, *Cristal Glas for Christian Women*, sig. A 2ᵛ.

63. Hoby, *Diary*, pp. 69, 74, 87.

64. Harrison and Leygh, *Deaths Advantage Little Regarded*, p. 79.

65. Clarke, *A Collection of the Lives of Ten Eminent Divines*, pp. 416, 491–92.

66. Gouge, *Of domesticall duties*, pp. 546, 258–59; Becon, *The Catechism*, pp. 4, 348. Robert Cleaver argued that a child's piety advertised the mother's worth; Robert Cleaver, *Bathshebas instrvctions to her sonne Lemvel . . .* (London: J. Beale for R. Jackson, 1614), p. 67.

67. Among those historians who see in religious instruction a meaningful role for women are Todd, *Christian Humanism and the Puritan Social Order*, p. 105; Roelker, "The Appeal of Calvinism to French Noblewomen in the Sixteenth Century," pp. 406–407; Greaves, "Foundation Builders: The Role of Women in Early English Nonconformity," p. 77; Houlbrooke, *The English Family 1450–1700*, p. 148; Travitsky, *The Paradise of Women*, pp. 9, 49–51. For a different point of view, see Schucking, *The Puritan Family*, pp. 87–88; Warnicke, *Women of the English Renaissance and Reformation*, p. 153; Thomas, "Women and the Civil War Sects," p. 347.

68. Rose Hickman, "Religion and Politics in Mid-Tudor England through the Eyes of an English Protestant Woman: The Recollections of Rose Hickman," ed. Maria Dowling and Joy Shakespeare, *Bulletin of the Institute of Historical Research* 60 (May 1982):97.

69. Clifford's will quoted in George Charles Williamson, *Lady Anne Clifford, Countess of Dorset, Pembroke and Montgomery, 1590–1676: Her Life, Letters and Work . . .* (Kendal: T. Wilson, 1922), p. 465.

70. Excerpt from Mildmay's journal is printed in Rachel Weigall, "An Elizabethan Gentlewoman: The Journal of Lady Mildmay, circa 1570–1617," *The Quarterly Review* 125 (1911):128.

71. Todd, *Christian Humanism and the Puritan Social Order,* p. 106.

72. Jocelin, *The Mothers Legacie to her unborn Child,* sig. B 34ᵛ (sic).

73. Hoby, *Diary,* pp. 62, 81, 85, 120, 125, 175. For further examples of women providing religious instruction, see Nicholas Guy, *Pieties pillar: or, a sermon preached at the funerall of Elizabeth Gouge* (London: G. Millar, 1625), pp. 45–46; Clarke, *A Collection of the Lives of Ten Eminent Divines,* pp. 491, 506–507; Houlbrooke, *The English Family 1450–1700,* p. 148.

74. Gouge, *Of domesticall duties,* p. 265; Guy, *Pieties pillar,* pp. 46–47.

75. Hoby, *Diary,* pp. 63, 117, 72, 100, and *passim.*

76. Clarke, *A Collection of the Lives of Ten Eminent Divines,* pp. 438–39, 489, 507–508.

77. W. K. Jordan, *Philanthropy in England 1480–1660* (London: George Allen and Unwin, 1959), pp. 222–24, 227–28, 353–55; W. K. Jordan, *Charities of Rural England 1480–1660* (London: George Allen and Unwin, 1961), pp. 96–98, 125–26, 138; Weigal, "An Elizabethan Gentlewoman," pp. 128–30; Wallace Notestein, *Four Worthies: John Chamberlain, Anne Clifford, John Taylor, Oliver Heywood* (London: Jonathan Cape, 1956), p. 160; Edward Rainbowe, *A sermon preached at the funeral of the right honorable Anne Countess of Pembroke, Dorset and Montgomery . . .* (London: R. Royston and H. Broom, 1677), p. 23.

78. Hoby, *Diary,* pp. 154, 159 and p. 243, n. 180.

79. Jasper Ridley, *John Knox* (New York: Oxford University Press, 1968), pp. 130 ff.

80. Collinson, *Godly People,* p. 284.

81. I am grateful to Paul Seaver for discussing this issue with me.

82. Collinson, *Godly People,* pp. 275. Cf. Richardson, *Puritanism in North-West England,* p. 111.

83. For comment on mother-daughter relationships, see Houlbrooke, *The English Family 1450–1700,* p. 187; Roelker, "The Appeal of Calvinism to the French Noblewomen in the Sixteenth Century," p. 412; Warnicke, *Women of the English Renaissance and Reformation,* p. 150 and cf. pp. 126–27.

84. Weigall, "An Elizabethan Gentlewoman," p. 130; see also pp. 128, 135.

85. Clifford, Anne, *The Diary of the Lady Anne Clifford,* ed. V. Sackville-West (New York: George H. Doran, 1923), pp. 23, 26, 29–32; Williamson, *Lady Anne Clifford,* pp. 58, 147–48, 153. Clifford in her will called her mother, Margaret Russell, "one of the most vertuousse and religiousse ladies that lived in her time." Williamson, p. 465.

86. Hoby, *Diary,* pp. 73, 130, and *passim.*

87. Patricia Crawford, "Menstruation in Seventeenth-Century England," *Past and Present* 91 (May 1981):65, 71.

88. Hickman, "Religion and Politics," p. 101; Cross, "He-Goats before the Flocks," p. 196.

89. Hoby, *Diary,* pp. 73, 131, 75 ff. For networks among female sectarians, see Greaves, "Foundation Builders: The Role of Women in Early English Nonconformity," p. 78; Ludlow, "Shaking Patriarchy's Foundations," p. 106. Warnicke sees isolation in household religion; Warnicke, *Women of the English Renaissance and Reformation,* p. 179.

90. Christopher Haigh, "The continuity of Catholicism in the English Reformation," *Past and Present* 93 (November 1981):65–66; John Bossy, "The Character of Elizabethan Catholicism" in *Crisis in Europe 1560–1660,* ed. Trevor Aston, p. 237. For a discussion of how Tridentine Catholicism undermined the household, see Todd, *Christian Humanism and the Puritan Social Order,* chap. 7.

91. Reay cites the figure of 1 or 2 percent by the 1640s; Barry Reay, "Popular Religion" in *Popular Culture in Seventeenth-Century England,* ed. Barry Reay, p. 111.

92. Angelo Raine, ed., *York Civic Records*, Yorkshire Archaeological Society 115 (1949):117–18, 130–37; Marie B. Rowlands, "Recusant Women 1560–1640" in *Women in English Society 1500–1800*, ed. Mary Prior, pp. 150–51.

93. Collinson, *Godly People*, p. 774; see Rowlands, "Recusant Women 1560–1640," p. 162.

94. Rowlands, "Recusant Women 1560–1640," pp. 151–55, 160; J. D. Hanlon, "These Be But Women" in *From the Renaissance to the Counter-Reformation: Essays in Honor of Garrett Mattingly* (New York: Random House, 1965), pp. 372–73.

95. See Rowlands, "Recusant Women 1560–1640," pp. 161, 174; Warnicke, *Women of the English Renaissance and Reformation*, pp. 170–71, 178.

96. John Mush, "Mr. John Mush's Life of Margaret Clitherow" in *The Troubles of Our Catholic Forefathers Related by Themselves*, 3rd series (London: Burns and Oates, 1877), 3:389–90, 381–82, 407, 418, 432; Rowlands, "Recusant Women 1560–1640," p. 164.

97. Mush, "Mr. John Mush's Life of Margaret Clitherow," pp. 375, 390–92, 372, 383.

98. Hanlon, "These Be But Women," pp. 389–90.

99. Quoted in Rowlands, "Recusant Women 1560–1640," p. 153. For the French example, see Roelker, "The Appeal of Calvinism to French Noblewomen in the Sixteenth Century."

100. Hanlon, "These Be But Women," pp. 377–79; Warnicke, *Women of the English Renaissance and Reformation*, p. 168.

101. Hanlon, "These Be But Women," pp. 374, 380.

102. For Clitherow, see Mush, "Mr. John Mush's Life of Margaret Clitherow," pp. 410, 354, 432. For Lady Falkland, see Sandra K. Fischer, "Elizabeth Cary and Tyranny, Domestic and Religious" in *Silent But for the Word*, ed. Margaret Hannay, pp. 231, 237. For Jane Wiseman, Warnicke, *Women of the English Renaissance and Reformation*, p. 173.

103. Joceline, *The Mothers Legacie to her unborn Child*, sig. A 3.

104. Usher, *Minute book of the Dedham classis, 1582–1589*, p. 35.

105. Collinson, *The Elizabethan Puritan Movement*, p. 93.

106. Rowlands, "Recusant Women 1560–1640," p. 171. Warnicke gives a full summary of Ward's activities and considers Ward possibly a feminist; Warnicke, *Women of the English Renaissance and Reformation*, pp. 174 ff.

107. For example, Elizabeth Gouge, wife of the Puritan minister William Gouge, was praised at her funeral since "shee most prudently and prouidently ordered the affaires of her house, wereby hee had the more leisure to attend his publike function." Guy, *Pieties pillar*, pp. 43–44.

108. I develop this argument further in Diane Willen, "Women in the Public Sphere in Early Modern England: The Case of the Urban Working Poor," *The Sixteenth Century Journal* 19 (Winter 1988):559–73. For the comment of others on this issue, see Ozment, *When Fathers Ruled*, p. 9; Schochet, *Patriarchalism in Political Thought*, pp. 58, 421 ff.; Susan D. Amussen, *An Ordered Society: Gender and Class in Early Modern England* (Oxford: Basil Blackwell, 1988); Margo Todd, "Humanists, Puritans, and the Spiritualized Household, *Church History* 49 (March 1980):30; M. Z. Rosaldo, "The Use and Abuse of Anthropology: Reflections on Feminism and Cross-cultural Understanding," *Signs* 5 (Spring 1980):389–417. I am grateful to Professor Penny Gold for sharing with me comments she made at the session "Implications for Women of the Public/Private Dichotomy: Sanctity, Work and Power in the Middle Ages and Renaissance," American Historical Association meeting, Chicago, December 1984.

109. Rowlands, "Recusant Women 1560–1640," p. 157.

110. See Reay, "Popular Religion," pp. 91 ff.; Keith Thomas, *Religion and the Decline of Magic* (New York: Charles Scribner's Sons, 1971), pp. 159, 165.

111. Haigh, "The Recent Historiography of the English Reformation," p. 999.

112. Reay, "Popular Religion," pp. 91–92, 111–112.

113. Clark, *English Provincial Society from the Reformation to the Revolution,* pp. 155–57; Haigh, "The Recent Historiography of the English Reformation," p. 1000; Reay, "Popular Religion," p. 96.

114. Collinson, *The Religion of Protestants,* pp. 189–241; Spufford, *Contrasting Communities,* pp. 253, 433, 437; Natalie Z. Davis, "Some Tasks and Themes in the Study of Popular Religion" in *The Pursuit of Holiness in Late Medieval and Renaissance Religion,* ed. C. Trinkaus and H. A. Oberman (Leiden: L. J. Brill, 1974), pp. 309–12, 336. For the best discussion of the two cultures, see Wrightson, *English Society, 1580–1680.* Paul Seaver argues that Puritanism could bridge "the high culture of the lettered and the popular culture of the illiterate masses . . ." Seaver, *Wallington's World,* p. viii.

115. A. L. Beier, "The social problems of an Elizabethan country town: Warwick, 1580–90" in *County Towns in Pre-industrial England,* ed. Peter Clark (New York: St. Martin's Press, 1981), p. 60; Paul Slack, "Poverty and Politics in Salisbury 1597–1666" in *Crisis and Order in English Towns 1500–1700,* ed. Peter Clark and Paul Slack (Toronto: University of Toronto Press, 1972), p. 166; John Webb, *Poor Relief in Elizabethan Ipswich,* Suffolk Record Society, 9 (1966):19–22; Carole Moore, "Poor Relief in Elizabethan England: A New Look at Ipswich," *Proceedings and Papers of the Georgia Association of Historians* 7 (1986):108–9; John Pound, *The Norwich Census of the Poor,* Norfolk Record Society, 40 (1971):7 ff.

116. See Spufford, *Contrasting Communities,* pp. 254–55.

117. Clark, *English Provincial Society from the Reformation to the Revolution,* p. 210.

118. Norman Moore, *The History of St. Bartholomew's Hospital* (London: Arthur Pearson, 1918), 2:341–42.

119. F. G. Parsons, *The History of St. Thomas's Hospital* (London: Methuen, 1932), 2:85; Moore, *The History of St. Bartholomew's Hospital,* 2:350–51.

SHERRILL COHEN

Asylums for Women in Counter-Reformation Italy

1. INTRODUCTION

The conventional view of the Counter Reformation of the sixteenth century, both in popular imagination and in historiography, stresses its identity as a movement that reaffirmed orthodoxy. To the extent that historians have examined the Counter Reformation's impact on women, they have largely illuminated its concern with a particular segment of the female population: nuns and exceptionally devout women in organized religious associations. The counter reformers attempted to cleanse the convents of long-time abuses, turning them into showplaces reflecting the respiritualized, reinvigorated Catholic church, and they approved the formation of a small number of new religious orders for women. The Protestant Reformation of the same era, on the other hand, has been seen as a revolution that brought many innovative gains for women: the possibility of legitimately serving as preachers, a devaluation of celibacy for both genders, and an upgrading of companionate marriage and the female role as teacher to her family.[1] Yet the Catholic reformist movements, both those of the early sixteenth century and the "official" Counter-Reformation phase that postdated the Council of Trent, fostered certain policies that in fact enlarged women's horizons. They sponsored alternative social asylums for ex-prostitutes and unhappily married wives that offered wider options to all women and were prototypes of important new social institutions for Western societies.

In the Catholic tradition women had long been treated as inferior members of the Christian body social while they were permitted some carefully delineated channels for rising to importance or power. Catholic theology and ecclesiastical structure put a premium on virginity, with virgins of both sexes seeking to match this ideal through holy celibacy and monasticism. But amid a religion and culture operating on the double standard, the weight of living up to the ideal fell more heavily on women, who had the Virgin Mary to look to as the shining exemplar of womanhood, than it did on men. The Church did not allow females to accede to the foremost positions of ecclesiastical or spiritual authority, as priests or preachers. Women did, however, play significant roles as heads of convents administering other women and as charismatic saints or holy figures admired for their spirituality and approached for counsel in social affairs. Throughout the Middle Ages, women sought greater leeway to be active in religious and ecclesiastical life outside of the Church's specified prescriptions. Their efforts were embodied by such figures as the legendary "Pope Joan," thought to have infiltrated her way to the papacy and lay religious communities like the *humiliate* of Italy and Beguines of northern Europe.[2]

Generally speaking, the era of Catholic reform and the Counter Reformation ushered in more such attempts by women and by the Church to maneuver beneficially within the established structures. Female religious activists like Saint Angela Merici in Italy, Mary Ward in England, and Saint Jeanne de Chantal and Louise de Marillac in France founded new communities or orders to enable women to actualize their religious values by helping others within the secular world. These women organized unenclosed communities and orders to serve the sick and poor and to educate. Other women like Saint Teresa in Spain and Saint Maria Maddalena de Pazzi in Italy played their role in Catholic reform by continuing and advancing the tradition of contemplative mysticism within enclosed convents. They promoted higher standards for devout monastic life. For its part, the Church resisted the Protestant challenge to the monastic ideal and instead reiterated that ideal and aimed to enforce it in reality. It approved the foundation of the dynamic new religious orders for women and encouraged increased religious education for girls. While the Church still valued the nun far above the wife engaged in active sexuality and childbearing, at Trent it did try to improve and sacralize the ways that marriages were arranged and experienced in early modern Europe.[3]

At the heart of the Catholic reform and Counter-Reformation movements lay a fervent philanthropic initiative. In place of the medieval Church's perceived corruptions and sanctioning of the purchase of divine grace through the sale of indulgences, the reformers wished to substitute a balance-scale of grace in exchange for true good works of mercy. By reaching out a helping hand to the poor and the distressed, they hoped to restore to Catholicism its integrity and humility. The needs of the poor glared forth in early sixteen-century Italy, which had been devastated by years of war, famines, and an invading French army and the syphilis and other diseases thought to come in its wake. There, Saint Ignatius Loyola and the Jesuits as well as representatives of the new Barnabite, Somaschi, Capuchin, and Oratorian orders (often collaborating with female activists) established large numbers of hospitals, orphan asylums, and schools—just as their counterparts Saint François de Sales and Saint Vincent de Paul did in France. In part through charity work the reformers carried out their apostolic drive to regenerate the religion, stave off defections to Protestantism, and guarantee the survival of Catholicism through the recruitment of the downtrodden, who were to be tutored in the faith. The sheltering and caretaking institutions founded by Catholic reformers did not simply mirror medieval charity donated to a passive "holy poor," but they embodied a new sort of transformative philanthropy that had the power to reinvigorate the Church and morally uplift the recipients of charity.[4]

One flank of the innovative sheltering institutions founded by Catholic reformers consisted of settlements for ex-prostitutes. Asylums for ex-prostitutes sprang up or revived all across Italy: in Rome in 1520, in Venice in the 1520s, in Milan in the 1530s, in Vicenza in 1537, in Verona by the 1550s, in Padua in 1558, in Treviso in 1559, in Mantua in the 1570s, in Siena in 1575, in Florence in 1579, in Bergamo in 1596, in Pistoia in 1604, in Crema in 1608, and in Brescia in 1611.[5] Their founders ranged from Verona's reforming bishop Gian Matteo Giberti to peripatetic Jesuits to many men and women of the laity. The notion of an asylum for women who wished to quit prostitution was not invented in the sixteenth century. Special religious orders and lay houses for penitent prostitutes had grown up sporadically throughout medieval Europe.[6] But the nature and role of these asylums differed in the medieval and early modern periods, dependent on the changing social position of the prostitute and changing attitudes toward her in those epochs.

In the Middle Ages, spiritual and lay authorities held ambivalent views toward prostitution. Christian theologians abhorred all premarital and extramarital sexual intercourse as sinful fornication. Yet theology, canon law, and medieval mores operated on the double standard that more readily allowed men than women to indulge in the sin of fornication. So that nuns, wives, and daughters could remain as pure as possible, another group of devalued women had to exist to absorb the unlawful sexuality. To avoid the worse evil of having all females subject to illicit fornication, religious and lay authorities, relying on the example set by Saint Augustine in the fourth century, realized that they had to tolerate the lesser evil of prostitution. From the mid-fourteenth century in cities in France, Italy, Germany, and elsewhere in Europe, they went so far as to subsidize prostitution in municipal brothels to deter the rape of respectable women or other ignominies such as male sodomy.[7]

At the end of the fifteenth and opening of the sixteenth centuries—times of crisis in public health, public order, and social relations—the tide of permissiveness toward prostitution turned. Legal regulations were harshened, subjecting prostitutes to tighter controls and often financial burdens in the form of taxes.[8] This change in policy was accompanied by a revived campaign to convert harlots and, especially in Italy, an explosion of institutional asylums for the former prostitutes, who were known as *convertite*. Pope Leo X's Bull of 1520 marking the inauguration of the Roman Convertite establishment relayed the spiritual basis for the conquest of prostitution:

> Our savior Jesus Christ, the son of God, when he took on human form, came, as he himself said, to save the sheep which had strayed. Hence, when the Pharisees and the publicans complained that he associated with sinners, he chose to recite the parable (now in the Gospel of St. Luke) of the sheep which had strayed and was afterwards found, so that he might show, as the same evangelist bears witness, that there is more joy in heaven over one sinner that repents, than over ninety-nine righteous people who have no need to repent.[9]

Indeed, conversion became a leitmotif of the entire Counter Reformation, with a rising call to purify a corrupt clergy and to recruit to the faith apostates to Protestantism and the unlearned poor. Especially striking as symbols of the need for conversion were those high-profile figures who remained outside of God's grace: prostitutes, Jews, and Moslems. In addition to the multiple foundations of asylums for ex-prostitutes, there were also widespread measures in doctrinal and civil policy to encourage the reform of *convertite*. Saint Carlo Borromeo, on behalf of the archbishopric of Milan, and later the Sacred Congregation of Bishops and Regulars, made special provisions to smooth the way for *convertite* to enter orders and to profess monastic vows more readily than other entrants.[10]

The Catholic reform movements of the sixteenth and seventeenth centuries also brought the proliferation of another set of important new institutions for women, establishments designed to prevent females from falling from virtue and turning to prostitution. Italian lay and clerical reformers, including such eminent figures as Ignatius Loyola, Carlo Borromeo, and Bishop Nicolò Sfondrati, sponsored an array of asylums willing to accept custody of females at risk. These included "refuges" (*rifugi*)[11] for orphans, poor girls, widows, and for women with marital troubles, who were dubbed *malmaritate*. The establishments went under the names of Fanciulle Abbandonate (Abandoned Girls), Vergini Miserabili (Poor Virgins), Zitelle Periclitanti (Imperiled Single Females), Casa di Soccorso (House of Assistance), Deposito (Depot), and Malmaritate. The custodial institutions existed in Venice (1539), Rome (1543), Bologna (mid-1500s), Modena, Trapani, Agrigento, Messina, Palermo (in the latter five settings, mid-1500s), Florence (late 1500s), Naples (1564), Cremona (1575), Milan (1570s), Brescia (late 1500s), Pistoia (1584), Vicenza (1600), Prato (1600s), and Turin (1684).[12]

The *convertite* houses and the custodial asylums (which collectively will be referred to as the alternative institutions/asylums) often overlapped in intent, function, and populations. Financing for the new asylums came from church and state and from private male and female donors who perceived the establishments as desirable religious and social policy, for "the honor of God and tranquility of our city."[13] Such benefactors believed that the institutions would recuperate the lost or endangered honor of females, steering inmates toward comportment matching the gender ideology values of the era.[14] The asylums ranged considerably in size, holding from under ten inhabitants to several hundred residents (the largest were bigger than most convents). Many females entered the alternative asylums on their own volition, and others arrived under coercion by their families or civil and religious officials. Although most inmates came from the working classes, the asylums occasionally sheltered females from the upper levels of society as well.[15] In addition to their declared purposes both sets of institutions also served as dumping grounds for anomalous females, girls and women with whom authorities and families simply did not know what else to do.

2. GENDER, RELIGION, AND SOCIAL WELFARE
IN THE SIXTEENTH CENTURY

The three predominant life options open to medieval women—marriage, monasticism, and prostitution—became riddled with problems in sixteenth-century Italy. On the heels of the fifteenth-century demographic recovery from the catastrophic plague of 1348, marital ages and rates fell off. Dowry prices soared, and females could not marry as readily as before. Families frequently forced daughters to become unwilling nuns in monasteries, severely overburdening the resources of Italian urban convents.[16] The many medieval cities, including Florence, that had subsidized civic brothels in order to deter sodomy or rape abruptly reevaluated these policies in the sixteenth century. As syphilis and other contagions infested Europe, frightened civic councilors adopted more stringent regulations designed to reduce the numbers of prostitutes.[17]

At the same time, whether it was demographic pressure, urbanization, unemployment, inflation from New World silver, war, plagues, or famines that tipped the balance in a specific locale, poverty became highly visible and acutely troubling in this era.[18] The emergence of the alternative institutions was related to women's limited options and to the economic difficulties of the period. The refuges seemed to offer a solution to problems prevalent in early modern Italian cities—unmarriageable women, overcrowded convents filled with surplus daughters, and the increasing stigmatization of prostitution. Furthermore, in the view of social authorities, the innumerable females in economic need merited institutional protection to preserve their virtue. In his brief of 1560 establishing Bologna's Opera dei Poveri Mendicanti (Refuge for Poor Beggars) Pope Pius IV portrayed whoredom as a result of immiseration, just as lay Tuscan commentators direly observed that poor girls cut off from institutional support "out of necessity quickly became prostitutes."[19]

Convents had served as the age-old refuges for displaced females, but they were not always reliable. In 1521, the father of Tuscany's future grand duke Cosimo I received two telling letters, one from agents of the bishop of Viterbo and one from the bishop himself:

> [The Bishop] tried to put [Signora Maria, the poor, pregnant woman you sent] in some monastery, but he could not put her anywhere. The nuns did not want to accept her without permission from their General, and she in no way wants to stay or remain with us. [We have resolved] to put her here in a room with some old woman [until further instructions].

> . . . it is not my charge to manage women, and not for anything do I want to do it because I have too much to do. I pray you to remove her immediately because I cannot attend to her. She is eager for things to be arranged. I await a reply about where I should send her.[20]

The traditional institutions for women—convents—were insufficient, early-modern social authorities realized. Clerical and lay activists, including ex-prostitutes themselves, embarked on an experimental course, establishing *convertite* refuges and other new asylums for females.

Socio-cultural institutions and sheltering asylums in Italian municipalities set the tone for what women's role was to be in those societies, whether females were to take a public role in society's mainstream or were to be relegated to separate spheres.[21] We must ask whether there was a point of intersection between the perspectives of early modern women and of societal authorities. It was not just former prostitutes for whom the prospect of new institutions held appeal. Respectable women too were interested in developing avenues for life and action more satisfying than those their society had offered in the past.[22] During the age of Catholic reform, excitement percolated among female spiritual luminaries. In the 1530s in Brescia, Angela Merici, a Franciscan tertiary,[23] founded the Company of St. Ursula, a noncloistered association for women who wanted to serve the causes of charity and education. The community consisted of 130 virgins and a number of widows supervising them. The Tuscan cleric Francesco Landini explained that Angela Merici's new group intended to

> assist and edify many young virgins, both rich and poor, who even though they feel a deep respect for the religious way of life, are nevertheless disinclined to shut themselves up within the narrow walls of cloisters, or bind themselves by vows; or who, again, cannot enter nunneries because of poverty, or do not wish to do so for other good reasons.[24]

Two core issues were at stake: the economic contingencies defining women's choices and the degree to which women could move away from the monastic ethos and its restrictions. After 1566, at the invitation of one of the most prominent counter reformers, Archbishop Carlo Borromeo, the group spread to Milan. In sixteenth-century Rome and seventeenth-century Florence, Isabel Roser and Eleonora Montalvo Landi, respectively, formulated plans to start female branches of the Jesuits, as Mary Ward had done clandestinely in England.[25] These religious women longed to put the message of the Gospel to work in the world, not behind convent walls.

The male and female civic activists who wished to ameliorate conditions for ex-prostitutes wrestled with the same questions. Veronica Franco, a well-known Venetian courtesan and poetess of the late sixteenth century wrote in a petition she intended to present to the Venetian senate:

> There are many women who, out of poverty or sensuality or for some other reason, lead a dishonorable life, but who are sometimes moved by the Holy Spirit to think of the miserable end, both in body and soul, to which for the most part they come by this means. They could easily withdraw from ill-doing if they had some reputable place to repair to, where they might maintain themselves and their children. For they are not allowed to enter among the Zitelle or Convertite if they have mothers, children, husbands, or other necessary responsibilities. It is, moreover, difficult for them to persuade themselves to pass, in a moment, from such a licentious existence to so strict and austere a way of life as that of the Convertite. Because there is no provision for such cases, they persist

in . . . this abominable crime among others: that women in need sell the virginity of their own innocent daughters.[26]

Again we find reform-minded women supporting new institutions and at-
tempting to come to terms with pressing issues: the limited electives available to the feminine sex, the economics of women's lives, the fate of girls in
peril, and the unsatisfying aspects of the monastic milieu.

The backers of many of the alternative institutions articulated similar
concerns. Despite the existence of Florence's medieval Monastery of the
Convertite (1330s), the patrons of the new Malmaritate house (1579) believed that the times required something else, something different, for

> Many [women] remain in sin since they are unable to become nuns because they
> have husbands . . . or even if they're free, because they do not want to become
> nuns. . . . For lack of help, they stay tied to the Devil. Or they convert and then
> quickly return to bad ways. If things were otherwise, they would convert and
> persevere.[27]

Below, we will explore the legacy of the early modern alternative institutions for females, drawing particularly on evidence from three Tuscan establishments: Florence's Monastery of the Convertite (1330s), the Florentine
Malmaritate (1579), which specialized in married ex-prostitutes, and Pistoia's settlement for *convertite*, Santa Maria Maddalena (1604).[28]

3. THE EARLY MODERN ASYLUMS FOR CONVERTITE AND IMPERILED FEMALES: NEW SOCIAL WELFARE INSTITUTIONS

The alternative asylums of the sixteenth and seventeenth centuries did not
on the surface seem very different from convents. Although the degree of
difference varied depending on whether administrators were lay or clerical,
all of the alternative institutions persuaded their inmates to engage in certain
religious observances, from participation in the sacraments of confession and
communion to attendance at sermons to prayer. Like convents, the asylums
all had sites where handwork, most likely sewing or weaving, was done.
Some of the asylums built large facilities akin to monasteries with common
spaces and multiple smaller chambers; other institutions occupied rented
secular houses divided into a number of rooms. The alternative establishments generally had internal governments along conventual lines, with
elected or appointed resident female supervisors and outside administrators
who visited the premises. Life in the asylums seemed to be characterized by
no more or less admixture of harmony and acrimony than in any monastery
of the time. Yet, although in physical atmosphere and regimen the alternative asylums closely resembled traditional and reformed convents, I will argue that these early modern establishments were a distinctly new kind of
institution. They advanced a new set of relationships concerning female control over property and women's autonomy.

WOMEN AND PROPERTY

In medieval Italy, while all of women's options—like those of men—were bound up with property, females had little legal right to control property. Civil law stipulated that at every stage of the female life cycle girls' and women's property lay officially at the disposition of a male, either a father, husband, son, male relative, or male guardian (*mundualdo*). Only a minority of women, particularly widows, exercised considerable discretion over their own wealth and goods. Females could indeed possess property in their own names, but at least in theory they had to obtain permission from males in order to manipulate that property. Females needed access to dowries to set themselves on either of the two honorable paths in life, marriage or monasticism.[29] Plebeian women supplied small dowries for marriage or joined convents as servant-nuns, paying off their conventual fees gradually through work or with wages from the cottage labor performed in monasteries. Both women in convents who had not taken vows and professed nuns still had to rely on a male representative, either a *mundualdo* or a conventual administrator, for transactions involving property. Medieval marriage and medieval monasticism accepted as normative a system of joint responsibility for female welfare. Relatives and benefactors from the community provided some support for girls and women. The females themselves were expected to contribute the rest, either as married women toiling unpaid in the family occupation or as spinsters, wives, widows, and nuns laboring for wages. The participation of married and single women in the paid labor force soared from the late sixteenth century onward in Italy's manufacturing center, Tuscany, and perhaps in other Italian regions as well.[30]

The early modern *convertite* houses and custodial institutions were tied to an emerging debate over women's relationship to property that would continue into subsequent centuries. At issue was the desirability of females having increased resources for their own economic support versus the threat of female economic and sexual independence unrestrained by the suasion of family or church or state. Church leaders like Archbishop Carlo Borromeo staked out one extreme position in the debate, as they pressed women to conform with the monastic ethos and submit to poverty, chastity, and cloister. At the other extreme were the lay bourgeois administrators of the Florentine Malmaritate house who prodded women to take greater financial responsibility for themselves by earning their upkeep and supporting themselves in the world.

The roots of Borromeo's position lay in the doctrinal conclave that launched the Counter Reformation, the Council of Trent (1545–63). Among other effects the decrees promulgated at Trent brought about wrenching changes in property relations at convents. Traditionally, income for the convent as a whole and for individual inmates derived from endowments, charity, and from the efforts of house members who labored at piecework and begged in the streets as alms-seekers (*cercatrici*). To fulfill their goal of respiritualizing the convents and eradicating the sexual license that had prevailed in some nunneries, the authorities at Trent produced regulations both to deter coerced monachation and to exact unblemished conduct from religious who had willingly professed vows. The churchmen set the age of consent for profession at sixteen, demanded that professed nuns and monks incorporate into the monastery any property and income, and called for strict cloister.[31] Local bishops and lay officials cooperated in setting numerical limits on the memberships of specific monasteries so that the convents' food supplies would be adequate to the populations housed. Here and elsewhere, civil and ecclesiastical aims coincided, but on other policies they clashed. As churchmen tried to curtail nuns' worldly contacts related to conventual labors in order to guard the women's chastity, they met with fierce opposition from nuns in individual monasteries and from lay authorities, who correctly anticipated the economic hardships that this would impose on the convents.[32] When Tuscany's Grand Duke Cosimo I tried to moderate the zeal of the ecclesiastical reformers by pleading the poverty of the nuns in his realm, he won no concessions from Pope Gregory XIII but only the reply, "Just as Divine Providence sent bread to Elijah, the desert hermit, and to Paul [in the beaks of] ravens, [God] will inspire benefactors to provide for these nuns."[33]

Lay activists and some clerics took a starkly different view. They promoted a contrasting ethos of greater female access to property. This tendency found its fullest expression in Florence, the seedbed of European textile manufacturing and venture capitalism. The merchants who established the Malmaritate house in 1579 especially for married *convertite* believed that economic ills caused prostitution, and they proposed an economic cure. Aberrant married and single women who entered the Malmaritate were to be recycled to the world as trained laborers, capable of earning their upkeep and benefiting the body social. Although the administrators there did not wholly relinquish the idea that spouses, relatives, and benefactors ought to help sustain females, the twenty or so Malmaritate inmates were expected to assume the greater part of the burden for their own support. The founders demanded that financially solvent entrants contribute toward the reasonable institutional fees of three *scudi* per month, so that the ex-prostitute inmates would not "usurp charity." Women too poor to do this at entrance would pay monthly taxes on the fruits of their labors at in-house cottage industries and retain the rest of their wages.[34] Because the burgher administrators believed that possession of property stimulated the development of moral character, they encouraged the *convertite* to save their earnings and to safeguard their own goods. With all entrants listing their possessions in inventories and storing them in individual locked chests, the women could trust that when it came time to depart, they would be able to take away what they had brought and what they had earned.[35] The Malmaritate regimen of training females for low-skilled jobs in the textile industry yielded society a cheap labor force. It profited the newly fledged workers as well. Although it did not thrust women out of the system of female subordination, it did offer them a step toward greater economic and social independence.

While both ecclesiastical and lay authorities saw value in a patriarchal system that took care of women, they expected women to contribute a certain amount, either a dowry or the fruits of labor, toward their own support. Yet the culture and social structures of early modern Europe put roadblocks in the way of women's true economic self-sufficiency. The same churchmen who wanted females to have ways of sustaining themselves other than prostitution ironically interfered with the nonsexual avenues of property accumulation that women found. In some cases, professed nuns may have found ways of getting around the Tridentine rules calling for an end to private property. Despite Trent's mandated inspections by ecclesiastical officials to monitor implementation of the reforms,[36] at least at Florence's Monastery of the Convertite the streetwise ex-prostitute nuns managed in the decades after Trent to retain individual title to their property. At the monastery, whose population fluctuated between one hundred and two hundred women in these decades, the chief administrator assisted professed nuns in the rental of lands and buildings that they owned.[37] The professed nuns at the Florentine Convertite also harvested personal savings from donations pledged to them and investments in the public debts, and they had the freedom to dispose of their property as they wished in their wills. They made loans, served as benefactors and guarantors for new entrants, and engaged in a wide variety of entrepreneurial schemes.[38] One professed nun at the monastery in the 1670s, the ex-prostitute Suor Bartolomea Leonora Corsini, entered into moneychanging contracts with male partners, changing foreign monies into the local currency at a 4 percent rate of interest.[39] *Convertite* houses had special reasons to indulge ex-prostitute inmates in order to encourage them to persevere in reform within the institution, but whether such lax enforcement of the Tridentine decree existed also at mainstream convents remains to be discovered.

A single impetus lay behind the Counter-Reformation church's directives concerning female institutional inmates and economic matters: the desire to bring all institutions, even those that were not convents, into closer conformity with the esteemed monastic ethos. Religious authorities knew that income-producing activities at the alternative institutions might interfere with spiritual exercises. The 150 residents at Milan's *convertite* house, Santa Valeria, had admitted to ecclesiastical inspectors that often they were too exhausted from spinning and housework to say their prayers.[40] Counter-Reformation leaders attempted to spread their restrictive policies on property and labor to the new alternative institutions. They sought to limit the contact institutional inmates could have with the outside in arranging labors or soliciting charity. The Milanese archiepiscopal regime headed by Carlo Borromeo prohibited street begging by the *convertite* at Santa Valeria in the

1570s, and it tried to bar the inmates of that house from earning individual wages for their piecework.[41] In 1646, ecclesiastical officials stopped members of Rome's Zitelle Disperse (1595), which could hold over two hundred girls, from contracting out as servants and from begging in the streets as alms-seekers.[42] As a general policy, the Church moved to replace an active means by which female inmates gleaned income with a more passive one. Rather than having inmates go to jobs outside or piecework within the asylums, the Church preferred to see female inmates adopt more of a religious function and await benefactions requiring the performance of religious rites in return.[43]

It is possible to make a broad distinction between the attitudes of lay reformers and ecclesiastical reformers in Italy as a whole. For institutional inmates to have real earning power would confer a degree of independence, something that the ecclesiastical officials viewed with trepidation. Although the ecclesiastical institutional administrators as well as the lay administrators ran work programs, such as the instruction in weaving at Pistoia's Santa Maria Maddalena,[44] they manifested greater ambivalence toward this facet of the regimen than did their lay counterparts. Under ecclesiastical supervisors, labor was sometimes designed to keep idle hands from doing the Devil's work, rather than intended to train workers to make a profit.[45]

At another level, however, all male leaders whether of church or state shared one assumption. They felt that although women should produce labor and income to benefit themselves and society, females should not themselves control this process or its profits. Prostitution offended religious and lay authorities not only because women violated the virtue of female chastity many times over, but also because in exchange for sex the women acquired money in hand, a form of power. Female control over property went against the grain of early modern gender ideology and the legal strictures of early modern societies. To stretch an old aphorism, medieval Florence fostered both the world's oldest profession and the Western world's oldest capitalism. What were the implications for the future when the rest of Europe became mercantile-capitalist Florence writ large? The very same controversy over women's potential economic empowerment versus the dictates of gender ideology would arise again in an overt way with nineteenth-century industrialization and the debates that accompanied women's entry into factory work.[46]

INSTITUTIONS AND FEMALE AUTONOMY

The *convertite* houses and custodial establishments that emerged in the sixteenth and seventeenth centuries represented a transitional phase within the evolution of different types of social institutions for female populations. Institutions may be distinguished from one another by who governs them, whether civil officials, clerics, or private citizens. They may also be distinguished by their predominant function—community for spirituality, workhouse, caretaking agency, school, or prison. Yet because both administrative jurisdiction and function were so multifaceted in the case of the medieval and early modern institutions for females, for our purposes we will focus on a different primary point of comparison: did inmates have the liberty to come and go between the fixed shelter and society at their own choice?

To understand the historical development of social institutions for females, we could set forth a schema as follows. Many medieval convents, third-order communities, and thirteenth-century orders and lay houses for penitent prostitutes were uncloistered and permitted some flow in and out, either official or de facto recidivism. Then, in the sixteenth century, the ecclesiastical authorities carrying out Tridentine policy tried to impose strict cloister on convents and on many other types of girls' and women's institutions too. Yet the *convertite* houses and custodial asylums that proliferated in that era offered a potent counter-image of more flexible social options for women. This tantalizing image became reality when the eighteenth-century schools and conservatories that evolved from the alternative institutions and from convents conceded to females fuller rights of autonomy concerning their fates.

Let us examine how the *convertite* and custodial establishments constituted a significant transition. We find that the Italian alternative institutions of the sixteenth and seventeenth centuries hewed to one of two models, the monastic model or the reinsertion model. The monastic model is exemplified by the post-Tridentine reformed monastery, in which the greater portion of the house's members—professed nuns—took vows to live a life of poverty, chastity, and obedience within the confines of cloister. The professed nun knew that she was expected to hold to those vows and live out her life at the monastery and that she would be retrieved if she sought to leave. Many of the alternative establishments, on the other hand, were predicated on a contrasting institutional identity, what we will call the reinsertion model. This institutional definition assumed that inmates could return to the realm of private property and licit sexuality—return literally to society. While convents permitted only for a minority of their population—novices who had not yet made profession of vows—the freedom to depart and to possibly reenter the convent at a later time, the new alternative institutions legitimated recidivism for all inmates.

The process of sorting out whether the new institutions were to resemble more closely one or the other of the two models provoked intense controversies among civil and ecclesiastical officials and institutional administrators, the latter coming from both lay and clerical ranks. The conflicts hinged on how much freedom of communication and mobility female inmates might have. Even in the alternative institutions that were not convents, inmates were subject to cloisterlike environments. Through supervision and locks on the outer doors, administrators limited residents' contact with the world in order to insure the sexual decorum of the inmates.[47] The regimens, in some cases, turned out to be more rigorous than either outsiders or female inmates expected. The Florentine citizen Pier Francesco da Diacceto funded a prostitute's enrollment into the Malmaritate in 1580, and when he discovered that he would not be allowed to speak to her as was his wont, he hurled rocks at the house's windows in protest.[48]

The question of how to treat departures was a foremost policy issue. At times, women wound up decamping from an unhappy family situation by entering an institution only to then be unable to leave the institution when they wanted to. This obstacle confronted Caterina Lanzini, who in 1618 obtained admission to Bologna's *soccorso* house, San Paolo, for a second time because she was "beautiful and in great peril, being in disgrace with her husband and other relatives." She hoped to stay for three months and afterward return to her husband but did not succeed in securing her release for three years.[49] One seventeenth-century Florentine institutional administrator aptly summed up the authorities' point of view when he spoke of "the dangers [unaffiliated females] court when they are at their liberty."[50] At the Pistoian *convertite* house Santa Maria Maddalena (1604), which hosted approximately twenty women, after an initial ten years in which inmates took their leave rather casually, the issues of departure and impending claustration generated heated polemics in the house's second decade. One incident drew the personal intervention of the grand duchess of Tuscany, and another case resulted in the exile of five inmates from the diocese and provoked two lay administrators to resign.[51] All of the turmoil grew in response to the fear of "scandals" that could result from the actions of women beyond official control who might bring "dishonor" to their families or civic community. Many administrators, however, willingly discharged inmates when they felt some surety that the girls and women would lead decorous lives on the outside. They authorized inmates to transfer to other institutions, permitted women to go to relatives, and helped women to reunite with spouses or to find husbands and marry.[52] At all of the alternative institutions an attitude of paternalistic guardianship prevailed. The supervision and aid directed at inmates could extend even beyond a woman's leavetaking. Florence's Malmaritate (1579), like Rome's Vergini Miserabili (1549) and Venice's Zitelle (1558), saw as part of its duties watching over released "daughters" of the institution.[53]

What did policies regarding departure and recidivism mean for the female inmates in these establishments? Some women welcomed restrictive institutional structures as an aid to self-discipline, like the Pistoian *convertite* in Santa Maria Maddalena who called for the house's transformation into a cloistered convent in 1621 and again in 1625.[54] Some inmates detested the sense of confinement or actual claustration and fled from it, sometimes forfeiting substantial sums of money in order to do so. Administrators duly recorded annotations such as this one from the early seventeenth-century casebooks of Florence's Monastery of the Convertite: "[Maddalena Martini] left . . . because she could not stand to be shut up so." Maddalena left to marry, and her earlier contemporaries in the Milanese *convertite* house Santa Valeria had likewise voiced their desire for husbands.[55]

Other females found satisfaction in institutional life for finite periods of time. Women reacted positively to administrative policies that encouraged recidivism. The Florentine Malmaritate (1579) invited the return of former inmates who lost employment, and the government of Tuscany offered dowry subsidies to recidivist *convertite*.[56] Occasionally strong-armed by the state into reentering but more often returning voluntarily, women made multiple essays at life in the alternative institutions. The prostitute Luisa Donnini who rejoined Florence's Monastery of the Convertite in 1661 had been in the house "other times."[57] Women turned up for repeat enrollments at Bologna's *soccorso* San Paolo (1589), which usually housed about fifteen to thirty residents.[58] Some women returned not so much to avoid succumbing to sin, but because the institution felt like a secure refuge, perhaps more like home than any place else. Maria Francesca of Cireglio, a woman who departed from Pistoia's Santa Maria Maddalena in 1623 to redeem her honor through marriage to her noble former lover, returned to the house nineteen years later when she was widowed.[59] The females who dwelled at the alternative asylums sought to come and go from institutions at their own self-determination. These women were not self-conscious participants in early modern feminism, the era's *querelle des femmes*.[60] They did not articulate challenges to the ideology of female inferiority and subordination. But they did pit themselves against attempts to keep them enclosed against their will.

Experiments with the reinsertion model multiplied throughout the sixteenth and seventeenth centuries. Myriad shelters for females sprang up based on the premise that inmates would probably exit, and such institutions tolerated recidivism. Rome's prototype house for *malmaritate*, Santa Marta (1543), required from inmates vows of temporary confinement. At the Roman Vergini Miserabili (1549), which had the capacity to shelter two hundred girls, the youthful entrants left at adolescence or womanhood to become wives and nuns, as they did also at the Venetian Zitelle (1558) and the Roman Zitelle Disperse (1595).[61] Archbishop Carlo Borromeo's Deposito and Soccorso in Milan (1570s) and Bologna's and Venice's *soccorso* houses (1589, 1590) intended to send their residents back into society. The average sojourn at the Bolognese institution lasted less than a year, and the administrators there allowed readmission of recidivists.[62] The thirty *convertite* at Verona's settlement (1530s) knew that they could return to society to be workers and wives. Inmates at the Sienese Convertite (1570), which housed thirty-one females, at Florence's Malmaritate (1579), and at Santa Maria Maddalena (1604) in Pistoia during its first decade held the same belief.[63] Like one seventeenth-century Florentine poorhouse official frustrated with overseeing rebellious inmates, certain administrators may have believed that "troublesome women perhaps commit more and worse sins being forcibly locked up, than those they would commit if they were at liberty."[64]

Yet during these two centuries, reformers also sponsored new foundations of *convertite* houses that were from the start monasteries, and churchmen tried to turn existing establishments into enclosed convents. In the 1550s, the Venetian Cardinal Francesco Pisani, who supervised a Roman settlement of penitent women living by the Augustinian rule, together with Pope Julius III oversaw the transformation of the Convertite of Venice (1520s) into a cloistered Augustinian convent which held between two hundred and four hundred women over the course of the next century. A new "Convento" for female sinners appeared on the scene in Bologna in 1559.[65] The Monastero delle Stabilite, founded in Florence in 1589, expected its working-class inmates to remain in the institution for life, and at Milan twenty years earlier the *convertite* house of Santa Valeria had begun to insist that its members take vows of stability and live in cloister. By 1646, administrators of the Roman Zitelle Disperse (1595) had curtailed residents' contacts with the world.[66] The Counter-Reformation church of this epoch was engaged in a massive drive to heighten discipline in religious life generally. In the latter half of the sixteenth century, Angela Merici's uncloistered association of women engaged in teaching and charity, the Ursulines, began to draw reactions of distrust as well as praise. By the seventeenth century, in most places, the group had been diverted from its original intent onto the safer path of formalization as a cloistered religious order. Everywhere in Catholic Europe, churchmen attempted to enforce claustration on often unwilling nuns and monastic vows on third-order communities.[67]

Thus, the same two centuries saw both an ongoing experimental bent that accommodated women's desires for more freedom of action and a reluctance to break with the familiar approach of claustration. What did these contradictory trends mean? For every step toward more open institutions, clerical and some civil authorities grew frightened and took a step back toward the familiar. Certain innovative administrators were ready to promote a policy of reinsertion, but they wanted to keep the female inmates shut in and under guard while at the alternative institutions. Sixteenth- and seventeenth-century ecclesiastical and civil authorities, with the collaboration of some citizens and families, would not countenance the freedom for women to come and go from institutional communities as they pleased and to live at their own self-direction. The brakes put on experimentation did not arise simply from a reluctance to break with the known. They appeared also because the compulsion to centralize triumphed over the instinct to experiment in Catholic reform. As the Counter Reformation rigidified, so did the Spanish empire's political domination of the Italian city-states, leaving less room for lay initiatives as well. But the experimentation with the *convertite* and custodial institutions for females pointed precisely toward the solution of more open institutions for women in the future.

The *convertite* houses and custodial establishments mirror major changes in the history of social welfare institutions in European societies. Their surge in prominence coincides with what has been called the "great confinement" of the poor, criminals, and the mentally disturbed. Institutionalization of the marginal, whether to simply exclude them or to rehabilitate and reintegrate them, increased tremendously in the early modern era.[68] In later centuries, the imperative to institutionalize continued apace, as social ills replaced heresy in the forefront of concerns for civic and state authorities.

The early modern alternative asylums were among the ancestors of later institutions for females that would serve both normative needs—schools—and problematic needs—prisons and halfway houses. Rehabilitative strategies that were first developed for the female inmates of alternative asylums gradually appeared as well in early modern and modern institutions for aberrant males or deviant segments of society. The alternative asylums were central players in a process of institutional evolution. As the asylums took over from the respiritualized, size-restricted convents the role of warehousing and disciplining errant females, the separate institutional identity of convents coalesced. As a means of coping with social aberrancy, the religious themes of sin and penitence would be gradually supplanted by more secular modes of guilt and expiation.[69] Not all of the new institutions for females were comfortable in executing the traditional mix of functions that the convents had performed. Some settlements tried at the outset to delimit the populations they would house. Others determined from experience that specialization was necessary, like the Soccorso in Cremona, which opened in the mid-1570s for *convertite, malmaritate,* and imperiled girls and decided within a decade to accept only endangered girls. Resistance to mixing in a single institution the functions of conserving and correcting became common among late eighteenth-century Italian officials, who were also increasingly drawing lines separating secular welfare institutions from religious ones.[70]

Institutional differentiation gained ground when schools for girls and female residence hostels distinctly split off from convents and other establishments. In Tuscany, the Enlightenment modernizer Grand Duke Pietro Leopoldo (later Emperor Leopold II) consolidated the convents in order to mold a large number of them into secular conservatories to educate girls or house homeless women.[71] This prince, in 1785, laid before all nuns in his realm the choice of taking on an activist teaching role outside of cloisters or continuing in a traditional monastic lifestyle. At his conservatories, including the surviving sixteenth-century Conservatory for Abandoned Girls in Pistoia, he guaranteed that "there will be liberty for [any oblate or inmate] to leave the community, without any other reason than her own inclination."[72] The *convertite* houses and custodial establishments of the sixteenth and seventeenth centuries bore a promise that was not completely realized, the expansion of electives for the female sex. With the differentiation of secular schools and female residence communities from convents and their other institutional antecedents, that promise came much closer to fruition.

4. CONCLUSION

The longevity of the alternative asylums testifies to the valuable function they performed for women and society. Florence's Monastery of the Convertite and Pistoia's house for ex-prostitutes, Santa Maria Maddalena, lasted until Napoleon conquered Italy and confiscated the property of religious and philanthropic institutions in 1808. Florence's Malmaritate house was administered by the civil police ministry from 1776 on and then was incorporated into a conservatory for females in 1808.[73] Alternative asylums elsewhere in Italy endured into the eighteenth and nineteenth centuries. Bologna's Santa Maria del Baraccano, where nubile girls of the lower echelons lived and saved money for dowries, only closed its doors in 1968![74] Even when alternative institutions shut down as independent entities, many times they reemerged phoenixlike as components of other institutions which were beneficial for women.

An outpouring of charitable support from the public enabled the alternative asylums to thrive. These newly organized settlements matched and in some cases surpassed traditional religious and welfare institutions in garnering financial assistance from civil governments and from private benefactors. As the sixteenth-century Malmaritate administrators in Florence stated, "Our endeavor is wholly based on charity."[75] Donors ranging from noblemen to widows of modest means contributed in cash, kind, and bequests to support the institutions as wholes and individual female inmates. They supplied entrance fees and sometimes annual stipends for inmates.[76] Male and female patrons invested their time as well as money and prestige, helping administer the institutions and visiting inmates to give them succor or practical aid.[77] The Italian public at large showed enormous enthusiasm for this quintessential Counter-Reformation philanthropic initiative of aiding moral reform and providing for social stabilization. Bourgeois females became involved in establishing and financing the institutions out of a mixture of motives. Gentlewomen could derive a sense of their own virtue and well-being from helping aberrant or endangered women. At the same time, they knew that they, too, might conceivably pass a sojourn at the asylums temporarily or permanently. They had a stake in making such institutions as livable as possible.

The influence of the alternative institutions stemmed not so much from the numbers of female inmates housed—a handful in one city, a few hundred in another—as from their structural and symbolic importance. Distinctly different from the ad hoc measures taken in the Middle Ages to shelter needy females, the early modern asylums were, rather, formal societal institutions recognized as existing for this purpose. The asylums had long-term significance: they spawned new sorts of secular residential communities for females in the form of schools and conservatories, and the *malmaritate* houses represented a novel way of criticizing and sidestepping marriages. The founders of the *malmaritate* houses identified a formidable social problem that had been little considered previously and posited a type of legitimate separation as the solution. At the same time that the Church was shoring up and sacralizing marriage, the religious leaders who countenanced the *malmaritate* establishments admitted the possible failures of marriage as a context for women's lives. They did so while Protestant theologians began to condone divorce in cases of adultery or abandonment. The eighteenth-century Florentine writer Marco Lastri stated that society needed institutions like the Malmaritate in order to be well regulated, since the Church forbade divorce.[78] For several centuries, until secular divorce won acceptance in most Catholic societies, the *malmaritate* houses with their institutionalization of marital grievance served as the Catholic alternative to divorce.

Thus, Catholic reform and the Counter Reformation disseminated throughout Europe the legacy of new social welfare institutions meant to be *utile publico*, "in the public interest."[79] Henceforth, more girls and women lived in institutional settings than ever before, and females resided in a much wider variety of institutions for their sex than had existed previously. Increasing institutionalization per se should be considered neither a gain nor a loss. While the regimens of the asylums proved a bane for some residents, other females may have found inside the institutions a refuge and opportunities that they would not have been afforded in the outside world. What determined the quality of the experience for the individual was whether women had the freedom to make institutions serve their own self-determined interests, as well as the interests of society. Today, we are witnesses to the expansion and multiplication of social welfare institutions for females, including battered women's shelters and institutional programs for pregnant and parenting adolescent girls. The definitions of who is problematic and the institutional solutions have changed, but the underlying phenomenon remains the same. In our own society, cultural ideology still marks the female gender; females continue to be the focus of social controversies concerning sexuality, work roles, and rights of autonomy over one's body and actions.

NOTES

An earlier version of this chapter was presented as a paper at the Shelby Cullom Davis Center for Historical Studies at Princeton University. I would like to thank Lawrence Stone, Natalie Zemon Davis, and Virginia Reinburg for their helpful comments on my drafts of the chapter. I also wish to express my gratitude to Ruth P. Liebowitz, who has led the way in studying early modern institutions for women and generously shared her data with me.

1. Eric Cochrane, "New Light on Post-Tridentine Italy: A Note on Recent Counter-Reformation Scholarship," *Catholic Historical Review* 56 (1970):309, 316; Jean Delumeau, *Catholicism between Luther and Voltaire: A New View of the Counter-Reformation* (London: Burns and Oates, 1977), pp. 21–23, 36–39; Natalie Zemon Davis, "City Women and Religious Change" in *Society and Culture in Early Modern France* (Stanford, Calif.: Stanford University Press, 1975), pp. 65–95; Jane Dempsey Douglass, "Women and the Continental Reformation," in *Religion and Sexism: Images of Woman in the Jewish and Christian Traditions*, ed. Rosemary Radford Ruether (New York: Simon and Schuster, 1974), pp. 292–318.

2. Eleanor Commo McLaughlin, "Equality of Souls, Inequality of Sexes: Woman in Medieval Theology," in *Religion and Sexism*, pp. 213–66; Vern L. Bullough, "Transvesticism in the Middle Ages," in *Sexual Practices and the Medieval Church*,

eds. Vern L. Bullough and James A. Brundage (Buffalo: Prometheus Books, 1982), pp. 50–51; Brenda M. Bolton, "Mulieres Sanctae," in *Women in Medieval Society*, ed. Susan Mosher Stuard (Philadelphia: University of Pennsylvania Press, 1976), pp. 141–58.

3. Ruth P. Liebowitz, "Virgins in the Service of Christ: The Dispute over an Active Apostolate for Women during the Counter-Reformation," in *Women of Spirit: Female Leadership in the Jewish and Christian Traditions*, eds. Rosemary Ruether and Eleanor McLaughlin (New York: Simon and Schuster, 1979), pp. 131–52; Eric Cochrane, *Florence in the Forgotten Centuries 1527–1800: A History of Florence and the Florentines in the Age of the Grand Dukes* (Chicago: University of Chicago Press, 1973), pp. 136–38, 295 on St. Maria Maddalena de Pazzi; Jean Gaudement, "Il legame matrimoniale nel XVII secolo. Legislazione canonica e tendenze laiche," in *Le funzioni sociali del matrimonio. Modelli e regole della scelta del coniuge dal XIV al XX secolo*, ed. Milly Buonanno (Milan: Edizioni di comunità, 1980), pp. 68–70. Notable among recent interesting works on women and religion in Counter-Reformation Italy is Judith C. Brown, *Immodest Acts: The Life of a Lesbian Nun in Renaissance Italy* (New York: Oxford University Press, 1986).

4. Outram Evennett, *The Spirit of the Counter-Reformation* (Cambridge: Cambridge University Press, 1968), especially pp. 26–28, 84–88; Brian Pullan, *Rich and Poor in Renaissance Venice: The Social Institutions of a Catholic State, to 1620* (Cambridge: Harvard University Press, 1971) and idem, "Catholics and the Poor in Early Modern Europe," *Transactions of the Royal Historical Society*, 5th ser., 26 (1976):15–34.

5. Pullan, *Rich and Poor*, pp. 375–93; Ruth P. Liebowitz, "Conversion or Confinement? Houses for Repentant Prostitutes in Late Renaissance Italy," paper presented at the Sixteenth Century Studies Conference, St. Louis, Missouri, 25 October 1980, p. 2.

6. Leah Lydia Otis, *Prostitution in Medieval Society: The History of an Urban Institution in Languedoc* (Chicago: University of Chicago Press, 1985), pp. 72–76.

7. James A. Brundage, "Prostitution in the Medieval Canon Law," *Signs* 1 (1976):825–45; Jacques Rossiaud, *La prostituzione nel medioevo* (Rome: Laterza, 1984), pp. 7–15, 77–78.

8. Otis, *Prostitution in Medieval Society*, pp. 40–45.

9. Translated by Pullan, *Rich and Poor*, p. 377.

10. *Acta Ecclesiae Mediolanensis*, 2 vols. (Milan: Paulo Pagnonio, 1843), 2:1200; Archivio di Stato, Florence, Conventi Soppressi 191:33, ff. 27v–28. Unless otherwise designated, all archival references cited hereafter are from Florence's Archivio di Stato.

11. Bigallo 1691, f. 35.

12. In addition to the sources in note 5, also Lucia Ferrante, "L'onore ritrovato. Donne nella casa del Soccorso di S. Paolo a Bologna (sec. XVI–XVII)," *Quaderni storici* 53 (August 1983):499–527, and in the same issue, pp. 383–497, Luisa Ciammitti, "Quanto costa essere normali. La dote nel Conservatorio femminile di Santa Maria del Baraccano (1630–1680)"; Daniela Lombardi, "Poveri a Firenze. Programmi e realizzazioni della politica assistenziale dei Medici tra cinque e seicento," in *Timore e carita: i poveri nell'Italia moderna*, eds. Giorgio Politi, Mario Rosa, and Franco della Peruta (Cremona: Libreria del Convegno, 1982), pp. 167–68 and idem, "L'ospedale dei mendicanti nella Firenze del seicento. 'Da inutile serraglio dei mendici a conservatorio e casa di forza per le donne'," *Società e storia* 24 (1984):308–309, n. 35, n. 39; Ruth P. Liebowitz, "Prison, Workshop and Convent: A House of Convertite in Counter-Reformation Milan," paper presented at the sixth Berkshire Conference on the History of Women, Northampton, Massachusetts, 1 June 1984, pp. 2–3; Luigi Bargiacchi, *Storia degli istituti di beneficenza, d'istruzione ed educazione in Pistoia e suo circondario dalle respettive origini a tutto l'anno 1880*, 4 vols. (Florence: Tipografia della pia casa di patronato pei minorenni, 1883–84), 2:253–56, 3:223–42; and Maria Elena

Vasaio, "Il tessuto della virtù. Le zitelle di S. Eufemia e di S. Caterina dei Funari nella Controriforma," *Memoria* 11–12 (1984):53–64.

13. Conventi Soppressi 191:10, f. 1.

14. Ferrante's "L'onore ritrovato" is very suggestive on this point.

15. Bigallo 1691, f. 39; Conventi Soppressi 126:62, unpaginated, list dated 1455–1620; Conventi Soppressi 191:10, ff. 20v–21; Liebowitz, "Conversion," p. 9; Ferrante, "L'onore ritrovato," p. 508; Lombardi, "L'ospedale," pp. 294, 302.

16. David Herlihy, *The Family in Renaissance Italy* (St. Louis: Forum Press, 1974), pp. 4–10; Pio Paschini, "I monasteri femminili in Italia nel '500," in *Italia Sacra* 2 (Rome: Antenore, 1960), pp. 36–37, 58; Richard C. Trexler, "Le celibat à la fin du Moyen Age: Les religieuses de Florence," *Annales, E.S.C.* 27 (November–December 1972):1333, 1339, 1345–46.

17. Pullan, *Rich and Poor*, pp. 375–81; Richard C. Trexler, "La prostitution florentine au XVe siècle: patronages et clientèles," *Annales, E.S.C.* (November–December 1981):1003–6.

18. Pullan, *Rich and Poor*, pp. 633–42; Thomas Riis, ed., *Aspects of Poverty in Early Modern Europe* (Florence: Europäisches Hochschulinstitut, 1981).

19. Ferrante, "L'onore ritrovato," p. 499; Arnaldo D'Addario, *Aspetti della Controriforma a Firenze* (Rome: Ministero dell'Interno, 1972), p. 309, n. 105.

20. Transcribed by Carlo Carnesecchi in Acquisti e Doni 292, unpaginated, at the dates 29 June and 13 July 1521.

21. On separate spheres, Judith R. Walkowitz, *Prostitution and Victorian Society: Women, Class, and the State* (Cambridge: Cambridge University Press, 1980), pp. 7, 117, 256.

22. Two recent books explore this theme in a later period. See Lee Virginia Chambers-Schiller, *Liberty, A Better Husband: Single Women in America; The Generations of 1780–1840* (New Haven: Yale University Press, 1984); and on England, Martha Vicinus, *Independent Women: Work and Community for Single Women, 1850–1920* (Chicago: University of Chicago Press, 1985).

23. A "tertiary" was a member of a medieval third-order, a religious association of laywomen or laymen loosely affiliated with a more formal monastic order. Tertiaries might reside with their families, in communal households with other tertiaries, or in monasteries. See Raimondo Creytens, "La Riforma dei monasteri femminili dopo i Decreti Tridentini," in *Il Concilio di Trento e la Riforma Tridentina*, Atti del Convegno storico internazionale, Trent, 2–6 September 1963, 2 vols. (Rome: Herder, 1965), 1:46–49.

24. Translated by Pullan, *Rich and Poor*, p. 394.

25. Liebowitz, "Virgins"; Cochrane, *Florence*, p. 212; H. O. Evennett, "The New Orders," in *The New Cambridge Modern History*, vol. 2: *The Reformation, 1520–1559*, ed. G. R. Elton (Cambridge: Cambridge University Press, 1958), p. 296.

26. Translated by Pullan, *Rich and Poor*, p. 392. I have changed his spelling to American usage. See Margaret (Tita) F. Rosenthal, "Veronica Franco: The Courtesan as Poet in Sixteenth-Century Venice," (Ph.D. dissertation, Yale University, 1985).

27. Bigallo 1691, f. 1.

28. See my book, *The Evolution of Women's Asylums: Ex-Prostitutes and Unhappy Wives* (New York: Oxford University Press, forthcoming).

29. Manlio Bellomo, *La condizione giuridica della donna in Italia* (Turin: Eri, 1970), pp. 27–28, 36–78; Ferrante, "L'onore ritrovato," p. 514; Thomas Kuehn, "Women, Marriage, and *Patria Potestas* in Late Medieval Florence," in *Tijdschrift voor Rechts geschiedenis* 49 (1981):128–33, 143–44 and idem, " 'Cum Consensu Mundualdi': Legal Guardianship of Women in Quattrocento Florence," *Viator* 13 (1982):310–18, 329–33; Diane Owen Hughes, "Domestic Ideals and Social Behavior: Evidence from Medieval Genoa," in *The Family in History*, ed. Charles E. Rosenberg (Philadelphia: University of Pennsylvania Press, 1975), pp. 139–42 on widows.

30. Judith C. Brown and Jordan Goodman, "Women and Industry in Florence," *Journal of Economic History* 40 (March 1980):73–80.

31. *The Canons and Decrees of the Sacred and Oecumenical Council of Trent, Celebrated under the Sovereign Pontiffs, Paul III, Julius III, and Pius IV*, trans. Rev. James Waterworth, (London: C. Dolman, 1848), pp. 237–38, 240, 246 (Session XXV, De Regularibus et Monialibus, Chapters II, V, XV).

32. Creytens, "La Riforma," pp. 66–79; D'Addario, *Aspetti della Controriforma*, pp. 132–44, 157–58, 162–67, 171, 281–97, 480–84.

33. Quoted in Enrica Viviani della Robbia, *Nei monasteri fiorentini* (Florence: Sansoni, 1946), p. 78. The pope's reference to Elijah is from 1 Kings 17:6 (NEB).

34. Bigallo 1691, ff. iv, 27v–29, 34–35v, 37rv, 40.

35. Bigallo 1691, f. 34.

36. *Canons and Decrees*, pp. 242–43 (session XXV, De Regularibus et Monialibus, Chapter VIII); Archivio Segreto Vaticano, Archivio sacra congregazione del concilio, Visite Apostoliche 37 (Florence, 1575), ff. 1rv, 49v–51.

37. For instance, Suor (Maria) Lavinia Barbigi received rent from a house she owned, as is documented in Conventi Soppressi 126:54, ff. 52, 64; Conventi Soppressi 126:69, unpaginated, 1 October 1640; Acquisti e Doni 230:4, f. 55. On the population of the monastery, Visite Apostoliche 37, f. 50 states that in 1575 the convent held 125 nuns and 10 novices; in Conventi Soppressi 126:63, an unpaginated inventory (ca. 1626) indicates a total of 204 nuns.

38. For the investments made by the monastery's mid-seventeenth-century abbess, Suor Maria Gratia Alberighi, Conventi Soppressi 126:53, ff. V, 31, 46.

39. Conventi Soppressi 126:66, 12 June 1679 and a thick file for the years 1697–99.

40. Liebowitz, "Prison," pp. 2, 10.

41. Liebowitz, "Prison," pp. 10–11.

42. Maria Elena Vasaio-Zambonini, "Miserable Virgins and Abandoned Maidens in Tridentine Rome: A Social History of Two Charitable Institutions in the Mid-Sixteenth and Early Seventeenth Centuries," (Ph.D. dissertation prospectus, New York University, 1984), pp. 5, 6.

43. What the Church intended did not uniformly transpire. In "Prison," pp. 11–12, Liebowitz notes that while Santa Valeria in the 1570s was becoming more conventual in form, economic exigencies would not permit a slackening of labor. Arduous work activities became "dominant in the life of the community" there. Santa Valeria, however, was a particularly harsh and grim *convertite* institution.

44. Conventi Soppressi 191:10, f. 8.

45. For an interesting look at convent workshops employing lay females and males in nineteenth-century Lyon, where the Church undertook the "socialization of the faithful for the industrializing world," see Laura S. Strumingher, *Women and the Making of the Working Class: Lyon 1830–1870* (St. Alban's, Vt.: Eden Press, 1979), pp. 51–64.

46. Ivy Pinchbeck, *Women Workers and the Industrial Revolution 1750–1850* (London: George Routledge and Sons, 1930), pp. 196–201; Margaret Hewitt, *Wives and Mothers in Victorian Industry* (London: Rockliff, 1958), pp. 48–61; Louise A. Tilly and Joan W. Scott, *Women, Work, and Family* (New York: Holt, Rinehart, and Winston, 1978), pp. 116–23.

47. Bigallo 1691, ff. 41v–42v, 52v, 65; Vasaio-Zambonini, "Miserable Virgins," pp. 3–5; Ferrante, "L'onore ritrovato," p. 502.

48. Acquisti e Doni 292, unpaginated, at the date October 1580.

49. Ferrante, "L'onore ritrovato," p. 513.

50. Quoted in Lombardi, "L'ospedale," p. 291.

51. Conventi Soppressi 191:10, ff. 8, 10, 15, 19–26; Conventi Soppressi 191:36, unpaginated, 1 and 15 September 1621, 16–17 December 1621.

52. Several pages of descriptions of departures from Florence's Monastery of the Convertite in the seventeenth century appear in Acquisti e Doni 230:4, ff. 44–47. On transfer between institutions and egress to wed, see Liebowitz, "Prison," p. 7; Ciammitti, "Quanto costa," pp. 487–88; Pullan, *Rich and Poor*, pp. 389–90, 393; Ferrante, "L'onore ritrovato," pp. 511–12.

53. Bigallo 1691, ff. 36v–38, 35rv, 39rv, 16, 18; Vasaio-Zambonini, "Miserable Virgins," pp. 2, 4; Pullan, *Rich and Poor*, p. 390. See also Ferrante, "L'onore ritrovato," p. 511, on releases of Bologna's Soccorso inmates *alla sigurtà* to reputable unrelated guardians.

54. Conventi Soppressi 191:10, ff. 21–23v, 27v.

55. For Maddalena Martini, Acquisti e Doni 230:4, f. 46; Liebowitz, "Conversion," p. 9.

56. Bigallo 1691, ff. 39v–40; Conventi Soppressi 126:55, ff. 159, 242, for a midseventeenth-century instance of a state subsidy granted to a woman reentering Florence's Monastery of the Convertite for the second time.

57. Conventi Soppressi 126:69, unpaginated, 7 April 1661.

58. Ferrante, "L'onore ritrovato," pp. 512–13, 501.

59. Conventi Soppressi 191:10, ff. 23, 24v, 26v; Conventi Sopprressi 191:36, unpaginated, 6 September 1642.

60. On the *querelle des femmes*, Joan Kelly-Gadol, "Did Women Have a Renaissance?" in *Becoming Visible: Women in European History*, eds. Renate Bridenthal and Claudia Koonz (Boston: Houghton Mifflin, 1977), p. 154; Ian Maclean, *The Renaissance Notion of Woman: A Study in the Fortunes of Scholasticism and Medical Science in European Intellectual Life* (Cambridge: Cambridge University Press, 1980).

61. Pullan, *Rich and Poor*, pp. 391, 389; Vasaio-Zambonini, "Miserable Virgins," pp. 3–6.

62. Liebowitz, "Prison," pp. 2–3; Pullan, *Rich and Poor*, p. 393; Ferrante, "L'onore ritrovato," pp. 500, 517, 512–13.

63. Pullan, *Rich and Poor*, p. 379; Liebowitz, "Conversion," pp. 2, 8.

64. Quoted in Lombardi, "L'ospedale," p. 299.

65. Pullan, *Rich and Poor*, pp. 377–78; Ferrante, "L'onore ritrovato," p. 500.

66. Viviani della Robbia, *Nei monasteri fiorentini*, p. 49; Liebowitz, "Prison," pp. 4–5; Vasaio-Zambonini, "Miserable Virgins," p. 5.

67. Pullan, *Rich and Poor*, p. 394; Liebowitz, "Virgins," pp. 139–43; D'Addario, *Aspetti della Controriforma*, pp. 296–97.

68. Although the generalization holds, the chronology varied for different marginal segments of the population. Systematic confinement of the poor began in the sixteenth century and widespread confinement of the insane not until the eighteenth century. On the "great confinement," Michel Foucault, *Madness and Civilization: A History of Insanity in the Age of Reason*, trans. Richard Howard (New York: Random House, 1965), pp. 38–64, and by the same author, *The Birth of the Clinic: An Archaeology of Medical Perception*, trans. A. M. Sheridan Smith (New York: Random House, 1973) and *Discipline and Punish: The Birth of the Prison*, trans. Alan Sheridan (New York: Random House, 1979). For an important critique that starts, as Foucault does, from the premise that institutionalization greatly increased in the early modern period, see Lawrence Stone, "Madness," *New York Review of Books* 29 (16 December 1982):28–36 and in vol. 30 of the same publication (31 March 1983):42–44, "An Exchange with Michel Foucault." See also Robert Forster and Orest Ranum, eds., *Deviants and the Abandoned in French Society: Selections from the Annales, Economies, Sociétés, Civilisations* (Baltimore: Johns Hopkins University Press, 1978); *Quaderni storici* (special issue) "Sistemi di carità: esposti e internati nella società di antico regime," 53 (August 1983).

69. Estelle B. Freedman, *Their Sisters' Keepers: Women's Prison Reform in America*,

1830–1930 (Ann Arbor: University of Michigan Press, 1981); David Garland, *Punishment and Welfare: A History of Penal Strategies* (Aldershot, England: Gower, 1985); Lombardi, "L'ospedale," pp. 305–306, on a late seventeenth-century institution for deviant male youth, p. 309.

70. Lombardi, "L'ospedale," n. 39, p. 303.

71. Viviani della Robbia, *Nei monasteri fiorentini*, p. 226; Bargiacchi, *Storia degli istituti*, 3:223–42. Reviewing a book on the history of American women's colleges, Diane Ravitch referred to the link between convents and schools for females: "The intention, in part, had been to create 'Protestant nunneries', but students seeking the joys of college life and faculty members seeking a measure of personal freedom eventually undermined the religious constraints placed upon them." See "Women's Schools: Sexed, Desexed and Resexed," *New York Times Book Review* 28 (October 1984):12.

72. Bargiacchi, *Storia degli istituti*, 3:238–39, quotes the Motuproprio of 21 March 1785, Art. 12. The oblates could not return to the same conservatory that they had once departed, but presumably they could enter another conservatory if they later wished to do so.

73. Conventi Soppressi 126:83; Conventi Soppressi 191:37; Marco Lastri, *L'osservatore fiorentino sugli edifizi della sua patria*, 3d ed., 8 vols. (originally published 1797; Florence: G. Ricci, 1821), 3:125–28.

74. Ciammitti, "Quanto costa," n. 72.

75. Bigallo 1691, f. 12v.

76. For Pistoia's Santa Maria Maddalena, see Conventi Soppressi 191:35, unpaginated, 10 April 1604, undated signed pledges, and 18 July 1653; for Florence's Monastery of the Convertite, see, for instance, Conventi Soppressi 126:70, unpaginated, Elisabeth de Paulis' donation of Monte di Pietà shares dated 5 November 1577 and a Florentine nobleman's donation dated 14 February 1610.

77. Conventi Soppressi 191:25, ff. 41v, 45v; Bigallo 1691, ff. 43v–47v; Pullan, *Rich and Poor*, pp. 386, 389, 390, 393; Ferrante, "L'onore ritrovato," pp. 504–06; Ciammitti, "Quanto costa," nn. 11, 48.

78. Gaudement, "Il legame matrimoniale," pp. 66–67 and Natalie Zemon Davis, "Ghosts, Kin, and Progeny: Some Features of Family Life in Early Modern France," *Daedalus* 106 (Spring 1977):103 on Protestant divorce; Lastri, 3:125.

79. Conventi Soppressi 191:10, f. 1v.

F. ELLEN WEAVER

Erudition, Spirituality, and Women: The Jansenist Contribution

The changes wrought by social, economic, and religious forces in the Reformation period in France have been studied from various aspects: for example, family structure, sexuality, social status, forms of spirituality, and education.[1] For the women in this essay the focus will be on education and spirituality. Since they were part of the rising bourgeoisie, the *petit nobilité*, social status forms the background of the study, which emphasizes the contribution of Jansenist women. Most of these Jansenist women were part of the privileged class, and their world was the world of the parliament and court of Paris.[2] As such they were well educated. They were also very religious, and were certainly affected by some of the religious changes effected by the Counter Reformation in France.

In post-Tridentine Catholicism, religion and education, particularly with regard to women, were not antagonistic. Supported by a significant amount of research François Furet and Jacques Ozouf state that it is anachronistic to consider that the Church of that epoch was the champion of the intellectual inferiority of women. On the contrary the Church multiplied recommendations that the education of girls be equal to that of boys. Any inequality which existed in the curriculum "was not caused by an intellectual condemnation of women, but by a furious will to segregate the sexes."[3]

Indeed, education of the young was a priority for the Counter-Reformation bishops, and the Jansenist bishops were among the most serious about meeting it. They were serious, also, about revitalizing prayer and reforming morals. Women were involved in this spiritual and intellectual renewal, which characterized Counter-Reformation France at many levels.

In France the Counter Reformation took root a generation later than in neighboring Spain. For example, Teresa of Avila, one of the great spiritual leaders of the Spanish Counter Reformation and founder of the reformed Carmelites, died in 1582. Teresa was a strong advocate of spiritual direction for women, and, indeed, she provided a model for the woman as director of women (and men, as well). The first community of Carmelites was established in Paris in 1604 by Cardinal Bérulle and another remarkable woman, Madame Acarie. Together they formed a kind of "spiritual salon" in the heart of Paris. An important member of this salon was François de Sales, the bishop of Geneva (Annecy, actually, since Geneva was in the hands of the Swiss/French reform), a model of the Counter-Reformation bishop.

François de Sales, author of *l'Introduction à la Vie Dévote*, was responsible, perhaps more than any other member of the "école française," for moving the spiritual renewal into the lives of the Catholic laity.[4] It is not insignificant that the "father" of French Jansenism, Jean Duvergier de Hauranne, Abbé de Saint-Cyran, and Mère Angélique Arnauld, reforming abbess of Port-Royal, the Cistercian abbey which became the center of the movement,[5] admired greatly and had some contacts with both François de Sales and Cardinal Bérulle. Saint Teresa was a revered model for Mère Angélique and the abbesses of Port-Royal who followed her.

Reform from the bishops down and the rise of spiritual direction for the laity were significant characteristics of the spiritual revitalization which made the seventeenth century one of the most brilliant chapters in the history of the Church of France.

This history was not without conflict, and the Jansenists were a storm center both politically and theologically. On the political front, since they came mainly from the parliamentary class, their ecclesiology was Gallican; that is, they defended the independence of the Church of France vis-à-vis Rome against those who viewed the Church as a monolithic structure headed by the pope in Rome. Members of the Society of Jesus, which was strongly aligned with the throne and vowed to defend the papacy, were their fiercest enemies.

On the theological front Jansenists and Jesuits were engaged in a debate over the definition of grace and freedom of the will which spanned the century. The debate was opened when the study of Augustine's doctrine of grace exponded in the *Augustinus* by Cornelius Jansen was condemned by the Jesuit-controlled Sorbonne. Jansen, from whom the Jansenists' name derived, was a close friend of Saint-Cyran, who introduced the *Augustinus* into France.

These political and theological battles are often the best remembered aspects of Jansenism. Yet the leaders of the group were also at the center of the intellectual, spiritual renewal outlined above. Of particular interest to this study, they were also feminists to the extent that they defended the right of the laity, including women, to participate in the offices of the Church and have access to Scripture and liturgical texts through translations.[6] The nuns of Port-Royal were part of the Jansenist movement of spiritual renewal from the beginning, and lay women were drawn into the movement and became prominent in its later stages.

Parallel to the movements of spiritual renewal, education, and Gallicanism in France in the seventeenth century there was a fascinating feminist movement.[7] If feminism is defined as the affirmation of the equal value of women and men as human beings and allowing women to share in the concerns, contributions to, and rewards of society along with men, then the Jansenist women were feminists, even though they did not subscribe to— even abhorred—some of the positions taken by the secular feminists of the age.

In addition to what we might term their "spiritual feminism," the Jansenist women reflect many of the characteristics of French Catholic culture of the age: a commitment to heightened levels of learning and serious spiritual renewal. But they also differ from women in other groups because of their identification with the Jansenist movement. Through education and spirituality, the ways in which these women shared in the ideals, erudition, the piety of the movement become evident.

The manuals of prayer written by the Port-Royalists illustrate how their ideal of spirituality and learning was translated into the lives of the men and women for whom these prayer books were written. Contemporary accounts present the Jansenist women living according to this guidance and shed light on the extent to which they, for instance, participated in the liturgy, and read Scripture. Finally, a more detailed account of two exemplary Jansenist women, Mademoiselle de Joncoux and Madame Angran de Fontpertuis, will complete this composite portrait of Jansenist women and the way they shared in Jansenist erudition and piety with the men.

MANUALS OF PRAYER FOR THE LAITY: ILLUSTRATIONS OF JANSENIST ERUDITION AND PIETY

The "erudite spirituality" of the Jansenists,[8] developed from a paradoxical view of human nature—the "misère/grandeur" of Pascal, a cultivation of erudition, and a consciousness of the rights of the individual conscience. It was a spirituality which appealed to, and indeed tended to form, an elite group within the Church. At the same time it led to a sense of the Church as a community in which the laity had their role to play and, for example, were encouraged to follow the prayers of the priest in the liturgy, the Mass as well as the daily offices such as vespers.

The Jansenists also sustained a great love of Scripture. The greatest work of scholarship of the group was the translation of the Bible, the so-called *Bible de Mons* (after the place of publication in Belgium). The laity were encouraged to read the Bible and to base their meditation and spirituality on it. Finally, Jansenism promoted a vision of the Church which was less hierarchical than the prevailing view, where the treasures of liturgy and scholarship were available to all, laity as well as clerics, women as well as men.

To judge from the many editions of the *Prières Chrétiennes en forme de Méditations* by Pasquier Quesnel, it must have been one of the most popular manuals used by the laity. The first edition was dated 1667, and the final revision was 1719, with many revisions and reprintings in between.[9]

Part 1 contains the "temporal cycle" of liturgical feasts from Advent through Pentecost, followed by the feasts of Holy Trinity, Corpus Christi, a feast to commemorate a Eucharistic miracle particular to Brussels, and the feasts of the Virgin Mary. Part 2 is the "sanctoral cycle"—that is, the feasts of the saints. The choice of saints is significant. Besides biblical figures there are only Saint Geneviève and Saint Denis, patrons of Paris; Saints Benedict, Bernard, and Bruno, founders of the monastic orders favored by the Jansenists—Benedictines, Cistercians and Carthusians;[10] Saints Teresa (of Avila) and Ursula, the first a major figure of the post-Tridentine reform of religious orders and model for the nuns of Port-Royal, and the second known for her instruction of young women; and finally the converted sinner and "desert mother," Saint Mary of Egypt.

For each feast there is a long prayer in the form of a meditation followed by a list of practices recommended for the day of the celebration. The moral rigorism of Jansenism appears in the practices, which include cultivation of a sense of unworthiness and a spirit of abnegation and sacrifice; emphasis on renunciation of the world; and prayers for charity, purity and humility.

The feast of Saint Mary of Egypt is a striking example of Jansenist erudition and piety. The devotion of the second longest chapter in the book to the feast of this "desert mother" is witness both to the attraction of the Jansenists to the early church (especially the desert fathers), and to their adaptation of texts for use of the laity.[11] According to the legend Mary fled the wicked city of Alexandria, where she had been an actress and courtesan, for the solitude of the desert to live out her days in prayer and penance. Following the "meditation prayer," which stresses the call to holiness of sinners like Mary, whom "the world regards with the greatest contempt and disgust," the meditation continues with an account of how, when her heart and body were buried in a profound abyss of corruption and vice, the Lord descended to search for this lost sheep.[12]

Mary, blind, insensible, drunk with the false delights of her loose life, thought she could forget God and abandon herself to sin. But—and here the theme of predestination appears—God did not forget her. She was written in the book of God's eternal love; she could not escape. When the moment written in the book of life came, God spoke: "and at [God's] word the light flashed out of the darkness—that glorious and triumphant light which dissipates the night of sin." The eyes of Mary's heart were opened and she saw the person of Jesus Christ. Seeing Christ she saw the glory of God, and of God's law which is the way, and of the grace which conducts the "elect" to the source of eternal light.[13] This powerfully written passage, is a clear example of election and a description of the effects of the grace of conversion. The image of light in darkness is a favorite of the Port-Royalists.[14]

The life of Mary the Egyptian, converted sinner, is then described at length. She retreated into the desert. There, taking as her guide the prophet Elias, she walked, not for forty days and forty nights, but for forty years, in solitude, fasting, vigils, and prayer. Finally, after forty-seven years, she was found by Abba Zozima. She made her confession and he received her into the Church. But, still not pure enough to receive the Body of Christ, she had to wait another year, adding to her penances a terrible hunger for the Eucharist. The prayer concludes with a long description of her fervent communion.

The life of Mary the Egyptian as retold by Quesnel is a paradigm of the Jansenist formula for holiness: election-conversion-penance-fervent communion. The prayer also illustrates graphically the doctrine of grace. The practices proposed for the reader repeat these emphases. The exercises for the feast are concluded by another example of Jansenist erudition: a recent translation of the *Litanies and Hymns of St. Mary the Egyptian* by Abbé de Rancé, founder of the Trappists.[15]

The longest office in the book, as might be expected, is for the feast of St. Augustine. At the end of the manual there are a series of prayers for special persons and occasions: for a mistress of novices, for a pregnant woman, a prayer for a good bishop (which can also be used during a vacancy of the Holy See to pray for a holy pope).[16] A very significant office is the "Prayer . . . for young people; and those who want to read the word of God, especially the Gospel."[17] The theme of the office is the words of Holy Scripture as the nourishment of every Christian, beginning in infancy, since:

> In the most pure centuries [that is, the Early Church], Lord, your Church had no problem about giving your adorable Blood in the Eucharist to nursing infants; can she not also put on the tongue and in the ears some of your words?[18]

It is noteworthy that here and elsewhere Scripture is compared to the Eucharist. In both the presence of Christ is encountered.

The first of the practices recommends that parents should have a complete Bible in the home and also should own several copies of the New Testament. The Bible is a precious furnishing that no Christian home should lack. It is an instrument for forming Christianity in souls and for producing true children of God.

Against the argument that many may be too poor to afford copies of the Bible, Quesnel uses a long quotation from John Chrysostom. Chrysostom asks: If a craftsman takes care above all to have tools necessary for his trade in order to earn a living for his family, how can parents neglect to have the tool necessary to craft the faith and the Christian virtues needed to earn eternal life?[19]

Quesnel urges parents to teach children respect for the Bible by calling their attention to the liturgical ceremonies which surround the Scripture readings in Church. Children learn from watching these ceremonies the respect with which the Word of God is to be treated. In the home other practices, such as kissing the Bible, help children understand that it is a book "full of mysteries." Children should be introduced to Scripture at an early age by listening to passages from the life of Christ, reading the New Testament as soon as they can, and learning psalms by heart.[20] What parents do for children in the home, pastors should do in the parish, especially for those children who do not have good home guidance.

The chapter ends with an appeal to the rich, be they members of the laity or clergy, to use their riches for the dispersion of the Word of God by putting the holy book of the Gospels into the hands of the poor. Quesnel exhorts not just spiritual directors, confessors, and preachers, but all those who have no other talent than familiarity with the Scripture, to share in the work of spreading the Gospel.[21] Following this chapter on the integration of Scripture into the spiritual life of the laity there is a section containing brief excerpts from the Bible and passages from the early Christian writers exhorting the people to read Holy Scripture.

This manual provides a striking illustration of all the ingredients outlined above as contributing to the Jansenist ideal of erudite piety: the emphasis on a life of moral rectitude; ample references to the work of grace in the Christian life with examples from the saints' lives; and the exhortation to Christians, regardless of condition, sex, or age, to make Holy Scripture the basis of their lives.

There is scant direct reference in Quesnel's *Prières Chrétiennes* to the liturgical life of Christians. Yet, the recommendation of church ceremonies as a way to teach children respect for Scriptures suggests attendance at liturgy from an early age. And, of course, the very fact of basing meditations on the liturgical year underscores familiarity with the offices. Others in the group did, however, furnish translations of texts and provide manuals to serve as guides to the liturgy.[22]

These texts not only presuppose an educated laity, but also serve to educate them further and to guide them in their participation in the liturgy and their appreciation of it. To determine the degree to which the laity actually followed this direction in their daily life as well as in their life of public worship we must glean what we can from contemporary accounts, realizing that, as in the case of any controversial movement, descriptions of the Jansenists suffer from possible exaggerations on the side of their defenders as well as their detractors.

CONTEMPORARY ACCOUNTS

At the Church of Asnières, a suburb of Paris, the priest Jacques Jubé initiated a liturgy which encouraged lay participation. According to the descriptions of the ceremonies there, he succeeded. The people sang the parts of the Mass intended for them, responded "Amen" to the priest's prayers, and so on.[23] The bishop of Auxerre, Charles de Caylus, who was an ardent Jansenist, published a pastoral letter in 1724 in which he urged the faithful to participate not only at communion but also throughout the Mass by uniting in mind and heart with the priest, who speaks in their name. It is the right and duty of the laity to unite their prayers with the priest's, he wrote, and consequently he exhorted them to make use of the French translation of the Ordinary of the mass.[24]

At St. Jacques-du-Haut-Pas, a Jansenist church in Paris, a liturgy similar to that at Asnières is described. Laffiteau, an enemy of the Jansenists, made an accusation that women performed the readings at vespers at St. Jacques.

Petitpied, one of the Quesnel group, responded that Laffiteau confused vespers with a Saturday evening teaching session for the children, at which one of the women reads the Gospel for Sunday and the children, who have studied it during the week, recite it from memory.[25]

Such references to the active participation of women in the liturgy are rare and, once found, need to be carefully analyzed. For example, a startling account is attributed to the niece of Abbé Duguet, Madame Mol, which describes how, like "the heretics of every age [who] have considered it a coup for the party to enlist women," among the Jansenists, "women mount the altar and say the Mass in priestly vestements." Further quotations, taken from Madame Mol's *Journal of the Convulsions*, describe how a certain Mademoiselle Danconi celebrates the holy Mysteries in "a manner so admirable . . . that one cannot but admire the dignity, the majesty, with which she celebrates this function." Another woman, the *Journal* continues, "has convulsions and says the Mass every day, which has authorized others to say it, because she did it with the approbation of the Doctors of the party."[26] Fact or fiction? Like many accounts in the literature of the eighteenth century at the time the Jansenist-Jesuit debates had heated up once more, it is not easy to sort out but it is not impossible. This description comes from a Jesuit tract which, it seems, first circulated in pamphlet form in 1738. It was authored anonymously by the Jesuits in an attempt to revive a story—the Jansenist journal *Nouvelles Ecclésiastiques* calls it a fable[27]—about the meeting of a group of conspiratorial Jansenists (St. Cyran, Antoine Arnauld, and others) at the Carthusian monastery of Bourg-Fontaine in 1621 to plot the overthrow of the Catholic church. The tract sets out to prove how the plot is being carried out through the democratization of the church by the Jansenists. The account of the women priests is just one example of the way ecclesiastical authority is being undermined by the party.

The *Nouvelles Ecclésiastiques* took up the gauntlet, pointing out that the quotation used above was indeed by Madame Mol. But the *Journal of the Convulsions* was so named in reference to the strange seizures accompanying devotion to the holy Jansenist deacon Pâris by those known as the "convulsionaries of St. Medard" (his burial place). It was Madame Mol's horrified account of what she considered profanations of the memory of the good deacon. "No one is ignorant of the fact that Madame Mol rose up against the convulsions," reported the *Nouvelles Ecclésiastiques*, "and she has been reproached for exaggerating the facts, far from diminishing them."[28] It appears, as was common in this war of words, that the Jesuits had taken what Madame Mol wrote in accusation of Mademoiselle Danconi and reported it as admiration.

And so the reply to "fact or fiction?" must be that there is some of both. In the case of the convulsionaries, it seems quite certain that women were given leadership roles. But this says nothing about the role of women in Jansenism, since the Jansenists, who at first were convinced that true mira-

cles occurred at the tomb of deacon Pâris, rejected the movement and dis-
owned it as soon as the phenomena included bizarre and hysterical
behavior.[29]

On the other hand, there is no question that Jansenist ecclesiology as it
evolved under the leadership of Quesnel in the eighteenth century defined
the Church as the assembly of the people, with the laity assuming an important role. Whenever the laity are recognized as having an active part in the
life of the Church attention is given to that portion of the laity who fill the
benches and often pay the bills: the women. Antoine Arnauld defended the
right of all the laity to the Scripture, and argued for the translation of Scripture and the offices of the Church into the vernacular, especially so women
would be able to read and understand them.[30]

Also, it is possible that in the prayer gatherings, which became more and
more common among the Jansenists as they were driven underground,
women as well as men read the Scripture aloud and commented on it. Was
this commentary a preached homily? One text, using as a source the anti-
Jansenist *Supplément des Nouvelles Ecclésiastiques*, reports on the clandestine
meetings of the *"Petite Eglise"* at Nantes: "During these meetings sometimes
there is only a reading, but most often there is a sermon . . . Women
preachers are especially successful."[31]

We know also that in the monasteries, when an exceptional situation prevailed, the women took charge. At Port-Royal, when the priests who had
been their spiritual directors went into exile, Mère Angélique de Saint-Jean
Arnauld d'Andilly wrote a treatise on spiritual direction, which could have
been called "How to Do Without a Spiritual Director." Her solution was for
the abbess to become spiritual director (and this could include care of matters of conscience) or for the individual nun to seek guidance in Scripture.[32]
The Carmelite monastery of Lectoure was placed under interdict in 1731
because of the refusal of the nuns to accept the *Unigenitus*. On Palm Sunday,
when they had no one to officiate, the prioress distributed palms blessed at
another church and the nuns, after chanting the Divine Office, recited aloud
the Mass and the Passion.[33]

As noted above, one of the more important changes brought about by
the Counter Reformation was emphasis on education. Many of the Jansenist
bishops established in their dioceses groups of lay women similar to those
described by Claude Lancelot in his account of a journey to Alet:

> They have no vows but those of their baptism. . . . They have no cloister, but
> live in a manner similar to nuns. . . . They go to church in the parish. . . . They
> are engaged to establish little schools and to teach Christian doctrine to mem-
> bers of their sex throughout the diocese. . . . They sleep in dormitories. . . .
> They have a common room where they say the daily office . . . They dress in
> secular clothing but very modestly, completely covering the lower arm.[34]

Since this account is dated 1644, the group described could very well have
had a copy of Jacqueline Pascal's *Reglement pour les Enfants*, written for care

of the girls educated at Port-Royal where she was a nun. This rule is very similar to the one developed by the "messieurs de Port-Royal" for their Little Schools. This similarity indicates that a generation before the publication of the manuals described above, women as well as men in the Port-Royal group were receiving a spiritual formation which centered on Scripture and the office. Jacqueline's rule includes not only guides for training in moral virtue, but also an initiation into participation in the Divine Office and ways to cultivate love of Scripture and meditation on it. A significant comment in the section on the children's instruction on the breviary is that those who come to the monastery school young often learn their entire psalter by heart, as well as the hymns of the breviary in Latin and French.

The *Nouvelles Ecclésiastiques* provides illustrations of how this Jansenist spirituality, the erudition and the scriptural-liturgical piety, was integrated into the lives of lay women of all walks of life.[35] There is, no doubt, an element of hagiography in these accounts. Most of the women are chosen as examples of the refusal of sacraments to holy people for the sole reason that they did not accept the *Unigenitus*. The accounts are, however, useful as descriptions of the qualities that the Jansenists admired in women. The accounts range from brief notices to long eulogies, but similar traits are praised throughout.

One of the longer notices, paraphrased here, can serve to characterize the exemplary Jansenist woman. Dame Marie-Thérèse d'Oraison, widow of Monsieur le Marquis de Valbelle, born from one of the oldest houses in Aix-en-Provence, died in 1752 at the age of 82. Her father had been remarkable for his unusual care for the poor tenants of his lands, and she followed his example. At a young age she received spiritual direction from Dom Jacques de St. Robert, a religious who was banished on account of his opposition to the *Unigenitus*. Dom Jacques acquainted her with the books of Port-Royal.

In 1700 at the age of thirty she married, and just as Mademoiselle d'Oraison had been a model for single persons, Madame la Marquise de Valbelle became a model of virtue for Christian wives. Widowed soon afterwards, she lived according to Saint Paul's instructions, occupied in prayer, retirement, penance, work with her hands, and service to the poor. She was generous in almsgiving, she found good positions for the children of her servants, and she paid the dowries for many of their daughters. When the anti-Jansenist bishop came to her diocese he demanded, through her confessor, that she give up reading the *Réflexions sur le Nouveau Testament* of Quesnel. She was "too enlightened" to be taken in, and she refused. From here on the account of her trials, of the refusal of sacraments, follows a familiar pattern except that, because of her exemplary life—or, more cynically, her high social status—on Easter Monday her parish priest gave her communion when she was carried into church in her *"chaise à porteurs, where no doubt he considered her more Catholic than in her bed."* When she died the New Testament, which she customarily carried with her, was found on her bedside table.[36]

An almost identical story is told of the wife of a merchant of Reims. The main difference is that, whereas Madame de Valbelle as a noblewoman cared for the people who served on her lands, Madame Elisabeth Sutaine, wife of Sieur Lacaille, shared her goods with her fellow townspeople. She is praised because in the midst of her concerns with the trade (she maintained the business alongside of her husband), she found time to pray, to study religion in depth, to give a Christian education to her daughter, and then to aid in the education of her daughter's many children. In this determination she and her daughter were aided by the good school teachers "of which the public had been deprived by persecution." (This suggests a clandestine Jansenist school.) Her house was a kind of store where the truly needy—the old, abandoned children, and others—found clothing, linens, and other necessities in health and in sickness.[37]

Education was a central concern in the lives of all of these women. There are some remarkable accounts of women who gave their lives to the profession of teaching. Catherine Cahouet died in 1751 in the diocese of Orleans at the age of 92. She had spent sixty years teaching in a school founded by the three Cahouet sisters. The five teachers in the school lived an almost monastic life, detached from the world, assiduous in their attendance at the divine office, frequenting the sacraments. The children were taught not only to memorize, but also to explain the catechism of Orleans. This instruction was augmented by the study of the New Testament. Every day the students recited verses which were explained in a way that elicited their respect for the Divine Word. Then, in every class a lesson was taken from the Gospel, but, instead of being given an explanation, the children were called on to explain it themselves. This exercise intended to teach them to seek in the sacred text the instructions Jesus Christ had for them. Thus they developed a taste for learning the epistles and gospels of the Holy Mass and the instructions for entering into the spirit of the Mysteries [of the Liturgy].[38]

This love of Scripture and liturgy is described in the life of a servant girl, Elisabeth Trochet of Nemours, who was refused absolution because she would not promise to give up reading the New Testament of Quesnel.[39] Similarly, the daughter of a rich merchant of Marseilles, Mademoiselle Besson, was called back to her family at the age of thirteen after education in a convent, and she consented to return only if she could continue her practices of piety, including the recitation of the Divine Office. She arose in the night to say matins and again at 5:00 A.M. to recite lauds. She continued to recite the office at the appointed hours throughout the day and also read and meditated on the Scripture. In the evening at prayer with the servants half a chapter of the New Testament was read, and on Saturday the gospel for Sunday was included. Afterward, Mademoiselle Besson continued alone to read from the Acts of the Apostles.[40]

The Jansenist women were not all recluses, however. Many spent time in the Bastille for their participation in the distribution of the Port-Royal books and the *Nouvelles Ecclésiastiques*. Madame de Blond, the widow of a professor of philosophy at the University of Paris, was arrested in 1720 and imprisoned with Madame Théodon. This, the *Nouvelles Ecclésiastiques* reports, made of the Bastille not only a kind of seminary (the reference is to the priests arrested for similar Jansenist activities and imprisoned there), but also a convent. Madame de Blond was suspected of being in contact with sources of the *Nouvelles Ecclésiastiques* abroad.[41]

Madame Théodon, who was imprisoned with Madame de Blond, was described as "the first of her sex to confess to the truth in chains." She was arrested in 1728 for possessing several pamphlets denouncing the Assembly of Embrun (where charges were brought against the Jansenist bishop, Soannen of Senez). Later it is noted that she gave much of her fortune to care for the exiles and kept several rooms in Paris for their use. She also supported clandestine presses and distributed the Port-Royal works.[42] Her life is told at length and provides another model of the Jansenist "holy woman."

Françoise Elizabeth Jourdain, the widow of M. Théodon, the director of the French Academy of Painting and Sculpture in Rome, was born in Paris but moved to Rome at an early age. Her Jansenist upbringing alerted her to the dangerous aspects of her husband's profession. An incident is recounted which provides a good illustration of rigorous morality. The editors of the *Nouvelles Ecclésiastiques* express the hope that this example will be useful to Christians who "keep without scruple and display with delight objects of art which religion reproves and modesty detests." Madame Théodon saw a chef-d'oeuvre of sculpture destined for one of the royal palaces in which the rules of modesty had not been followed. She withdrew it, preferring to lose a large amount of money rather than to allow indecent art to appear in public.

Left a widow with a large fortune, after her two children entered religious orders, Madame Théodon established a home for the formation of young women, to train them for the care of the sick and teaching. Her active support of the Jansenists was combined with a style of life which was increasingly austere. She ate only once a day and for many years took her repose sitting in a chair, interrupting her sleep at intervals for the recitation of the office.[43]

At the other end of the social scale is Marie Reaubourg, a peddler who was arrested for the discovery in her possession of 900 copies of *Nouvelles Ecclésiastiques*. An account is given of her heroic refusal to divulge the secret of the location of the presses on which they were printed. She was condemned to five years of banishment from Paris, and she simply remained in her place of exile until death. Of her piety we are told that she assisted daily at Mass without neglecting any of her duties.[44]

TWO EXEMPLARY
JANSENIST WOMEN

From this sketch of the lives of a number of women (of whom I know only what is recorded in the *Nouvelles Ecclésiastiques*), I conclude with two women whom I have chosen as exemplars. These two women have left ample evidence of their reality, primarily in letters to and from them, but also in their "literary remains." To a remarkable degree each of them fits the model I have attempted to construct in this study of Jansenist erudition and piety and its traces in the notices on women in the *Nouvelles Ecclésiastiques*.

Françoise-Marguerite de Joncoux may have owed her fiery intelligence to her origins in that same region, Auvergne, which produced Blaise and Jacqueline Pascal. She left plenty of evidence of her lively wit and bold loyalty in her long descriptions, of her visits to the archbishop of Paris to plead the cause of the nuns of Port-Royal.[45] It is not easy to discern the ingredients of her personal piety. She says very little about herself in her letters. When this tiny, well-groomed woman set forth in her little two-wheeled, servant-drawn cart on her journeys to visit prelates and magistrates and other persons qualified to aid the cause of Port-Royal she always carried a book, we are told. But we are not told what she read. That she was pious there is no doubt. We can surmise that she had chosen her celibate state, for, in spite of her somber, "bark-colored" garb, her open, cheerful manner left the impression of a vibrant, attractive woman, not a bitter recluse.

But if we can only conjecture about Mademoiselle de Joncoux's prayer life, there is no question about her qualifications for inclusion in the category of erudite Jansenists. Beginning with what must have been a deep native intelligence, her mind was cultivated through her studies of literature and philosophy. A major indication of her scholarly ability was her translation into French of the notes of the Latin translation of Pascal's *Lettres provinciales* by Nicole. This translation into Latin, which Nicole published in 1658 under the name of Wendrock along with the commentaries he added, popularized the *Lettres* throughout Europe. It also added fuel to the fire which continued to flame until, forty years later, the Jesuit Père Daniel decided to reply to Pascal. Since he aimed many of his attacks at the commentaries in the Wendrock, that work became central to the new controversy. Père Daniel's work was available to the public in French. Mademoiselle de Joncoux determined to make the Wendrock accessible also: hence her translation of Nicole's notes into French.[46]

She also collaborated with leaders of the Jansenist party in the composition of apologetic tracts and a history of the movement.[47] There is some evidence that she did research for the friend of the Jansenists in Mons, Dr. Philippe-Ignace Save, as background for an essay he wrote on the baptism of monsters.[48] When Sainte-Beuve refers to her as the soul of the little Jansenist Sanhedrin,[49] he may be reflecting a name given her by the group who acclaimed her as their "nouvelle Debora." In every way, Mademoiselle de Joncoux typifies the women who were attracted to the intellectual aspects of Jansenism and who used their own scholarly talents to contribute to erudite Jansenism.

Angélique Crespin du Vivier, Madame Angran de Fontpertuis, belonged to an earlier generation, but was friendly with Mademoiselle de Joncoux, who probably regarded her as a kind of elderly relative. Madame de Fontpertuis fits the description given above of Madame de Valbelle. She belonged to the lesser nobility, the *noblesse de rôbe*. Left a widow with a young son after six years of marriage, she devoted the rest of her life to support of Port-Royal. She appears to have been fairly wealthy, if we can judge from the considerable support she provided the nuns and later the men in exile and the frequent journeys she made on their behalf.

Madame de Fontpertuis also fits the model of Jansenist women remarkably well. Like Madame de Blond, Madame Théodon, and Marie Reaubourg, she had a hand in smuggling the Port-Royal books from the clandestine presses into Paris.[50] We find in her letters evidence of all the marks of Jansenist piety: "I am presently alone," she writes from her chateau Fontpertuis in the diocese of Orleans, "and I taste the advantages of solitude with great pleasure."[51] In the many letters written to her by Soeur (then Mère) Angélique de Saint-Jean Arnauld d'Andilly and Antoine Arnauld, these heroes of Jansenist asceticism often warn her against too much austerity in her life, too rigorous a fast, too many night vigils.[52]

But of central interest here is the entry of Madame de Fontpertuis into the circle of erudite Jansenism. In a series of interesting letters to Madame de Fontpertuis, Monsieur du Charmel of the Oratory of Troyes discusses their respective literary efforts. He notes that in his exile he is writing litanies of the Good Shepherd. He had hoped that she would write the annales of Port-Royal, to be completed by Mademoiselle de Joncoux ("votre petite amie"), who should do the section on the last days. Instead, he comments in 1707,

> you have made good use of your retirement by consecrating it to the Breviary which is a tissue of Holy Scripture. This strikes me as a prodigious work, not only in the 2,500 pages which compose it, but in the selection and ordering [of scriptural texts?].[53]

In 1709 du Charmel mentions that his litanies do not compare with the great task Mme. de Fontpertuis has undertaken: the breviary, which she has not mentioned for some time, but which he supposes is finished. In 1710 he makes reference to a "diurnal," which is an extract of the breviary, noting that she has told him that the breviary was finished and bound in 1708. He presumes that what she refers to is the manuscript, which she has adorned with a magnificent binding.[54]

It is possible that Madame de Fontpertuis' *Diurnal* was never published. From 1710 until her death in 1714 her energies and material resources were more and more absorbed by the care of the nuns of Port-Royal, who were dispersed in 1709 before the destruction of the monastery in 1710. Perhaps she never carried through her plans to publish the *Diurnal*. Whatever its final fate, it has assured her a place among the erudite Jansenists. A breviary whose texts are woven from Scripture alone brings together the love of Scripture and liturgy in a significant way. Whatever may have drawn Madame de Fontpertuis to Port-Royal in her youth, in her old age she had been formed in the spirituality of Port-Royal, and she made her contribution to its literary history.

CONCLUSION

The question of the effect on women's lives of the changes brought about by the Counter Reformation is a complex one. Two of these changes, emphasis on education and spiritual direction for the laity, clearly affected the lives of women.

The case of the Jansenist women is an interesting one. Their spirituality was formed by their Jansenist directors, and it was a form of piety which endured.[55] This spirituality differed from pre-Reformation types, such as devotions to the saints, pilgrimages, the rosary.

It differed also from other post-Tridentine types in Catholicism. The Jesuit-sponsored devotion to the Sacred Heart of Jesus, for example, focused on the Eucharist. Yet rather than encouraging the laity to follow the prayers of the priest, to pray the psalms, to read and meditate on Scripture, and otherwise to enter into the liturgical prayer of the Church, the eucharistic devotions focused on the consecration at Mass. Laity were encouraged to attend services of benediction of the Blessed Sacrament, to visit Jesus in the Blessed Sacrament and to say prayers of reparation, to make novenas, to receive communion on the first Friday of every month, and so on.

Jansenist spirituality differed from Jesuit spirituality particularly in that it depended on education, or at least on careful instruction so that participation in the prayer of the Church was intellectually as well as emotionally founded.

Although not all Jansenist women were literate, the majority were. And those who were educated shared all aspects of the movement with the men. They certainly used the manuals examined here. In the home and in the instruction of children they shared responsibility for developing knowledge of and appreciation for Scripture, liturgy, and Christian doctrine. Women as well were appellants and suffered for their refusal to accept the *Unigenitus*. It is doubtful that the women exercised leadership roles in the liturgy, outside of the peripheral underground assemblies of the convulsionaries, but neither did laymen in the Catholic church of that era.

It would be too much to say that the Jansenist movement was feminist. Yet, without declaring themselves to be part of the feminist movement of their age, the Jansenist women did live very independent, self-motivated lives and enjoyed equality within the group. Furthermore, as noted in the writings of Arnauld, the leaders of the movement showed remarkable respect for women. Could not this equality in the realm of spirituality and intellectual life be considered another aspect of the feminism of the seventeenth century in France?

We can affirm neither that women were drawn to the movement because of the opportunities it afforded them nor that they were particularly attracted to the special blend of erudition and piety that made up Jansenist spirituality. Most of the women were part of the group because they were born or married into it. Their husbands or fathers were part of that social group, mainly parliamentarian, from which the Jansenists were drawn. But whatever drew them to Port-Royal, they became loyal supporters of the cause, contributed in many ways, and were formed spiritually by the contact.

This study illustrates, through one case study, the effect on women of the Counter-Reformation emphasis on education and spiritual direction of the laity. In fact, the Jansenist women, it seems to me, were in a remarkably integral way precisely the Catholic laity the reforms of the Council of Trent aimed to produce: a laity that was educated, especially in the doctrines of the church, that led morally upright lives, and that worshipped out of devotion and conviction rather than social habit. This may be the final paradox in Jansenism: the Counter-Reformation movement that was declared heretical produced, at least in its women, a kind of paradigm of Catholic reform.

NOTES

1. A list of all the significant works here would be too long. A few examples follow: in the area of family history the review *XVIIe siècle* (1974) was devoted to "Le XVIIe siècle et la famille"; Robert Forster and Orest Ranum edited a collection of selections from *Annales, economies, sociétés, civilisations,* translated by Elborg Forster and Patricia M. Ranum, *Family and Society* (Baltimore: Johns Hopkins University Press, 1976); also important are Jean-Louis Flandrin, *Familles: parenté, maison, sexualité dans l'ancienne société* (Paris: Hachette, 1976) and *Family and Sexuality in French History,* ed. Robert Wheaton and Tamara K. Hareven (Philadelphia: University of Pennsylvania Press, 1980). Carolyn C. Lougee has raised significant questions about the relationship between feminism and antifeminism and social mobility in *Le Paradis des Femmes: Women, Salons, and Social Stratification in Seventeenth Century France* (Princeton: Princeton University Press, 1976). For a study of the relationships between a religious order of women and the economy and society see Roger Devos, *Vie Religieuse Féminine et Société. L'origine social des Vistandines d'Annecy aux XVIIe et XVIIIe siècles,* (Annecy, 1973). For a few other references see F. E. Weaver, "Women and Religion in Early Modern France: A Bibliographic Essay on the State of the Question," *The Catholic Historical Review,* vol. LXVII, no. 1 (January 1981).

2. There were notable exceptions, for example, the servant Elisabeth Trochet and Marie Reaubourg, the peddler, who are described below.

3. François Furet and Jacques Ozouf, *Lire et ecrire: l'alphabétisation des français de Calvin à Jules Ferry* (Paris: Les Editions de Minuit, publié avec le concours de CNRS, 1977), p. 86.

4. One of the best discussions of the development of the *école française* spirituality remains Louis Cognet, "Les origines de la spiritualité française au XVIIe siècle," *"Culture" Catholique* (Paris: Editions du Vieux Colombier, 1949).

5. For a resume of the history of Port-Royal see F. E. Weaver, *The Evolution of the Reform of Port-Royal: From the Rule of Citeaux to Jansenism* (Paris: Editions Beauchesne, 1978), pp. 31–36. Major studies include Sainte-Beuve, *Port-Royal,* 3 vols. (Paris: Editions Gallimard, 1953), and Alexander Sedgwick, *Jansenism in Seventeenth-Century France: Voices from the Wilderness* (Charlottesville: University of Virginia Press, 1977).

6. A good example is Antoine Arnauld, *Défense des versions de l'Ecriture Sainte, Des Offices de l'Eglise et des ouvrages des Pères. Et en particulier de la nouvelle traduction du Bréviaire. Contre La Sentence de l'Official de Paris du 10 Avril, 1688.* (Cologne: chez

Nicolas Schouten, 1688). For a full discussion of this aspect of Jansenist scholarship see F. Ellen Weaver, "Scripture and Liturgy for the Laity: The Jansenist Case for Translation," *Worship* 59, No. 6 (Dec. 1985), pp. 510–21.

7. There are numerous studies on this movement. A general study is Jean Rabout, *Histoire des féminismes français* (Paris: Stock, 1978).

8. For a more complete definition of this concept see F. Ellen Weaver, "Port-Royal," in *Dictionnaire de spiritualité* (Paris: Éditions Beauchesne, 1985), vol. XIII, cols. 1931–1952.

9. I have used *Prières Chrétiennes en forme de Méditations. Sur tous les Mystères de Notre Seigneur & de la Ste Vierge & sur tous les Dimanches & les Fêtes de l'Année*, Nouvelle édition (Paris, 1733).

10. Saint Bernard was considered the "second founder" of the Cistercian order. Port-Royal was a Cistercian monastery and Saint Bernard was an honored "father" of the order. Citeaux (the Cistercians) was a medieval reform of the Benedictine order. Thus, the Rule of Benedict was the basic rule of Citeaux, hence of Port-Royal. St. Cyran greatly admired the Carthusians, founded by St. Bruno, because they imitated the life of the desert fathers.

11. The story of Mary of Egypt would have been available to the Port-Royalists in the *Acta Sanctorum* edited in Antwerp in 1643. This is confirmed by a recent publication of the catalogue of Isaac-Louis Le Maistre de Sacy (major translator of the Bible, cousin of Antoine Arnauld, one of the first group of Port-Royalists), *Une Grande Bibliothéque de Port-Royal*, edited by Odette Barenne (Paris: Etudes Augustiniennes, 1985). The *Acta Sanctorum* is listed there, p. 52.

12. *Prières Chrétiennes*, p. 211.

13. Ibid., p. 212.

14. Pascal incorporated it in his seal, which shows rays of light escaping from behind a cloud.

15. *Prières*, pp. 235–39.

16. Ibid., pp. 284–349.

17. Ibid., pp. 462–92.

18. Ibid., p. 466. The reference is to giving communion from the cup to infants at baptism, a practice which still exists in the Orthodox Church and churches which follow the Eastern Rite. Quesnel quotes Cyprian.

19. Ibid. pp. 471–72.

20. Ibid., pp. 473–78.

21. Ibid., pp. 490–91.

22. A good example of this genre is the book attributed to Nicolas Le Gros as compiler and editor, the *Manuel du Chrétien, contenant Le Livre des Pseaumes, le Nouveau Testament, & L'Imitation de Jesus Christ, Avec l'Ordinaire de la Messe* (Cologne, 1742). The companion work to Le Gros is *L'Année Chrétienne ou les Messes des Dimanches, Feries et Festes de toute l'année. En Latin et François. Avec l'Explication des Epistres et des Evangiles, & un Abregé de la vie des Saintes dont on fait l'Office* (Brussels, 1687) by Nicolas LeTourneux. This multivolume commentary contains not only the Ordinary but also the Proper for all the feasts of the year in Latin and French. *L'Année Chrétienne* became controversial because the Mass texts given were from the missal translated by Voisin, which was condemned in 1660. Arnauld discusses this condemnation and the grounds for declaring it illegal in *Defense des Versions*. LeTourneux was also author of the small and valuable *de la Meilleure manière d'Entendre la Sainte Messe* (Paris, 1688), which was certainly intended for the laity. In it LeTourneux recognizes that there are other ways to follow the Mass (for example, some say their rosary, some recite prayers, some meditate on subjects suggested by their directors), but he maintains that the best way is to read attentively, in the spirit of the Church, the prayers the priest is reciting at the altar (pp. 13–14).

23. The story of Jubé is found in L. Bouyer, *Liturgical Piety* (Notre Dame, Ind.: University of Notre Dame Press, 1966), pp. 53–54, who quotes Dom Guéranger, *Institutions Liturgiques* (Paris, 1841), vol. II, pp. 249–55. Interestingly enough, Bouyer, one of the proponents of the modern liturgical movement, praises Jubé whereas Guéranger denounces him, especially for reciting the prayers of the canon in an audible tone. Thus we find in the present liturgical movement a return to the position of the Jansenists. The primary source of the description of the Jubé liturgy is found in Blin [le P. Jacques de la Baune, S.J.], *Les reflexions sur la nouvelle liturgie d'Aniers* [sic] (N.P., 1724) and Jean Grancolas, *Observations sur l'examen du cérémonial d'Asnières, ouvrage ou on accusait le curé Jubé et le docteur Petit-pied d'avoir altéré ce cérémonial* (Paris, Bibliothèque de Ste Geneviève, MS 1305, no date).

24. *Nouvelles Ecclésiastiques*, 17 vols. (N.P., 1728–81), 1751 pp. 49–50 [hereafter noted as *N.E.*, year, page/s].

25. Bibliothèque Nationale, Paris. MS fonds français 24, 877. *Lettre à M. l'abbé de Vessière au sujet de plusieurs faussétés avancées par M. Laffiteau, Evêque de Sisteron dans son "Histoire de la Constitution Unigenitus"*, p. 633.

26. *La Réalité du Projet de Bourg-Fontaine demontrée par l'Execution*, 2 vols. (Paris, 1755), Vol. II., pp. 300–302. The author has been established as Henri-Michel Sauvage, S.J.

27. *N.E.* 1758, pp. 73–77.

28. *N.E.* 1750, pp. 88.

29. One of the best studies of this episode is B. Robert Kreiser, *Miracles, Convulsions, and Ecclesiastical Politics in Early Eighteenth-Century Paris* (Princeton: Princeton University Press, 1978). For the reaction of one prominent Jansenist, Nicolas Petit-pied, who first defended and later renounced the miracles at St. Medard, see pp. 122–24 and 343–44.

30. *Defense des versions de l'Ecriture Sainte*, pp. 29–31, 153–56, *et passim*. See also n. 7 above.

31. A. Bachelier, *Le Jansénisme à Nantes* (Paris, 1973), pp. 189–90.

32. A critical edition with notes is soon to be published. F. E. Weaver, "Spiritual Direction of Women at Port-Royal," *Cistercian Monastic Women: Hidden Springs*, Vol. III of *Medieval Religious Women* (Kalamazoo, Mich.: Cistercian Publications, forthcoming).

33. *N.E.* 1731, pp. 102–03.

34. National Archives of Utrecht, MS P.R. 8, Claude Lancelot, "Relation du voyage d'Aleth, 18 Dec. 1644." See also the reference to the "Régents" in the diocese of Chalons-sur-Marne in J. Matet and R. Pannet, "Vialart de Herse . . . Le sense et les limites d'une réformation," *Le Christianism populaire* (Paris, 1976), p. 149.

35. See F. E. Weaver, *The Evolution of the Reform of Port-Royal: From the Rule of Citeaux to Jansenism* (Paris, 1978), where I have explored the lives of monastic women. It is interesting to note that the total number of lay women mentioned in the *N.E.* is 254 by my count. One hundred ninety-seven lay men are mentioned (of course, the total number of men is much higher, but most of those mentioned are clerics) and most are mentioned only as members of the parliaments involved in the political struggles of later Jansenism or as doctors called in to witness to the miraculous healings during the period of the convulsionaries of St. Medard.

36. *N.E.*, 1753, pp. 85–87.

37. Ibid., 1750, pp. 131–32.

38. Ibid., 1754, pp. 62–63.

39. Ibid., 1732, p. 222.

40. Ibid., 1740, p. 125.

41. Ibid. 1728, pp. 229–300; 1729, pp. 31–32; 1745, p. 48.

42. Ibid., 1728, p. 129; 1731, p. 70.

43. Ibid., 1740, pp. 89–90.

44. Ibid., 1731, p. 106; 1732, pp. 95, 153–54; 1752, p. 186.

45. See, for instance, the account of her interview with Cardinal de Noailles in a letter to Mère St. Anastasie Du Mesnil, prioress of Port-Royal in its last days, reproduced in Saint-Beuve, *Port-Royal* (Paris, 1955), vol. III, pp. 802–6.

46. It would be out of place here to describe the new phase of the battle stirred up by the publication of the *Entretiens de Cléandre et Eudoxe* by Père Daniel. (Ironically this work was eventually placed on the *Index* alongside Pascal's *Lettres*.) What is important to note is that we owe to Père Daniel's *Entretiens* the translation of the *Notes de Wendrock* by Mademoiselle de Joncoux, as she tells us in the Preface to the first edition (c. 1700). (I have used the edition of 1766, p. lxxxix.) This translation of the notes and commentaries of the Nicole-Wendrock, reprinted in 1739, was as popular and highly praised as the original.

47. *Historie du Cas-de-Conscience* (Nancy, 1705) with Jean Louail, and the *Histoire Abregée du Jansénisme* (Cologne, 1698) with Jacques Fouillou.

48. E. Jacques, "Médecine et spiritualité: un médecin belge oublié, ami de Port-Royal, Philippe-Ignace Save (1659–1702)," *Revue d'Histoire Ecclésiastique*, vol. LXXV, no. 2 (April–June 1980), p. 336.

49. *Port-Royal*, vol. III, p. 806.

50. Mention of Madame de Fontpertuis's smuggling activities is found in *Archives de la Bastille. Documents inédites récueillis et publiés* par François Ravaison (Paris, 1876), vol. VIII, pp. 43–44, 56.

51. Archives of Utrecht, MS P.R. 596, Letter to Feydeau (July 1694). I have visited the site of her chateau at Lailly-en-Val, just across the Loire from Beaugency. Although the original chateau is replaced by a nineteenth-century building in seventeenth-century style, the ancient moat, the dove cote, and the spring which gives "Fontpertuis" its name are still there. It is a lovely solitude, indeed.

52. Arnauld's letters can be found in *Oeuvres d'Arnauld* (Paris, 1775–83), vols. II, III, and IV. Those of Angélique de Saint-Jean are conserved in a good manuscript collection at the Bibliothèque de la société de Port-Royal (Paris), MS P.R. 358–61.

53. Bibliothèque de Troyes, MS 2334.

54. To date I have been unable to discover a copy of either the breviary or the *Diurnal*. A recent visit to the site of the chateau de Fontpertuis, Lailly-en-Val dashed my hopes of finding archives of the family. The chateau was destroyed by fire in the eighteenth century, and what few archives remained were dispersed in an auction when the nineteenth-century owner declared bankruptcy. At the archives in Utrecht, however, there is a file of correspondence between Madame de Fontpertuis and Bigres (a name often found in approbations given by the Sorbonne) which refers to a *Diurnal*. A note on the manuscript says that the *Diurnal* was composed by Madame de Fontpertuis and that Bigres has approved it. At Utrecht there is also a letter from a Monsieur Lauthier dated 1709, which gives Madame de Fontpertuis instructions on how to apply for the publication permission. He advises her to go to the house (*libraire*) of Helie Josset with her *Diurnal ou heures journalières tirées de la Sainte Ecriture*. Madame de Fontpertuis, it appears, followed Lauthier's advice. The *Diurnal* is registered by Josset in 1710 and Lauthier's name appears on the permission. (Bibliothèque Nationale, MS fonds français 21,949, "Registres pour l'Enregistrement des Privilèges 1710–1716," p. 527, 8 janvier no. 104, "Privilege General, Josset, 968.")

55. Even today, in the Old Catholic Church of Utrecht, which was formed from a schism in 1726 and which had as its theologians at the time the Jansenists who were in exile there, the spirituality of the lay people is exactly as described here. A fascinating talk on this spirituality of the Church of Utrecht was presented by J. A. G. Tans at a Colloque Port-Royal held at Amersfoort, Holland, October 1985.

Contributors

SHERRILL COHEN received the Ph.D. in history from Princeton University in 1985. A fellow of the American Council of Learned Societies in 1988–89, she is writing a book, *The Evolution of Women's Asylums: Ex-Prostitutes and Unhappy Wives*. Cohen has worked as a social policy analyst and is co-editor of *Reproductive Laws for the 1990s*.

DAVID P. DANIEL is director of library services and professor of historical theology at Concordia Seminary, St. Louis. A specialist in the Reformation in the Austrian Habsburg lands, he has published *The Historiography of the Reformation in Slovakia* (1977) and articles on related subjects.

GRETHE JACOBSEN, who received her Ph.D. from the University of Wisconsin, Madison, in 1980, is a senior research fellow at the faculty of law, University of Copenhagen, engaged in research on women, guild statutes, and town laws in Denmark from 1400 to 1600. She taught previously at the University of Copenhagen and was Fulbright Scholar-in-Residence at Western Michigan University, 1986–87.

SUSAN C. KARANT-NUNN, professor of history at Portland State University, Oregon, is author of *Luther's Pastors: The Reformation in the Ernestine Countryside* (1979) and of *Zwickau in Transition, 1500–1547: The Reformation as an Agent of Change* (1987).

SHERRIN MARSHALL is associate dean for academic affairs and associate professor of history at Plymouth State College, New Hampshire. She is the author of *The Dutch Gentry 1500–1650* (1987), as well as co-editor of and contributor to *The Process of Change in Early Modern Europe: Essays in Honor of Miriam Usher Chrisman* (1988). Marshall is engaged in a study of Protestants, Catholics, and Jews in the Dutch Republic.

MILAGROS ORTEGA COSTA, born in Barcelona, Spain, received her Ph.D. from the Five College Cooperation Program at the University of Massachusetts, Amherst in 1974. Ortega Costa is author of the *Proceso contra Maria de Cazalla* (1978) and numerous translations and articles. She has taught at Smith and Mount Holyoke Colleges, and is now professor of Spanish at Salem State College, Massachusetts.

F. ELLEN WEAVER received the Ph.D. from Princeton University in 1973 and is assistant chairwoman of the department of theology at the University of Notre Dame. Author of *The Evolution of the Reform of Port-Royal* (1978), Weaver has written on liturgy and liturgical reform in early modern France, as well as on women's history.

MERRY E. WIESNER, associate professor of history at the University of Wisconsin, Milwaukee, is the author of *Working Women in Renaissance Germany* (1986) as well as many articles in women's history. Her current project is a study of women's defense of their public role in early modern Europe.

DIANE WILLEN, associate professor of history at Georgia State University, is former executive secretary of the North American Conference on British Studies. Author of *John Russell, First Earl of Bedford* (1981) and articles in women's history, Willen is working on a book, *Godly Women in England: Puritanism in Practice*.

Index

Numbers in italics indicate an illustration.